CAMBODIAN EVANGELICALISM

WORLD CHRISTIANITY

Dale T. Irvin and Peter Phan, Series Editors

ADVISORY BOARD:
Akintunde E. Akinade
Adrian Hermann
Leo D. Lefebure
Elaine Padilla
Yolanda Pierce

Moving beyond descriptions of European-derived norms that have existed for hundreds of years, books in the World Christianity series reflect an understanding of global Christianity that embodies the wide diversity of its identity and expression. The series seeks to expand the scholarly field of world Christianity by interrogating boundary lines in church history, mission studies, ecumenical dialogue, and interreligious dialogue among Christians and non-Christians across geographic, geopolitical, and confessional divides. Beyond a mere history of missions to the world, books in the series examine local Christianity, how Christianity has been acculturated, and how its expression interacts with the world at large. Issues under investigation include how Christianity has been received and transformed in various countries; how migration has changed the nature and practice of Christianity and the new forms of the faith that result; and how seminary and theological education responds to the challenges of world Christianity.

OTHER BOOKS IN THE SERIES:

Krista E. Hughes, Dhawn Martin, and Elaine Padilla, eds., *Ecological Solidarities: Mobilizing Faith and Justice for an Entangled World*

Aminta Arrington, *Songs of the Lisu Hills: Practicing Christianity in Southwest China*

Arun W. Jones, ed., *Christian Interculture: Texts and Voices from Colonial and Postcolonial Worlds*

Edward Jarvis, *The Anglican Church in Burma: From Colonial Past to Global Future*

Jifeng Liu, *Negotiating the Christian Past in China: Memory and Missions in Contemporary Xiamen*

CAMBODIAN EVANGELICALISM

Cosmological Hope and Diasporic Resilience

Briana L. Wong

The Pennsylvania State University Press
University Park, Pennsylvania

Library of Congress Cataloging-in-Publication Data

Names: Wong, Briana L., author.
Title: Cambodian evangelicalism : cosmological hope and diasporic resilience / Briana L. Wong.
Other titles: World Christianity (University Park, Pa.)
Description: University Park, Pennsylvania : The Pennsylvania State University Press, [2023] | Series: World Christianity | Includes bibliographical references and index.
Summary: "Amplifies and analyzes the stories of Cambodian converts to evangelical Christianity, emphasizing the ways in which they have experienced hope and purpose in the wake of overwhelming tragedy and loss"—Provided by publisher.
Identifiers: LCCN 2023022268 | ISBN 9780271095479 (hardback) | ISBN 9780271095486 (paper)
Subjects: LCSH: Christian converts—Cambodia. | Christianity—Cambodia.
Classification: LCC BR1185 .W66 2023 | DDC 270.09596—dc23/eng/20230522
LC record available at https://lccn.loc.gov/2023022268

Copyright © 2023 Briana L. Wong
All rights reserved
Printed in the United States of America
Published by The Pennsylvania State University Press,
University Park, PA 16802–1003

The Pennsylvania State University Press is a member of the Association of University Presses.

It is the policy of The Pennsylvania State University Press to use acid-free paper. Publications on uncoated stock satisfy the minimum requirements of American National Standard for Information Sciences—Permanence of Paper for Printed Library Material, ANSI Z39.48–1992.

For my family,
and for all those around the world
who have welcomed me as their own.

Contents

Acknowledgments ix
List of Abbreviations xii
Editorial Note on Khmer Language
and Interview Conventions xiii

Introduction 1

chapter 1 National and Transnational Contexts of
Cambodian Evangelical Christianity 12

chapter 2 Conversion 40

chapter 3 Cosmology 65

chapter 4 Spirituality 89

chapter 5 Transnational Ministry and Mutual Mission 115

Conclusion 143

Epilogue: Reflections on the Ethnographer's
Identity in World Christianity 149

Notes 161
Bibliography 169
Index 180

Acknowledgments

At its inception, I conceived of this project as an inquiry into the work of Christian missionaries and aid workers operating within Cambodian refugee camps along the border with Thailand. As I began researching this topic, I started exploring the idea with Cambodian evangelicals who had lived through this period and who had been active in the church communities that arose within the camps. During a phone conversation with one Cambodian ministry leader whom I met through family friends, I asked him about his memories of the mission work that took place in the refugee camps, particularly that which Christians from elsewhere in Southeast Asia had initiated. Instead, he launched into a story of which, up to that point, I had been unaware—a story of vibrant communities of Cambodian evangelicals, many of them new converts, meeting for Cambodian-led church services so large that many could not fit within the church building and had to encircle it while listening to the sermons outdoors on loudspeakers. As a result of this conversation, I decided that rather than focusing on Cambodian refugees as recipients of mission, I would explore the compelling stories of Cambodian evangelicals themselves, the ministries they formed and led, and the way their Christian faith has impacted their lives and communities in the wake of the trauma of war and genocide.

I am profoundly grateful to all who have contributed to the formation of this book. First, I would like to thank Richard Fox Young for his keen insight and steadfast support from start to finish, as well as Afe Adogame and Raimundo Barreto, for adding depth to my project through their consistently sound counsel over the years. I also very much appreciate Erin Raffety's generosity in offering important feedback on an early version of this manuscript.

The patience and expertise of my Khmer language instructors enriched my ethnographic fieldwork and afforded me entrée into communities and relationships that otherwise would have remained inaccessible to me. Many thanks to my teachers Chhany Sak-Humphry, Sisotha Oeur, Sophea Chouk, Manith Nguon, Chan Hopson, Sanghak Kan, and Hok Sreymom for propelling me forward in my pursuit of this beautiful language. My project was enhanced through support from the Center for Khmer Studies (CKS), The

ACKNOWLEDGMENTS

United Methodist Church, the Louisville Institute, and the Forum for Theological Exploration (FTE). I am grateful to the selection committees who decided to help fund my research, as well as to all those who wrote recommendation letters on my behalf. I would also like to thank Samedy Suong, Samedy Top, and Sreypich Tith for the benefit of CKS affiliation during my stay in Phnom Penh in the spring of 2019, including visa sponsorship, assistance in locating an apartment in the city, and the opportunity to visit headquarters in Siem Reap to share about my research.

For the archival portion of my project, I greatly appreciated the assistance of Jitra Samsa, formerly of the Church of Christ in Thailand archive at Payap University in Chiang Mai; Susan Needham, who kindly provided access to the CamCHAP collection at the Historical Society of Long Beach; and Sita Sharon Mullenix at the Christian and Missionary Alliance archive in Colorado Springs.

I would like to thank my mentors and colleagues from Princeton Theological Seminary, Wake Forest University School of Divinity, Phillips Theological Seminary, CKS, the Louisville Institute, the Asian Theological Summer Institute, FTE, the Wabash Center, and the World Christianity Unit at the American Academy of Religion. I am especially grateful for the encouragement of Ruth Amwe, Edwin Aponte, Kenneth Appold, Jacalyn Barnes, Lisa Barnett, Brenda Bertrand, Joe Bessler, Lisa Bowens, Peter Capretto, Arthur Carter, Warren Carter, Katherine Casey, Emily Chesley, Byung Ho Choi, Alexander Chow, Lisa Davison, Lisa Dellinger, Elabo Amidu, Lucy Franklin, Elizabeth O'Donnell Gandolfo, Jessica Garber, Hans Harmakaputra, Melanie Harris, Derek Hicks, Anne Joh, Stanley John, Kevin Jung, Afia Sun Kim, Henry Kuo, Kwok Pui-lan, Bo Karen Lee, Peace Pyunghwa Lee, Sun Yong Lee, Tat-siong Benny Liew, Annie Lockhart-Gilroy, Kathy McCallie, Janice McLean-Farrell, Emily Mitchell, Sarah Morice Brubaker, Carmen Nanko-Fernandez, Kenneth Ofula, Shalon Park, Phoebe Quaynor, Paul Rajashekar, Don Richter, Thomas Seat, Jayakiran Sebastian, Sandy Shapoval, Katy Shevel, Margarita Mooney Suarez, Jonathan Tan, Christopher The, Stephanie Mota Thurston, Allie Utley, Grace Vargas, Anne Carter Walker, Ralph Watkins, Avery Welden, Nicola Whyte, Corey Williams, Chelsea Yarborough, See Yin Yeung, and Gina Zurlo.

In the midst of all the chaos surrounding the COVID-19 pandemic, Wake Divinity and Phillips Seminary provided safe, peaceful, and inspiring opportunities to write. I am forever grateful to President Jonathan L. Walton of Princeton Theological Seminary, formerly the dean of Wake Divinity, and to President Nancy Pittman and Dean Lee Butler of Phillips, for welcoming me and allowing me the time and space to write while being surrounded by such wonderful academic colleagues. Alyson Anderson, my editorial and research assistant at Wake, supplied invaluable support on this project, for which I am tremendously thankful. The faculty members and students at both Wake and Phillips encouraged me in this project in ways I never could have anticipated.

I greatly appreciate the willingness of Penn State University Press to include this book in its World Christianity series. I extend my heartfelt thanks to series co-editors Peter Phan and Dale Irvin for believing in this project, as well as to acquisitions editor Kathryn Yahner and managing editor Laura Reed-Morrisson for making it a reality. I would also like to thank my two anonymous readers for taking the time to offer their insights on how to improve the manuscript.

To my Cambodian evangelical friends in Philadelphia, Long Beach, Paris, and Phnom Penh, I owe an enormous debt of gratitude. Without their willingness to entrust their stories to me, this project would have been impossible. I hope that my work will honor their experiences and the overwhelming generosity with which they welcomed me into their lives. In addition to my interlocutors, I would like to thank all the family friends, friends of friends, and all those who live adjacent to Cambodian evangelicalism who paved the way for my research and significantly enriched my experience in the field. Among these are Cambodian Buddhists; Cambodian Catholics; Cambodian evangelicals living in areas other than my main field sites; non-Cambodian members and leaders of predominantly Cambodian churches in the diaspora; and long-term residents of Cambodia hailing from Australia, Hong Kong, Korea, Nigeria, the Philippines, South Africa, Switzerland, the United Kingdom, and the United States.

I could not have made it far without the family and friends from around the world who buoyed me with their prayers, including when I encountered Yellow Vest rioting in Paris and fell sick in Phnom Penh. I am overwhelmed by the loving support of my community, including Washington Crossing United Methodist Church, St. Paul United Methodist Church, the Rev22 group, and all those kindred spirits who celebrated each incremental victory and uplifted me in difficult times. Finally, I am thankful to my family on both sides—including my grandparents, aunts, uncles, cousins, and honorary family members—who have cheered me on in my studies over the decades, and especially to my parents, Barry and Michele Wong; sister, Naomi Wong; and grandmother, Phyllis Garror, who have constantly reminded me of who I am and who I am called by God to be.

Abbreviations

CMA	Christian and Missionary Alliance
IPA	International Phonetic Alphabet
IRB	Institutional Review Board
KHOV	Khmer Old Version (of the Bible)
KSV	Khmer Standard Version (of the Bible)
MEP	Missions Étrangères de Paris
OMF	Overseas Missionary Fellowship (1964–1993); OMF International (1993–present)
WCC	World Council of Churches
WCD	World Christian Database
WHO	World Health Organization

Editorial Note on Khmer Language and Interview Conventions

The modern Khmer script features thirty-three consonant symbols, twenty-four dependent vowels—with each dependent vowel having two distinct pronunciations—and twelve independent vowels. Numerous Khmer transliteration and transcription systems have been created, but none is used ubiquitously. In this book, I have transcribed Khmer words according to the International Phonetic Alphabet (IPA). This IPA transcription will enable readers unfamiliar with the Khmer language not only to understand how these words sound when spoken but also to search for their nuanced English definitions in the online SEAlang Library Khmer Dictionary, which draws on the resources of the 1977 and 1997 versions of Robert K. Headley's *Cambodian-English Dictionary*, along with the classic *Chuon Nath Khmer Dictionary*. When citing the work of other authors, I have left transliterated Khmer terms as they currently stand, in the interest of avoiding confusion.

Readers will note that I often resort to paraphrasing my interlocutors' stories rather than quoting them at length. This is explained further in the introduction. For lengthier segments of my interlocutors' responses, I offer paraphrases set in italics, indicating that the text in question is not a direct quotation but nevertheless captures the essence of the speaker's intent. Such quotations also omit grammatical errors and irrelevant interjections.

INTRODUCTION

This book is a book about stories—specifically, about the testimonies that reveal the ways in which Cambodian converts to evangelical Christianity have drawn on their newfound faith to make sense of their traumatic collective past in the wake of the Cambodian genocide (1975–79). Based primarily on ethnographic fieldwork carried out between June 2018 and June 2019 in the metropolitan areas of Philadelphia, Pennsylvania; Los Angeles, California; Paris, France; and Phnom Penh, Cambodia, this book explores questions of religious identity and the search for meaning within the context of transnational Cambodian evangelicalism, particularly with respect to conversion, cosmology, spirituality, and mission. During my field research, I held interviews, had informal conversations, or did both with several dozen Cambodian evangelical adults and spent approximately three months participating in the communities to which they belonged in each of these areas. Although I did have to grit my teeth and make a few cold calls, I typically relied on the personal connections of my existing interlocutors in the search for new study participants. By the time I arrived in Phnom Penh, my final destination, I had already received the names and contact information of many key interlocutors there through connections with their friends and family members whom I had met in the previous cities in which I had been carrying out my fieldwork. Expatriates from Norway, the Philippines, and the United States, all friends of friends, were also of tremendous assistance in serving as gatekeepers to the gatekeepers,

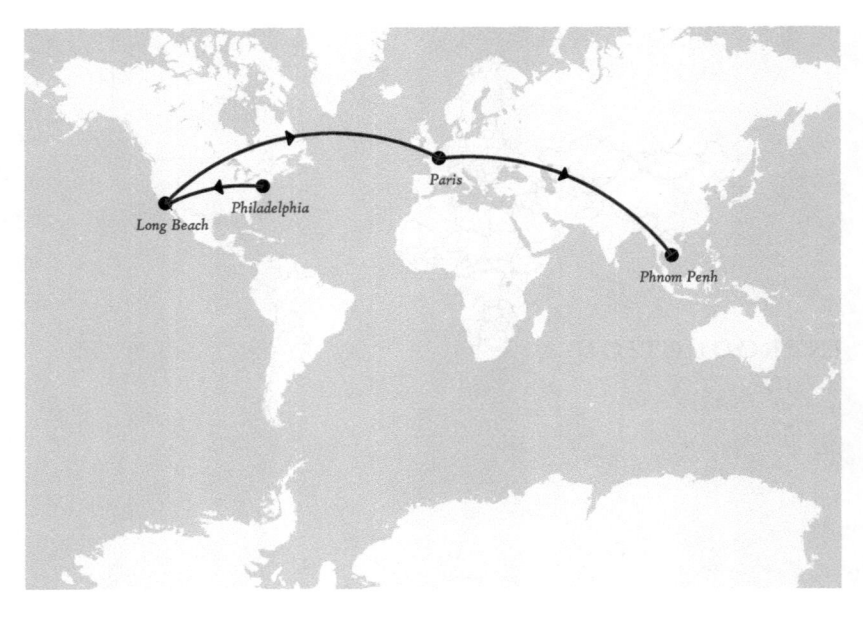

Trajectory of my research.

if you will. Many individuals falling into this category introduced me to Christian communities in Phnom Penh and vouched for my trustworthiness after they themselves had met with me and assessed my motives. The service they provided in this vein was crucial to my gaining entrée into numerous field sites.

During interviews, I typically met with interlocutors individually to ask questions about how it came to be that they had converted to Christianity and how they understood their present religious identity. A member of one Long Beach church requested that I consider offering interviewees the option to meet with me in groups of two or three for the sake of solidarity and emotional support, especially as many of the testimonies involved revisiting painful and traumatic memories. I was glad to oblige and grateful for the recommendation, as several interlocutors did indeed ask to meet with me while accompanied by spouses, friends, or ministry partners. Interviews with my interlocutors took place in a variety of settings, including at their houses, at restaurants, at the mall, and, once, at a Swensen's ice cream parlor.

When initiating interviews, I asked to meet with each interviewee for one hour. Some interlocutors were unable to meet for the entire hour, while others were keen to continue sharing their stories for upward of two or three hours. I made a conscious effort to create opportunities for my interlocutors to speak about that which was most salient to them when reflecting on their own faith. Only rarely did I complete the entire list of interview questions with any given interlocutor; much more often, a few questions occupied us for the entire interview. Not infrequently, my interviewees took the majority of the time to answer my seventh question: "How did you become a Christian?"

Participant observation, including copious informal conversations with Cambodian evangelicals, accounts for the bulk of my fieldwork interactions. At least as ethnographically generative as the interviews were worship gatherings I attended in each location. I also spent time getting to know the community through a variety of events outside of church services. In each city, I met one-on-one or with small groups of interlocutors for appointments other than interviews, such as for a meal or a visit to an individual's place of business, in order to build relationships and trust. Many were enthusiastic about meeting me in the donut shops, churches, museums, and taxis where they spent their working hours. I also attended a variety of gatherings organized by Cambodian evangelical groups outside of regular Sunday services. These included adult education courses, prayer meetings, dinner parties, holiday events, and Bible studies. I considered myself almost always "on call" during my fieldwork, as, at any moment, I might receive a text or a Facebook message inviting me to join an interlocutor at the movies or a café. Saturdays and Sundays were frequently my longest days, as my interlocutors were often off from work and eager to show me around their world.

Although this book does indeed analyze and engage concerns of a theological nature, I do not argue in favor of any particular theological viewpoint. My goal is instead to highlight the perspectives and experiences of my interlocutors. Part of the decision to depend primarily on living texts, rather than on written texts, stems from the fact that during the Cambodian genocide, Pol Pot's Khmer Rouge government abolished schools, targeted literate individuals, and prevented many of its subjects from learning to read or write. Rather than drawing mainly on texts about Cambodian evangelicals, I wanted to listen to their own voices, sharing their own perspectives.

Although I did meet some Cambodian Christians who were unable to read, all those who sat with me for interviews were at least moderately literate in one language or more. This could be considered a limitation of the study due to my general dependence on snowball sampling and on my modest fluency in Khmer, especially during the earliest period of my fieldwork.[1] Another limit of the study concerns my decision to interview only adults.[2] In the diaspora, this meant that most of my interlocutors were refugees born in Cambodia or in refugee camps. This limitation became even more consequential once I entered Cambodia itself. Young people—those under thirty—make up almost two-thirds of the population.[3] In Phnom Penh, I often found myself, at age twenty-eight, among the oldest individuals at a church service on a Sunday morning. When I met with the all-Khmer leadership team at Word Made Flesh Church, a congregation associated with a northern European ministry organization, the church's pastor, Somlain, told me that the majority of his parishioners were teenagers. Tragically, the age disparity between the churches in Cambodia and in its diaspora is connected to the loss of approximately one-fifth of the population during the Cambodian genocide.[4] In Pastor Somlain's words, "In Cambodia, it's a lot of teenagers, because the Khmer Rouge kill[ed] off all the [educated] people."

At another of the churches I visited in Phnom Penh, the pastor invited the congregation to divide into small groups after the service one Sunday to discuss questions pertaining to the sermon. After we had done so, I noticed quickly that I was the only adult in my group, with everyone else falling between the ages of fourteen and seventeen years old. I found these young people's observations profound, and their level of engagement impressive. They also expressed undying patience with my still-halting Khmer as we chatted after the service, which was an added bonus. Their contributions to the development of Cambodian evangelicalism are significant, and I look back on that time somewhat wistfully when I think of the fact that I was not in a position to interview them or others of their generation.

Furthermore, I acknowledge that any research approach that entails asking people to share memories associated with harrowing experiences that occurred several decades in the past is rife with difficulties, including the likelihood of certain historical inaccuracies. In the researching and writing of this book, I have tried to hold in tension the validity of my interlocutors' experiences, on the one hand, and the commitment to the highest level of accuracy as possible under the circumstances, on the other. I have not claimed as historical anything I know to be untrue but given that my focus has been on my interlocutors' understanding of their own religious experiences and identities, I have not found it necessary to attempt to disprove or delegitimize any memories with which my interlocutors have entrusted me.

As described in the editorial note above, I often resort in this book to paraphrasing my interlocutors' stories. I made a methodological decision soon after beginning my research to refrain from audio recording. The early choice to avoid using recording technology has to do with the painful associations certain Cambodian genocide survivors have had with recording devices. Judith Hamera, a professor at Princeton University, recounts with great remorse an anecdote featuring a time when one of her Cambodian interlocutors in Long Beach, California, appeared to be significantly triggered upon seeing Hamera's tape recorder. Hamera learned ex post facto that the Khmer Rouge had employed tape recorders to collect the so-called confessions they coerced out of their prisoners and gathered that this context likely contributed to her interlocutor's intense response.[5] Indeed, Kang Kech Ieu (alias Duch), the overseer of the infamous Tuol Sleng Prison, admitted that prison authorities made prisoners "repeat their confessions before a tape recorder."[6] The tape recorder has been remembered as an instrument of torture for those threatened, beaten, subdued, and forced to voice confessions, often to actions they had not committed. Maha Ghosananda, the renowned former Buddhist Supreme Patriarch of Cambodia, famously and, perhaps allusively, asserted that at the attainment of nirvana, "all karma is erased, just as we erase the tape on a tape recorder."[7] The simile of the tape recorder in this context makes for a particularly powerful analogy in light of the Cambodian genocide and the trauma that survivors continue to endure. Bearing this history in mind, I concluded that it would be preferable to take notes with a pen and notepad, rather than relying on a recording device. My notes, consequently, could not be used to reconstruct entire interviews verbatim. For lengthier segments, the paraphrases are set in italics. These paraphrases omit grammatical errors or casual interjections that could distract the reader or result in an inaccurate portrayal of the speaker's mien.

Importantly, I have avoided delineating details that would be likely to expose my interlocutors or their families to undue risk. For example, I have not made my interlocutors' political views and activities a primary focus of this book. Eve Monique Zucker offers a compelling description of obstacles, suspicion, and outright police interference she faced during her Cambodian fieldwork.[8] Although providing more information on my interlocutors' various political views would have made for a particularly rich analysis—for their views were often disparate, even within the same geographical vicinity—I refrain from delving too deeply into this aspect of my interlocutors' lives for the sake of their protection and peace of mind.

I do not, however, seek to obscure information to the extent of creating composite characters; each interlocutor named in this book, though identified only by a pseudonym, is a real person. Nevertheless, I recognize, as Carol Mortland does, that especially when speaking of situations involving conflict or controversy, "identities can be easily revealed and people harmed."[9] In this book, I have done my utmost to prevent such harm from occurring, although it has required the omission of certain otherwise pertinent details.

Finally, it goes without saying that finishing my ethnographic research for this project in 2019 simultaneously represented an opportunity and a limitation. On the one hand, if I had begun fieldwork the following year instead, it almost certainly would have been cut short by the COVID-19 pandemic, which brought the world to a halt in many ways. Having the chance to complete my fieldwork prior to the impending lockdown, unbeknownst to me or to anyone at that time, provided me with the opportunity to travel internationally; to meet with interlocutors inside their church buildings, homes, cars, and places of work, as well as at restaurants; to cook and eat with large groups for community gatherings; to ride behind interlocutors on their motorcycles; to give and receive hugs; and to engage in a host of other social activities previously considered mundane, if not universal, but soon thereafter rendered risky by the pandemic. On the other hand, the COVID-19 pandemic has impacted nearly every aspect of life the world over, and the practice of Cambodian transnational evangelicalism is no exception.

Overview of the Argument

Chapter 1 sets the tone for the rest of the book by acting as a segue between mission history and the development of indigenous evangelicalism within the Cambodian community. This chapter brings into sharp relief the influence of Cold War politics, especially relating to the Vietnam War, on the lives of Cambodian Christians, thereby shedding light on many of my interlocutors' faith testimonies by situating central events within their relevant historical contexts. The nation's Catholic and evangelical communities, respectively, often faced governmental favor—or suppression—at opposite times due to the conflation of Vietnamese heritage with Catholicism and of American political allegiance with evangelicalism. The US carpet-bombing of Cambodia, in addition to the much-loved Norodom Sihanouk's support for the Khmer Rouge, contributed to Pol Pot's ascent to power. Among those who fled the atrocities of the Khmer Rouge regime and its aftermath, a small evangelical community expanded rapidly within refugee camps along the Thai border and spread thence throughout Cambodia and its diaspora.

Chapter 2 considers the reasons Cambodian Christians have provided concerning their decision to convert from Buddhism to Christianity. Drawing from my interlocutors' accounts of their own conversion processes, I unpack a multistep concept of conversion, in which converts might choose to identify with their new religion for a series of reasons, the earliest of which might strike the reader as unexpectedly practical—for example, the desire for food, friendship, resettlement in a new country, entertainment for their children, or all the above. Richard Fox Young helpfully places Robert Hefner's idea of self-identification[10] on a chronological continuum with Robin Horton's "intellectualist theory,"[11] the latter of which Young identifies with "cognitive reorganization."[12] Young thus demonstrates that converts might first begin identifying with a new religious community out of a sense that it might somehow enhance their well-being, but without really knowing why, and only later, if ever, come to a fuller understanding of the tenets of the new religion. Despite the material benefits that many Cambodian Christians around the world have recalled seeking upon conversion, there is still substantial social and economic risk involved in this decision to identify with what is still often considered among Cambodians a Western religion antithetical to Khmer culture. In the face of this cost, many converts attribute the coalescence of their new Christian identity to a desire for personal forgiveness and, not infrequently, to divine intervention. I call special attention to Cambodian Christians' not-uncommon accounts of having perceived appearances of the Christian God either during the genocide or in the refugee camp period that followed it. For some Cambodian former refugees, the memory of these perceived appearances of God have brought about a sense of purpose through the assurance that one's survival was neither by accident nor by one's own agency, but by providence, thereby offering a sense of relief from survivor's guilt.

Chapter 3 opens with a comparison between cosmology and spirituality. I characterize the former as something akin to the roster of beings that a religious community believes inhabit their world, and the latter as the community's prescribed and perceived patterns of interactions with such beings. I then address the phenomenon of multiple religious belonging in Cambodia and its diaspora, involving an amalgam of elements derived from Khmer and Chinese traditional religions; Brahmanism; Buddhism, in both its Mahayana and Theravada varieties; and both Catholic and Protestant Christianity. Combining the idea of "multiple religious belonging" with that of "believing without belonging,"[13] I explore what I call multiple religious believing without multiple religious belonging, in which Cambodian evangelicals identify primarily with their new religious community but retain a belief system shaped by a cosmology involving key elements of Cambodian Theravada Buddhism and indigenous religions.

In chapter 4, I claim that the cosmology I described in the previous chapter promotes an array of spiritual practices that occupy Cambodian evangelicals' lives—and their conversations on theological matters—demonstrating the freedom seen in accessing and interacting with the Christian God in a personal way. Many interlocutors shared experiences of having been tormented by evil spirits and of God's assistance in keeping these powers at bay. Part of maintaining loyalty in relationship with God, according to my interlocutors, is allowing God to transform one's character and patterns of behavior. I reflect in this chapter on the interconnectedness of relationship, gift giving, and merit in a Cambodian religious context—with special reference to the Buddhist tale known as the *Vessantara Jataka*—in an attempt to contextualize this pastoral admonition, echoed in various forms throughout my fieldwork. For people who have experienced grievous loss, adoption has special meaning. The idea of being adopted by the God who owns everything inspires freedom to give generously in response to their experience of the generosity of God, thereby attaining a sought-after sense of relationality following the isolation so many endured as a result of the war. The feeling of security derived from the belief in God's bounty and availability for relationship has led many Cambodian evangelicals to view their interactions with God as rather casual and informal, to emphasize exclusive loyalty to God, and to expect their lives to be transformed spiritually and materially as a result of their relationship with God.

Chapter 5 makes the case that through transnational ministry, expedited through the power of digital media, Cambodian evangelicals today find purpose in their past suffering. A circular pattern of mutual mission exists within the Cambodian diaspora itself, by which I mean that Cambodian evangelicals frequently travel with the intent to carry out mission-oriented activities within Cambodian communities other than their own, without the churches in one geographical location or another being designated as mission senders or receivers in any mutually exclusive terms. During my fieldwork, it was quite common to hear of Cambodian pastors flying from the United States to Cambodia for the encouragement of the churches there, and vice versa. Adding a new dimension to the transnational network, social media has greatly facilitated the process of transnational ministry, making it possible for evangelicals in Cambodia to view church services taking place in California, thanks to Facebook Live, and to chat with friends and family members between services or during Bible study via Facebook Messenger. This increase in digital modes of spiritual expression has opened up new opportunities for women and laypersons to participate in theological reflection and the spiritual development of their local and transnational communities.

Preliminary Findings

In each location, my interlocutors were eager to share how they had decided to convert to Christianity. The conversion story quickly became the jumping-off point for nearly all my interviews, with many other ethnographic details flowing out of that initial testimony. A recurring theme that ran through many of my interviews and informal conversations with my interlocutors was that of their memories of interacting with spiritual beings, both benevolent and malevolent. Another common element of such conversations was the strikingly consistent emphasis on purpose amid suffering, with interlocutors in all four locations—men and women, clergy and lay, old and young—calling special attention to what they understood to be the impact of the restorative presence and plan of the Christian God in their lives. My main argument in this book is that Cambodian evangelicals' personal conversion stories, beliefs surrounding cosmology and spirituality, and mutual, transnational ministry practices suggest that conversion to Christianity has served as a means for survivors of the Cambodian genocide, along with their children, to interpret their individual and collective experiences through a lens of hope, expressed through multidirectional mission.

Scholarly Contribution and Relevance

Little scholarly work has been done on transnational Cambodian Christianity. Research on Cambodia over the past forty years has concerned itself, by turns, with questions of politics, then of cultural studies, and, presently, of emotional healing. The Khmer Rouge period was shrouded in secrecy—to such an extent that much of the early writing on this era, according to

Anne Ruth Hansen and Judy Ledgerwood, was fraught with "a justifiable confusion about what empirically happened between 1975 and 1979."[14] Prior to the fall of the Khmer Rouge regime, and even for a number of years thereafter, the Western world was at a loss as to what to make of the revolution and allegations of mass violence in Cambodia. In the 1980s, Western academic publications on Cambodia generally concerned themselves with political history.[15] Historians Michael Vickery, David Chandler, and Ben Kiernan, together considered "at the forefront" of research on the Cambodian genocide,[16] turned their attention during this time toward detailing the history of communism in Cambodia, along with the political ascent of Pol Pot. The mid to late 1990s saw a burgeoning interest in Khmer cultural studies, in which scholars from a variety of disciplines were determined to work toward cultural preservation efforts with survivors in the diaspora.[17] Many of the publications illuminating the experiences of Cambodian refugees in the diaspora have been ethnographic studies. Nancy J. Smith-Hefner produced excellent work based on time spent with Khmer Americans in Lowell, Massachusetts,[18] which has the second-highest Cambodian population in the United States, smaller only than that of Long Beach, California.[19] Smith-Hefner is one of the few scholars who have included evangelical communities in their studies of refugees from Cambodia. Kathryn Poethig focuses on transnational Cambodian evangelicalism among former refugees returning to the homeland in her essay concerning the concepts of conversion and "heavenly citizenship" among Cambodian Americans.[20] Khatharya Um, formerly a refugee herself, has conducted ethnographic work inquiring into issues relating to emotional healing from the trauma of the genocide.[21] Her research attends to the plight of both perpetrators and victims; between the two, the line is often blurry, as even those who never joined the Khmer Rouge were often forced to commit acts that haunt them to this day.[22] On the same theme, Eve Monique Zucker has shown that Christianity has contributed to emotional healing in Cambodia—including in the experiences of former Khmer Rouge soldiers. In fact, in a village she features in her study on postconflict recovery in Cambodia, all the Christians were former Khmer Rouge soldiers who converted during the early 1980s on the border with Thailand or during the 1990s or early 2000s in response to a local minister's work after coming back to the communes.[23] Zucker's inclusion of Christianity, however minimal, is strikingly rare among scholars studying Cambodia. John Marston and Elizabeth Guthrie, pardoning themselves for excluding Christianity from their collected volume on Cambodian religions, acknowledge that "perhaps the chief gap in this volume is the absence of Christianity." Marston and Guthrie explain that although the subject is "still little studied ... recent conversions related to the return of refugees from border camps and evangelization by overseas Cambodians may yet prove to be an important social development."[24]

Vickery dedicates a few sentences to the rapid expansion of Christianity within the refugee camps in Thailand,[25] but the main sources detailing this phenomenon tend to fall into the category of journalistic writing, missionary memoirs and correspondence, and survivor stories, almost always mediated through a Western lens. Take, for example, the memoirs of genocide survivors Barnabas Mam,[26] Rany Chan,[27] and Sophal Ung.[28] Each of these authors provides meaningful, firsthand accounts of Christian life during and immediately after the Democratic Kampuchea period. Even so, both Mam and Chan wrote their stories alongside Western coauthors—Kitti Murray of the United States and Andrée-Marie Sigrist of France, respectively. Ung, now a prominent evangelical leader, shared his experiences with the American Randy Clark through a series of video-recorded interviews, on which Susan Thompson drew as she penned Ung's biography.[29] The experiences detailed in such sources are inspiring and noteworthy, but the analysis afforded by an academic treatment offers a significantly different approach. Brian Maher and Uon Seila have provided a helpful historical account of the development of Christianity in Cambodia and its diaspora in relation to Western mission,[30] but the niche I aim to fill involves more of an emphasis on indigenous Christian thought and practice than on mission per se. Through the present book, I seek to address the need for a full-length ethnographic study of Cambodian evangelicalism as a transnational phenomenon.

Chapter 1

NATIONAL AND TRANSNATIONAL CONTEXTS OF CAMBODIAN EVANGELICAL CHRISTIANITY

Historical Overview

Before analyzing conversion to evangelical Christianity in the Cambodian cultural context, it would be helpful to take into consideration the story of Christianity's entry into Cambodia in the first place. This brief historical overview of Christianity in Cambodia, beginning with the arrival of evangelical missionaries and including key moments of Cambodian Catholic history is not intended to be exhaustive, but rather to place this topic within its larger historical context. The first missionaries to land in Cambodia were Portuguese Dominicans from Malacca, in the Malay Archipelago, arriving in 1555. In the seventeenth century, Roman Catholic priests came from France and started a church in Cambodia. A group of Dutch Calvinists, the first Protestants in Cambodia, were killed in Phnom Penh in 1643 while trying to establish a branch of the Dutch East India Company. In the nineteenth century, the French Catholic priest Marie-Joseph Guesdon translated a set of passages from the gospels for use in the Khmer liturgy. In 1863, when Cambodia became a French protectorate, the Catholic Church received total freedom of operation.[1] Catholicism did not see much growth among the Khmer population during this time, but a faithful community developed primarily among Catholics of Vietnamese origin, some of whom had fled persecution under Emperor Tu Duc.[2]

In 1921, missionaries representing the Christian and Missionary Alliance (CMA) began witnessing conversions among the ethnic Khmer people of South Vietnam, known as the Khmer Kraom, who speak the Khmer language, though often "with a detectable Vietnamese accent."[3] The CMA missionaries working among the Khmer Kraom started translating the books of Luke and Acts into Khmer around this time.[4] Two years later, two CMA missionary couples received permission to minister in Cambodia. Arthur and Esther Hammond began translating the Bible into Khmer in Phnom Penh,[5] with the help of numerous translation consultants, the earliest of whom were Buddhists.[6] The first project was the New Testament translation, completed by 1933. The Old Testament translation was finished by 1940 but was not published until 1953.[7] David and Muriel Ellison moved to Battambang in northwest Cambodia in 1923, and there they established a Bible school in 1925 for the purpose of educating ministers and preparing them to lead the nation's initial set of local evangelical churches.[8] The Christian population of northwestern Cambodia began to grow as numerous Khmer Kraom who had converted in South Vietnam in the early years of the CMA mission relocated to Battambang.[9] During this time, the new, revelation-based religious movement known as Caodai was growing rapidly in Vietnam, where by 1928, it reportedly had gained a million followers. The accuracy of this statistic has been disputed as a potential "exaggeration for promotional purposes," but the religion's undeniable expansion certainly piqued the interest and, eventually, the ire of the French in Vietnam, who ultimately expelled certain Caodai practitioners to Madagascar in 1941. Caodai, which combines Chinese and Vietnamese indigenous spiritual practices with a form of "medium-led 'spiritism'" common in France during the colonial period,[10] also made its way into Cambodia. For this reason, Cambodia's King Sisowath Monivong in 1930 officially prohibited religious practices of any kind other than Buddhism and Roman Catholicism. Despite this broad interdiction, evangelicals continued preaching and establishing small congregations in Cambodia.[11] As a result of the prohibition, the students at the Bible school in Battambang were arrested and imprisoned.

Over a decade later, Vichy France (1940–44) installed Prince Norodom Sihanouk as king of Cambodia in 1941. From 1945 to 1952, the Issaraks, an anti-French independence movement inspired by the Vietminh communists, and by Thailand's victory in the Franco-Thai war, staged a series of uprisings in Cambodia. After achieving independence from France in 1953, the nation was known as the Kingdom of Cambodia until 1970.[12] Sihanouk expelled all North American missionaries in May 1965 due to suspicion against the United States, while French Catholics and Protestants, including members of the French CMA (Alliance Chrétienne et Missionaire de France) continued their ministries in Cambodia.[13] After having to depart suddenly, North American CMA missionaries feared for the future of the nascent Khmer Evangelical Church, which comprised a total membership of fewer than one thousand Christians.[14]

Meanwhile, the 1960s would become quite an important period for the Catholic Church in Cambodia, when French missionary priests from the Missions Étrangères de Paris (MEP) began a revitalization project there. The Vietnamese predominance within the Catholic community in Cambodia had been established centuries prior to the arrival of the MEP. Catholics from Vietnam had been living in Cambodia from the middle of the seventeenth century, before the French colonization of Cambodia. Despite the small size of their community, Vietnamese Catholics constituted all but 5 percent of Cambodia's Catholic population.[15] Later, in the nineteenth century, Catholics in the area of present-day Vietnam known as Cochinchina fled to Cambodia to evade persecution from 1858 to 1862, during the reign of Emperor Tu Duc. In 1863, Norodom, king of Cambodia, welcomed 1,200 such refugees from Cochinchina and invited them to settle in Russey Keo at the north of Phnom Penh.[16] By this time, Catholics of Vietnamese origin accounted for 7–8 percent of the Vietnamese community in Cambodia.[17]

As the Catholic Church of the 1960s constituted primarily Vietnamese membership and French leadership, journalist Arnaud Dubus described the church as possessing "a doubly foreign face."[18] In 1969, Bishop Yves Ramousse of Phnom Penh made the decision "to render the liturgy more fully Khmer, gradually establishing Khmer as the language used for the liturgy of the Word."[19] In one church in the province of Kampong Cham in southeastern Cambodia, Vietnamese language services took place in the church building, and Khmer services, in a classroom in the parochial school associated with the church.[20]

The project to indigenize Catholicism in Cambodia was born out of tragic circumstances. As is mentioned above, the Catholic and Vietnamese populations in Cambodia were often conflated, due to significant overlap in the two communities. Ethnic Vietnamese in Cambodia, including but not limited to the Catholics among them, became vulnerable to targeted attacks during the Cambodian Civil War of 1970–75. In March 1970, while

NATIONAL AND TRANSNATIONAL CONTEXTS

Prince Sihanouk was traveling internationally, the National Assembly voted him out of office, and Lon Nol, Sihanouk's prime minister, assumed control of the government. In response to his unexpected ouster, Sihanouk took charge of an opposition coalition,[21] the National United Front of Kampuchea (FUNK), which was supported by North Vietnam.[22] Most of the fighters in Sihanouk's resistance movement had previously been in opposition to him as supporters of Saloth Sar (alias Pol Pot), leader of the Communist Party of Kampuchea, of which the members and followers were known as the Khmer Rouge. The Catholic population underwent great persecution during this time, due at least in part to their largely Vietnamese heritage and the support of North Vietnam for the Cambodian resistance.[23] Lon Nol proceeded to arrange for the removal of ethnic Vietnamese inhabitants of Cambodia. His government massacred thousands and expelled to South Vietnam an estimated 200,000 of Cambodia's approximate total of 450,000 civilians of Vietnamese origin.[24] Dubus estimates that the total number of ethnic Vietnamese expelled was closer to 250,000; among them were 54,000 Catholics, including numerous priests, nuns, and French missionaries. As a result, the Catholic Church in Cambodia was "brutally emptied of the majority of its faithful."[25]

In the early 1970s, the Benedictine community at a monastery in the southern province of Kep translated a number of songs into Khmer, borrowing Latin or French melodies. François Ponchaud completed a translation of the Old Testament into Khmer in 1973 and then began working on the New Testament. Later that year, he joined an ecumenical committee supervised by the United Bible Society's David Clark,[26] and which consisted otherwise of four evangelicals from the Cambodian branch of the CMA—the Khmer Evangelical Church (KEC)—and Ponchaud himself. This committee managed to draft a translation of the New Testament but had only just begun the editing process by the time of the Khmer Rouge takeover in 1975.[27]

It is important to acknowledge, however, that this revival of Khmer culture within the Catholic Church in Cambodia cast a grave shadow. Thien Huong T. Ninh identifies the MEP priests' "Khmerization" endeavors as categorically "anti-Vietnamese." Efforts to develop a more culturally Khmer form of Catholicism had the effect of alienating Vietnamese Catholics in Cambodia. Vietnamese Catholics found themselves faced with the choice of venerating either Khmer or European representations of the Virgin Mary. Vietnamese Catholics living in Cambodia today have become accustomed to images of Mary depicted as a European woman to the extent that they identify such images as "the 'true' representations that have been passed down through many generations by their ancestors" and as "a reminder of their belonging to a universal Catholic community that is beyond Cambodia." According to Ninh, Vietnamese Catholics in Cambodia today, many of whom are stateless persons, typically experience marginalization even within their own religious community in Cambodia. Without the stability of citizenship, they rely on Cambodian Catholic leadership for support and protection, which puts them in a vulnerable position that makes it difficult to advocate for greater cultural sensitivity. The legacy of the Khmerization programs has put them in the position of needing "to constantly prove their belonging within the Church."[28]

Meanwhile, in the spring of 1975, the civil war continued raging in Cambodia between the American-backed Lon Nol government and Pol Pot's Khmer Rouge rebel forces.[29] The Khmer Rouge increased in power, due partly to the leadership, at least in name, of Sihanouk—who was still wildly popular throughout much of rural Cambodia[30]—and also due to deep dissatisfaction with Lon Nol,[31] whose pro-American stance did not falter even after the United States wrought destruction throughout much of the Cambodian countryside. In secret, the United States carried out a carpet-bombing campaign in Cambodia from 1969 to 1973, ostensibly in an effort to destroy Viet Cong fighters who had spilled over the Vietnamese border into Cambodia. Cambodians living in rural areas, incensed at the devastation of their homeland but unsure of whom to blame, often believed the Khmer Rouge accusations that the Cambodian government had dropped the bombs.[32] The Khmer Rouge then succeeded in leveraging the American attacks to foment greater antigovernment sentiment.[33] Historian Ben Kiernan explains that Communist Party officials had intentionally misled young survivors of the bombings, convincing them that "'the killing birds' had come 'from Phnom Penh (not Guam), and that Phnom Penh must pay for its assault on rural Cambodia.'"[34] Without sufficient access to news outlets, Cambodian families living in the countryside found themselves vulnerable to the Khmer Rouge's version of the story, which seamlessly conflated Lon Nol's Phnom Penh government and the Americans who supported it. Thus, the Khmer Rouge blamed the bombing on the Lon Nol government and used the antigovernment sentiment that arose in response to these claims as a recruitment tactic.[35] Kiernan asserts that the American carpet-bombing was "probably the single most important factor" in the political ascent of Pol Pot.[36]

As the nation of Cambodia was being destroyed from the inside out during the civil war, its Christian community, both Protestant and Catholic, was undergoing unprecedented growth. According to Don Cormack, an Anglican priest who was involved in ministry alongside Khmer Christians for many years in Cambodia and Thailand, a "lay-centred movement [comprising] scores of new 'house churches' multiplie[d] across the city [of Phnom Penh] and significant church growth [was] seen in provincial centres, also."[37] American Missionaries from the CMA, whom Sihanouk's government had expelled in 1965, worried over what might happen to the evangelical churches in Cambodia following this expulsion. The question surfaced among them, "Will the church in Cambodia stand?" To their surprise, when the missionaries returned in 1970, welcomed by Lon Nol's government, they found that the evangelical community in Cambodia had not only survived but flourished. The denomination's 1971 annual report declares joyously that the years between 1965 and 1970 "rained persecution and suffering upon these believers only to drive their roots deeper in the grace of God and firmly prove their faith in Jesus Christ." The CMA's 1971 report continues: "Thrilling conversions have prodded the church to greater witness and work. Weekly, souls are led to Christ by both clergy and laity. A strong lay group has emerged to set the pace in church leadership and soul-winning. A hunger and openness to the gospel is unprecedented. All levels of society are responding—school teachers, students, doctors, soldiers, government officials, and laborers. Other prominent officials are presently interested and very friendly."[38] The growth of the evangelical community in Cambodia continued throughout the war. In 1973, Major Taing Chhirc, a Cambodian student and military official who had been studying in England, spoke before the Keswick Convention and OMF Singapore, a group dedicated to evangelistic ministry, and pleaded for Christians outside of Cambodia to pray for his country's Christians and to send missionaries. The response from OMF came almost immediately, as the organization deployed a group of five missionaries to partner with the Khmer Evangelical Church (KEC) in 1974.[39] Barnabas Mam, a well-known Cambodian pastor and former refugee himself, refers to the two years leading up to 1975 as a period of "revival" in Cambodia.[40]

In April 1975, the Khmer Rouge captured Phnom Penh and, after establishing a new communist government, implemented policies that resulted in what is commonly known today as the Cambodian genocide, during which the new Khmer Rouge government killed approximately 1.7 million people—21 percent of the country's population.[41] Among those who lost their lives were "virtually all the Christian leaders."[42] Between 1975 and 1979, the Khmer Rouge turned all of Cambodia into what anthropologist

Alexander Laban Hinton has called "a giant prison camp in which basic rights and freedoms were severely curtailed in the name of revolution."[43] Indeed, Pol Pot himself is said to have "boasted at one point that his goal was to make Cambodia 'one big work camp.'"[44] Renaming their new totalitarian state "Democratic Kampuchea," the Khmer Rouge sought to establish a pure, agrarian society, free from all foreign influences and class disparity. In the process, Pol Pot sought to systematically eliminate everything and everyone he suspected might hinder the accomplishment of this objective. Anything perceived as foreign or elitist—including practicing Christianity or Islam, wearing glasses, or speaking English or French—could put one at risk of execution.

The ironically named Democratic Kampuchea government carried out a forced evacuation of Cambodia's cities and relocated the urban population to newly created labor camps in rural areas. The Khmer Rouge separated families with the goal of undermining connections of kinship and replacing such bonds with an unyielding commitment to "the Party Organization, Ângkar."[45] The Khmer Rouge organized adolescents into gender-specific work groups where they lived, ate, and slept alongside their team members. Under this new arrangement, young people were required to stop addressing their parents and other elders with the terms of respect they had been raised to use, and to adopt alternative terms devoid of any allusion to status differential.[46] The Khmer Rouge shut down schools, suppressed religious activity, abolished banks and markets, and maintained tight surveillance over social life in the labor camps.[47]

The Khmer Rouge persecuted members of Cambodia's Chinese,[48] Vietnamese Catholic,[49] and Cham Muslim minorities with peculiar intensity until the Vietnamese army invaded Cambodia in 1979 and brought an end to Pol Pot's regime. Some scholars have called special attention to the overwhelming suffering the Cham underwent during the Cambodian genocide. The Cham, who live on both the Cambodian and the Vietnamese sides of the Mekong Delta, account for just under 2 percent of the population in Cambodia and are over 90 percent Shafi'i Sunni Muslim.[50] There are numerous theories pertaining to the original geographical homeland of the Cham. Most scholars agree that the Cham originated from the ancient kingdom of Champa in central Vietnam. Individual Cham have claimed to have come initially from a variety of locations, including Cambodia, Malaysia, and elsewhere in the Islamic world. Anthropologist Philip Taylor suggests that perhaps they have multiple sites of origin; for example, some of his interlocutors believed that the original inhabitants of the Mekong Delta were

Malays, and that Cham from Champa later joined them and intermarried. Islam as practiced by the Cham tends to be mixed with indigenous religious practices, evinced in the widespread, even if internally controversial, practice of praying to Cham saints.[51] Kiernan calls special attention to how the Khmer Rouge compelled the Cham to raise pigs and to eat pork—in violation of Islamic law—on pain of death.[52]

In considering the atrocities suffered by the majority of the Khmer population in addition to those the Khmer Rouge intentionally meted out against the Chinese, Vietnamese, and Cham, scholars and others have called into question the appropriateness of applying the term "genocide" to the Cambodian crisis of 1975–79. International criminal law professor William Schabas has famously pointed out that "genocide, as defined in the [Geneva] Convention, requires the intentional destruction of a 'national ethnical, racial or religious group.'" In that light, Schabas rhetorically asks, "Which group was it in Cambodia?"[53] More recently, the Extraordinary Chambers in the Courts of Cambodia, also known as the Khmer Rouge Tribunal, ruled in November 2018 that the term "genocide" was indeed apt to describe the Khmer Rouge killings between 1975 and 1979 because of the targeting of Cambodia's Vietnamese and Cham populations.[54]

I have decided to use the term "genocide" to refer to the mass killing that took place in Cambodia during this period—including that of Khmer by other Khmer—even while acknowledging that the definition set forth in the Geneva Convention is an imperfect fit for the situation in question. While one solution could be simply to refer to these atrocities as acts of continued warfare, rather than of genocide, I find that doing so would obscure the one-sidedness of the killing. Similarly, I find the oft-recommended substitute term "autogenocide" to be problematic—more so than "genocide"—in that it implies exclusive culpability on the part of the Khmer people, thereby removing any sense of responsibility from other parties, including the United States which, through its now infamous carpet-bombing campaign, likely contributed significantly to the rise of the Khmer Rouge. In choosing to use the term "genocide" in this case, over against "autogenocide," I align myself with Khatharya Um, professor of ethnic studies at the University of California, Berkeley, who suggests that "autogenocide" connotes "self-infliction" in a way that unduly hides the Western, and particularly American, role in laying the groundwork for the atrocities.[55] Viet Thanh Nguyen also echoes this sentiment. Even while describing the "horror" in Cambodian society that "consists not only of being victimized but also of victimizing others," Nguyen notes "the responsibility of the French in colonizing

Cambodia, the Americans in bombing the country, the North Vietnamese in extending their war through the country, [and] the Chinese in supporting the Khmer Rouge even with knowledge of their atrocities."[56]

The genocide was brought to an end by the Vietnamese army, which invaded Cambodia on December 25, 1978, and expelled Pol Pot from Phnom Penh on January 7, 1979, installing a new government the following day with onetime Khmer Rouge commander Heng Samrin as its leader.[57] During and after this period, thousands of Cambodian refugees fled to camps along the border with Thailand.[58] Before 1979, 35,000 Cambodian refugees entered Thailand. By the end of 1980, an additional 150,000 had entered. By the end of 1985, 250,000 more arrived, making for a total of 435,000. Between 1991 and 1993, 360,000 repatriated to Cambodia.[59] Over 100,000 resettled to third countries, primarily between 1979 and 1984.[60] A high birth rate accounts for there being a higher number of Cambodian refugees who departed Thailand in the 1990s than those who had entered in the 1970s and 1980s. For example, for the twelve-month period starting in December 1981, the Khao-I-Dang Holding Center, known as "the second largest Khmer city in the world, after Phnom Penh," had a crude birth rate of 54.4 per 1,000 population, with 2,323 births recorded during this year.[61]

This period was transformative with respect to Cambodian religious life, as many refugees living in the camps converted from Buddhism to Christianity and were mentored in their new faith by fellow Cambodian refugees. Historian Michael Vickery notes that "disaffection [with Buddhism] was massively apparent among the refugees in camps in Thailand, where in 1980 there were more registered Khmer Christians than in all of Cambodia before 1970."[62] According to Cormack, an evangelical community "of several thousand" people thrived under the leadership of Cambodian pastors and lay leadership inside the camp.[63] Barnabas Mam recalls that he and his ministry partners founded "fifteen seedling churches" in Thailand and "nourished them in anticipation of a return" to Cambodia.[64] Indeed, refugees who had become Christians prior to entering the camps often "took the lead in some of [the] church groups in the camps: they visited, distributed literature, conducted Bible courses and liaised with missionaries who came in regularly from nearby towns," according to Van Arun Rasmey and Mathews George Chunakara.[65] The majority of Cambodian refugees in Thailand stayed in camps along the border under the control of a variety of "liberation armies" until 1993, when most repatriated to Cambodia.[66]

In the period immediately following the Vietnamese army's overthrow of the Khmer Rouge government, the new Vietnamese-allied government in Cambodia made an effort to suppress Christianity.[67] Because the United States and the eventually victorious North Vietnam had been on opposite sides of the Vietnam War, the new government in Cambodia was suspicious of evangelical Protestantism, which they associated with the United States. According to the biography of evangelical leader Sophal Ung, the "genocide did not end when the Khmer Rouge were driven out," because "the Vietnamese continued to imprison, torture, and kill political prisoners" whom they deemed "a threat." Ung himself was among those beaten and imprisoned, accused of being "a Christian from America working for the CIA."[68] Cambodia's government, led by Prime Minister Hun Sen, reinstated Buddhism as Cambodia's state religion in 1989,[69] and subsequently recognizing Christianity in 1990, after fifteen years of suppression.[70] After having been nearly extinguished in Cambodia under Pol Pot, Christianity began to gain significant traction among primarily Buddhist Cambodian refugees,[71] and even among former Khmer Rouge members,[72] in the camps along the Thai border.

Throughout the 1990s, new missionaries from around the world brought a diverse batch of additional denominations and organizations to Cambodia. Among them are the Assemblies of God, the New Apostolic Church, the Southern Baptist Convention, the Church of Jesus Christ of Latter-day Saints, and the Foursquare Church, with this last church claiming to be "the fastest-growing church in Cambodia." Mainline Protestants, such as Methodists and Presbyterians, hailing from France, Malaysia, Korea, Singapore, Switzerland, and the United States, also entered Cambodia during this period. The independent New Life Fellowship Phnom Penh, founded by the American Eric Dooley, started in 1993 and has since grown to become one of Cambodia's largest churches. Numerous other nondenominational churches affiliated with various global networks have arrived since that time. Additionally, a number of indigenous Cambodian networks have emerged, including Living Hope in Christ Church (LHCC), founded by Barnabas Mam and Paulerk Sar in 1995. Over five hundred new churches have roots in LHCC.[73]

In Cambodia and in the Western countries in which Cambodian refugees resettled following the war and genocide, Christianity has grown in part due to the mission-focused efforts of former refugees who themselves had converted in the border camps. Of course, one must note that not all Cambodians who played a role in the development of the nation's Christian community were refugees; there were also those, including among my interlocutors, who remained in Cambodia throughout the civil war, the genocide, and the period immediately following the Vietnamese invasion, who demonstrated notable commitment to the growth of Cambodian Christianity. Even so, the importance of the refugee camp period in the explosion of Cambodian Christianity should not be underestimated. Mam refers to Thailand as "the greenhouse of the Cambodian church," due to the significance of the Christian movement that took shape in the camps.[74] In many cases, the Cambodian heritage churches thriving throughout the diaspora, in places like the United States, France, and Australia, are the direct result and continuation of the ministries that Cambodians conducted while still refugees in Thailand.

It is important to note that for all its growth, the Christian community in Cambodia accounted for only an approximate 2.56 percent of the nation's total population of over fifteen million in 2015, while the vast majority remains Buddhist.[75] This phenomenon is not unusual in mainland Southeast Asia. The late anthropologist Charles Keyes, in his essay "Why the Thai Are Not Christians," asserts that Christianity's inability to establish a foothold in Thailand is largely due to the inextricable, centuries-long connection between Buddhism and the Thai state. As evidence, he adduces the Thai watchword "To be Thai is to be Buddhist." Keyes claims that potential converts are generally inclined to adopt a new religious worldview if it can provide a preferable approach to the one to which they had been accustomed when it comes to dealing with problems in the world as they know it. When confronted with the choice between Buddhism and Christianity, he maintains, many Thai people have chosen to remain Buddhists because they do not believe that Christianity has shown itself to offer more coherence than Buddhism, and because Buddhism does not require its adherents to relinquish their former beliefs.[76] Taking into consideration the great similarities across the predominantly Theravada Buddhist societies of mainland Southeast Asia, exemplified in such analogous slogans as "to be Cambodian is to be Buddhist"[77] and "to be Lao is to be Buddhist,"[78] it is quite possible that the dynamic that Keyes has identified in the Thai context is at play more broadly.

Some might wonder, in that case, why it would be worthwhile to study an expression of Christianity with such a small number of adherents, especially when time could be spent exploring those forms of the religion that are gathering significantly more momentum elsewhere in the Global South. Martha Frederiks has suggested that the history of Christianity ought to include research centered on communities in which Christianity has constituted "a negligible minority" of the broader population. Indeed, there is no reason why Christian communities located within countries where the religion never rose to the level of majority or plurality must be considered unworthy of scholarly attention. Frederiks has made the case that the exploration of Christianity in areas where it has remained "a negligible minority" is part of what it means to study Christianity through the lens of intercultural history rather than that of mission history.[79] The impulse to focus on areas where Christianity accounts for a sizeable percentage of the population often seems to come from the desire to highlight, measure, and evaluate the effectiveness of missionary endeavors, usually carried out by Western individuals and organizations. The field of World Christianity, on the other hand, historically has distinguished itself through its commitment to calling attention to the beliefs, practices, and initiatives of Christian communities in the Global South, whose experiences often have been obscured by the dominant narrative of the West.

In this book, I aim to amplify the voices of Cambodian Christians whose stories have only rarely appeared in books that feature the history of Christianity. The appeal of studying Christianity where it is "a negligible minority," however, lies not only in the diversity it brings to the field but also in its potential to answer a question. The question, initially posed by Fenella Cannell, which has long been foundational to one of World Christianity's adjacent fields, the Anthropology of Christianity, asks, "What difference does Christianity make?"[80] When looking at Christianity where it has become a majority religion, we may find that people often identify as Christians because it is expected or even assumed, and that their religious identity makes only a minimal difference in their lives, perhaps barely coming to mind on an average day—in other words, people identify as Christian without obvious motivation for doing so, other than having been born into a Christian family. Studying Christianity where it is a small minority serves to illustrate what it is that people find so attractive about Christianity, such that they are now willing to jeopardize their social standing, familial bonds—and, in certain cases, physical safety—as a result of their conversion.

In conversations surrounding the risk of conversion, it is important to acknowledge that the present-day concerns of Cambodian converts to Christianity tend not to rise to the level of those experienced by certain Christian communities elsewhere in Asia—including China, where many Christians worship privately in unregistered churches, and where even registered churches have seen their crosses torn down by government bulldozers; India, where Dalit Christians have been excluded from the affirmative action–style reservation system established to redress the oppression against the Dalit community at large; Myanmar, where ethnic minorities identifying primarily as Christian "have reported campaigns of forcible conversion to Buddhism"; and Vietnam, where ethnic minorities belonging to majority Christian groups have experienced "significant restrictions on religious freedom," including "arbitrary arrests"[81]—let alone in Afghanistan or Iran. Although most Christians in Cambodia do not fear for their physical safety as a result of their conversion, choosing to convert to Christianity nevertheless can be seen as a cause for rejection by one's family or community due to a perceived abandonment of one's Khmer heritage and identity. For my interlocutors, most of whom were ethnic Khmer or Sino-Khmer, Christianity was not the majority religion of their people, but they found in their conversion the promise of hope and purpose in the wake of overwhelming suffering.

Evangelicalism in the Transnational Cambodian Context

I employ the term "evangelical" with a lowercase *e* in this book for the sake of clarity, given that the Cambodian churches within the CMA use the qualifier "Evangelical" with a capital *E* to refer to churches within their own denomination. I use "evangelical" primarily as an emic term; that is, I use the word to describe individuals and communities who have chosen to identify with it. Admittedly, the term "evangelical" is a contentious one and has become increasingly so after the 2016 and 2020 American presidential elections, as well as the storming of the United States Capitol on January 6, 2021. In recent years, there has been a marked shift among communities of Christians in the Global North and in the Global South who have chosen to eschew the "evangelical" label on account of its cultural and political associations, even if their own theological commitments have not changed. Even so, it remains the most accurate word to use to describe these congregations—in large part, because it is how they typically chose to characterize themselves.

Western evangelicals in recent decades have often pointed to David Bebbington's "Evangelical Quadrilateral," according to which the following four categories are considered to characterize evangelicalism: *conversionism*, "the belief that lives need to be changed"; *biblicism*, "a particular regard for the Bible"; *crucicentrism*, "a stress on the sacrifice of Christ on the cross";

and *activism*, "the expression of the gospel in effort."[82] Of course, it is important to acknowledge that evangelicalism has developed cultural and political meanings alongside the theological one that must also be considered. It remains to be seen whether and to what extent Cambodians identifying as evangelicals will align themselves with the cultural and political expressions of evangelicalism that have gained prominence in recent years; but with respect to theology, my fieldwork has led me to believe that on the whole, Cambodian evangelical theology fits quite well with that underscored by Bebbington.

Conversionism, the ideal of seeing lives changed in response to the person and message of Jesus, was shared among all the individual Christians and church communities I encountered during my fieldwork, although heated debate often surrounded precisely how a properly changed life ought to look, as chapter 4 will address more fully. In practice, with certain notable exceptions, the process of conversion among Cambodian evangelicals often relied heavily on family networks, such that it did indeed take on a communal orientation. For many of my individual interlocutors, however, I feel it is worth recalling that experientially and in their own memory, the process of choosing to convert felt like an exercise in personal agency, especially in retrospect. The maintenance of family relationships—or any number of other practical motivations—often accounted for the early stages of identification with Christianity, while other, potentially more intellectual and theological factors, come into play when the convert is deciding whether to remain in the new religious community. Importantly, salient within my interlocutors' conversion stories was the notion of God entering into human space and acting on their behalf, eliciting a response of continued interaction with God. As with intellectualization and commitment, the development of a relational orientation toward God could occur at any point in the conversion process. Often, attention to this relational dynamic surfaced more than once in a convert's faith testimony.

Biblicism took on a shape unfamiliar to most Western evangelicals. There is no doubt that commitment to the Bible—and to the most literal interpretation of it as possible—was widespread among my interlocutors. One person who most dramatically exemplified this biblicism was Ting Xiu, a Cambodian woman of Chinese descent living in Long Beach, who invited me to interview her in the fall of 2018. Immediately after my arrival at her home, a compact in-law unit situated behind a larger house, she gestured for me to sit on the couch and wait for her as she promptly disappeared into the kitchen. As I waited for her to return, I began soaking in my surroundings.

What first caught my attention was the presence of standard pieces of white printer paper adorning her walls, bearing in red and blue marker pen ink the handwritten words of various Bible verses in Khmer: Psalm 119:105,[83] John 3:16,[84] John 14:6,[85] Philippians 4:4,[86] and Revelation 22:12–13.[87] This last quote hung inside the door separating the living room from the tiny foyer. On one wall, multiple verses appeared together, the eight-and-a-half-by-eleven sheets of paper connecting in the form of a cross.

An observer familiar with evangelicalism of the sort Bebbington describes might walk into Ting Xiu's home and infer that she had posted the Bible verses on her wall as a way to remind herself daily of the words themselves. Indeed, the content certainly mattered to Ting Xiu, as she drew on the Bible for guidance in making sense of the grief she had endured in her life. Full of emotion, she told me her story:

> My brother went to the Khao-I-Dang camp in Thailand in 1981. From there, he went to New Zealand and wrote to me about the spiritual God in a letter. The Christians in Cambodia kept their worship a secret at that time. I went around to find a church. I walked around, asking, "Where is the church? Please tell me." One day, I walked and asked the right person. I have believed in God since September 1990.
>
> The first church I attended was a Nazarene church. They didn't have a church building. They worshiped at a house. I believed in God for one month and then got baptized. After I had been baptized three months, the pastor saw that I believed and asked me to preach and teach about God. I had been running a lumber business but stopped in 1992 so that I could serve God full time. During that time, my husband's side of the family didn't like me. They said, "She's crazy! Why did she stop working for her business and go to Jesus?" In 1994, my husband died. People said that it was because I believed in Jesus that my husband had died. I asked the people in the neighborhood who believed in Jesus to help me. It was the church people who took my husband to the hospital.
>
> Later on, my house caught fire. People said it was because I believed in Jesus. My life was like Job's. I trusted God and didn't understand why he didn't come through for me. I wanted to know, "Why?" I ran outside and prayed aloud to Jesus to help me as my house was burning. People thought I was crazy. Partway through, as the house continued to burn, I prayed, "Thank you, Jesus, for taking my house." The people said that the reason my house had caught fire was because I believed

in Jesus. This was such a hard time. There were several verses that were important to me around this time, like Romans 8:28, Romans 5:3–5, and the book of Job.

Evidently, Ting Xiu drew on both the Old Testament and the New Testament for inspiration and comfort in painful seasons of life, but there is more to the story.

Given Ting Xiu's background as a Chinese Cambodian, it is also important to acknowledge that there are additional lenses no less meaningful through which to view her expression of biblicism. Ting Xiu affixing Bible verses on each wall and door can also be interpreted through the lens of expressing allegiance to God and seeking God's protection. In both Khmer and Chinese culture, images hung on the wall often carry spiritual significance. Carol Mortland notes that in Khmer Buddhist homes, "Photographs of deceased parents or grandparents are often propped on the family altar or hung high on the wall, additional inspiration for thoughts of tradition and the ancestor spirits."[88] The question of filial piety proved a major sticking point in conversations between Cambodian Christians and their Buddhist friends and family members. Larry, a Cambodian American parachurch minister who had converted to Christianity as an adolescent, put it bluntly: "In Cambodian culture, the parents are the gods."

Chinese families also typically mount ancestral tablets on an altar on the wall. David S. Lim has written about how ethnic Chinese Christians have tried to go about honoring their parents in a way they feel would be appropriate in a Christian context. He offers an example of the Taiwan Presbyterian Church, which "endorsed hanging on the central wall a picture of Christ, the Ten Commandments, and Bible verses on large sheets of paper that are carefully framed." Lim also notes, "An enlarged and framed photo of the deceased is also hung in a prominent place in the house, but not on the spot once occupied by the ancestral tablets."[89] Thus, in Ting Xiu's context, hanging Bible verses on her wall was a way of declaring commitment to God, to the exclusion of venerating one's own ancestors.

Kristin Kobes Du Mez has written about White American evangelical consumer culture, which includes the use of Christian-themed decorations in one's house with the aim of emphasizing one's evangelical identity. This culture, according to Du Mez, involves the avid consumption of magazines, books, music, radio and television shows, movies, conferences, clothing, and decorations. Du Mez asserts that it would not be uncommon to find those identifying as evangelical who are unfamiliar with the key doctrines typically associated with their brand of Christianity but who are culturally shaped by "evangelical popular culture," including the computer generated *VeggieTales* films for children, radio programs by Focus on the Family, and various types of rock-and-roll- or hip-hop-style Christian Contemporary music.[90] Indeed, there is a certain overlap between the use of Bible verses as wall art in Cambodian and White American expressions of evangelicalism, in that individuals within each community have used Christian-themed decorating as a way to call attention to their status as evangelicals. It is important to note, however, that for Cambodian evangelicals like Ting Xiu, such a decorating choice is relationally costly, as it identifies her with a marginalized group within her ethnic community. Her verse sheets, which she created herself with inexpensive materials, clearly do not place her within the target market of those selling evangelical home decor, including the thousands of items that appear on Amazon when searching "Bible verse wall art." She did not need to purchase a certain brand or associate herself with a particular program in order to assert her religious identity.

Another important aspect of the practice of posting Bible passages in one's home has to do with the placement of such passages. In indigenous Khmer cosmology, spirits are believed to occupy physical space, such that they are thought to make use of doors and other openings, much as humans do. Depending on whether one desires the presence of a given spirit, the notion of spirits' ability to navigate through doorways can elicit either comfort or horror. Sucheng Chan writes that in Khmer culture, a person suffering from mental illness is often thought to need both Western medical professionals and Khmer indigenous spirit priests, [kruu], to provide relief. Some [kruu] invite those suffering from mental illness to sleep for several days within the same room that hosts the altar of the priest's own guardian spirit. As the patient is sleeping, the [kruu] or a family member remains in the room, sleeping close to the door in order to prevent unwanted spirits from entering.[91] In hanging Bible verses on her door, Ting Xiu was making a move to protect her home spiritually. The specific verses she chose to place on the door read, in English, "See, I am coming soon; my reward is with me, to repay according to everyone's work. I am the Alpha and the Omega, the first and the last, the beginning and the end."[92] In selecting this verse as the one marking the entrance, it seems that Ting Xiu wanted to invite Jesus into her living space, even as she found assurance in the words themselves, which identified him as the one with authority to carry out justice in response to each human's actions—an outcome which, in Buddhism, is believed to take place through the karmic restitution system, rather than at the hands of any deity or other being. In these words was vindication, perhaps, for one who had faced ridicule and accusations of wrongdoing on account of her conversion.

As for crucicentrism, my interlocutors certainly emphasized the value of Christ's death on the cross, to which they attributed salvation from the consequences of sin. The details of this salvation constitute an important example of hybridity, to be discussed in chapter 3. Continuing with the example of Ting Xiu, it was by no coincidence that she arranged her scriptural wall art in the shape of a cross. The cross, like the Bible, is associated with spiritual power and protection in Cambodian evangelicalism. One difference between the theological leaning of Cambodian evangelicals and those of some of the other Global South evangelical communities described by Brian Stanley is that for Cambodian evangelicals, belief in the significance of the cross in eliminating sin, rather than merely overcoming the power of evil spirits, retained tremendous relevance among my interlocutors. In the wake of the Cambodian genocide and the ways in which the Khmer Rouge coerced so many to participate in acts that have haunted them for decades, evangelical survivors of this atrocity have placed great emphasis on the cross as the point of access to forgiveness from sin and an escape from karma.

Activism, in the sense of being outwardly oriented with evangelism as a priority, is the focus of chapter 5. The Keswickian form of Christianity that the CMA missionaries brought to Cambodia in the 1920s, and which flourished there in the first half of the 1970s, centered on mission, which remains a priority for Cambodian evangelicals today. One point to highlight is that for Cambodian evangelicals in the United States, the goal of seeing transformation come to broader American society is shaped by the cultural trappings of the Religious Right, as well as by the refugee experience. Support for Donald Trump, motivated in part by his rhetoric in favor of Israel and against communism, superseded his actions against refugees. The improvement of American society, including through an increase in conversions to Christianity among non-Cambodian Americans, was a priority for my interlocutors in the United States, although the language barrier often limited direct evangelism—the sharing of one's own understanding of the Christian message. Instead, my Cambodian American interlocutors engaged in activism through prayer, which they believed would be effective in bringing about the transformation of their neighborhoods and the country as a whole.

Anthropologist Edwin Zehner, whose Thai evangelical interlocutors have much in common theologically with the Cambodian Christians I encountered both in Cambodia and in the diaspora, discusses his interlocutors' process of deciding which aspects of their preconversion cultural and religious practices they felt comfortable to incorporate into their practice of evangelical Christianity, which he depicts in a way largely compatible with Bebbington's understanding.[93] Zehner characterizes the particular principal values of Thai evangelicalism as being centered on agreement concerning concepts such as God's eternal nature, creationism, the Trinity, the divine-human nature of Jesus Christ, the idea of Jesus having died for the sins of humanity, the effectiveness of faith in Christ for entry into heaven, and the reality of Satan and his opposition to God.[94] The same held true for my interlocutors, although, as with the Thai evangelicals with whom Zehner worked, there were sometimes competing understandings within individual congregations regarding how best to interpret these concepts. More discussion of the types of theological reflection and debate that emerged surrounding orthodoxy and orthopraxy in the Cambodian evangelical context appears in chapters 3 and 4.

Overview of Field Sites

In order to honor the privacy of the past and present members of the churches featured in my study, I have used pseudonyms not only for the individual members but also for the churches they attended. I also refrain from identifying any specific churches by their respective denominational affiliations, as this information could make it easier for the pastors' and parishioners' identities to be discovered. In the diaspora, each of the churches I visited bore a name indicating its geographical location (i.e., city or neighborhood) and denomination. The denominations to which these churches belonged all originated in the West: the Christian and Missionary Alliance (CMA), the Church of the Nazarene, the Religious Society of Friends (Quaker), the Seventh Day Adventist Church, the Southern Baptist Convention, and the United Methodist Church. Not every denomination above had a presence in each diaspora city, and in certain cities, some denominations were represented by more than one congregation. Frequently, the word "Cambodian" appeared in the names of the respective diaspora churches I visited, unless the church formed part of a larger, multiethnic congregation. In one unique instance, a church in the United

States with a majority Cambodian membership, and with a Cambodian pastor at its helm, did not explicitly identify itself as a Cambodian church in its title but reflected only the name of the neighborhood, which was ethnically and racially mixed.

Despite the points of significant distinction between the various communities who welcomed me during my field research, I noticed certain important commonalities, as well. One element of religious life I encountered in all four of my major field sites was the presence of the CMA hymnal, actually a combination of an older hymn book and a newer one, both in CMA churches as well as congregations associated with other denominations or groups. The first segment of the combined hymnal contained *Tomnuk Domkerng* (translated literally, "Lyrics to Glorify")—the earlier hymnal consisting of Western songs translated into Khmer—and the second segment, *Tomnuk Khmer Borisot* (translated literally, "Khmer Holy Lyrics")—the newer hymnal consisting of indigenous Khmer songs. Sarin Sam, a Cambodian evangelical pastor and songwriter, began to compile *Tomnuk Khmer Borisot* in 1983, while living in the Khao-I-Dang refugee camp in Thailand. Barnabas Mam collaborated with him on this project, sending numerous "Cambodian folk and traditional hymns."[95] Alice Compain, a British missionary working with the Thai branch of OMF International, served as the coordinator of the Khmer hymnal project, which was published by the CMA in 1985 as a companion to *Tomnuk Domkerng*.[96]

Many of the differences between the congregations I visited fell along denominational lines. For example, I met female pastors within denominations and networks that affirmed women's leadership in the church, but other churches prohibited women from preaching or receiving ordination. With respect to the organization of individual services, some churches followed the same liturgical formula every week, and others were more fluid. At one of the more liturgically flexible churches I visited in Long Beach, one woman's testimony lasted longer than expected, such that there remained only five minutes at the end of the service for the pastor to deliver the sermon. Some churches regularly shared in the Eucharist together, while one Quaker congregation, in keeping with the tradition of the Society of Friends, celebrated neither communion nor baptisms. For the diaspora churches that included communion in at least some of their services, it was almost always bread and grape juice—not wine—that constituted the elements, and at one church in Cambodia, communion consisted of a fried potato snack standing in for Christ's body and a ginseng energy drink, for his blood. Many Cambodian evangelicals, both in Cambodia and in the diaspora, consider alcohol consumption to be a sin, except in extenuating circumstances, such as the occasional glass of wine to ease the grief after losing a parent or to seek temporary relief from menstrual pain.

Another key difference had to do with the role of spiritual expressions known in more charismatic settings as the gifts of the Holy Spirit. In this book, I use the term "charismatic" to describe a theological orientation that believes that these "gifts" or "charismata" described in the New Testament may—or even must—be used in the present. In the West, I am aware that some Christians will casually categorize as "charismatic" all individuals or communities who believe in the overlap between the physical and the spiritual, but this broader conceptualization does not fit well with Cambodian cosmology, including in evangelical settings. While most, if not all, of my interlocutors demonstrated belief in some interaction between the physical and spiritual realms, some churches were more overtly supportive of what they considered a "charismatic" viewpoint, while others were less supportive, and some were outright against it. According to Larry, an interlocutor from Long Beach who eventually moved to Phnom Penh, the major hallmarks of a charismatic outlook are "instant healing" and speaking in "tongues." By his estimate, most of the Cambodian churches in Long Beach were not charismatic, although there were some exceptions. Pastor Samedy, a Phnom Penh pastor whom I originally met in Philadelphia, appeared to draw the line at the idea that God speaks to individuals who listen in silence for divine revelation. Lambert, a church leader in Paris, identified faith healing as a point of potential suspicion. He clarified that he had no qualms about the idea of supernatural healing in general—he believed that God had every right to respond to prayers for healing—but that it was the notion of an individual pastor's having a "gift of healing" that was worrisome. On the other end of the spectrum, Pastor Somlain and his colleagues in Cambodia looked to healing as a primary ministry tool, hoping that those experiencing the healing or watching it take place would learn about the power of the Christian God and consider converting to Christianity as a result.

In Phnom Penh, the churches with which I had the most contact belonged not to historical denominations but rather to newer networks or organizations that self-identified as nondenominational, even though these organizations functioned rather similarly to how denominations typically do. Two large, independent churches, each with attendance in the thousands, occupied the poles of church life in Cambodia's capital city. These congregations were renowned within the diaspora church, as well. Cambodian

Christians all over the world could watch their sermons and musical worship sessions online. Interestingly enough, their actual names were so similar as to be frequently confused, although the congregations themselves could not have been more different, apart from their considerable size and influence. The first, with a formal atmosphere appealing to an older generation of churchgoers, was founded by a local pastor who had once led the Cambodian branch of an American parachurch organization. Multiple choirs in uniforms color-coded according to age group and gender took turns leading carefully rehearsed hymn selections. The elderly pastor, dressed in a suit and tie, commanded the respect of the congregation as he solemnly delivered his sermons. At the second megachurch, youthful Khmer ministers, led by the church's White American founder, wore colorful dress shirts without coats, paired sometimes with blue jeans, exuding casual confidence and dynamism. Flashing lights and dancing musicians contributed to the energetic, even playful worship environment, redolent of a Christian rock concert. The term "charismatic" captures with equal accuracy the vibrant worship style and the theological underpinning of this church, at which glossolalia, that is, speaking in tongues, is not only an option but an expectation.

These two large churches, though the most visible among congregations in Cambodia, represent rare exceptions. For this project, I spent most of my time with three smaller congregations in different locations throughout the capital. The first of these congregations, Descending Dove Church, was a Cambodian evangelical community with approximately forty attendees per week. It formed part of a larger church comprising multiple congregations, founded by Filipino missionaries who had trained Descending Dove's current leadership. This multicongregational church was itself part of an international network of churches. The other two congregations, Knowledge of Christ Church and Life in the Spirit Church, each drew about twenty attendees per week. Although the services at each church took place in Khmer and were operated by Cambodian leadership on the ground, foreign financial and theological impact could be identified if one traced back far enough along the chain of influence. For example, several of the pastors I met in Cambodia had been trained at the same Bible school, which employed both Khmer and foreign faculty and staff. Each congregation belonged to an overarching, nondenominational organization in Australia, the Philippines, or the United States, and their leaders maintained close contact with their missionary mentors.

In addition to diversity in approaches to spirituality, there were several other key differences between the instantiations of Cambodian evangelical culture that I encountered in my various field sites. For instance, nearly everyone of Cambodian heritage I met in the United States had been either a refugee or the child of a refugee who had escaped Cambodia during or after the genocide. In France, by contrast, there was a significant population of individuals who arrived as students or interns before the Cambodian Civil War (1970-75) and who enjoyed a certain amount of socioeconomic comfort. In Cambodia, some of my interlocutors had been refugees who returned to their homeland, and others had remained in the country during the genocide or were born after it had passed.

According to G. D. M. Wijers, a former researcher at the University of Wageningen who carried out an ethnographic study among Cambodians in France, approximately 40,000 Cambodian refugees legally received asylum in France at the time of the fall of Phnom Penh in 1975. Some of these were Cambodians who had managed to escape before the Khmer Rouge had meted out the brunt of their atrocities, and others had been students and interns living in France on a temporary basis.[97] Sucheng Chan, professor emeritus at the University of California, Berkeley, writes that only 5 percent of the 158,000 refugees who eventually resettled in the US had arrived by 1975.[98] Even in France, it is important to acknowledge that the majority of refugees arrived in 1978 and after. Wijers writes that although the earliest Cambodian refugees in France—those who left Cambodia before the fall of Phnom Penh, and those who had already been studying or interning in France—represent the "most prominent" among refugees in Paris, the majority arrived later. Beginning in 1978 and continuing until the Khmer Rouge's defeat in 1979, France received approximately "a thousand Cambodian refugees per month."[99]

In the diaspora, the Cambodian churches served as communities dedicated not only to worship but also to cultural preservation. My interlocutors in Philadelphia and Long Beach often dressed in traditional Cambodian attire, and their music almost always came from the combined Khmer hymnal. Men were more likely than women to come to church in Western clothing, but sometimes, men could be seen wearing shiny, silk shirts in the Cambodian style. Women, more often than not, wore [sampʊət], that is, wrap-around skirts, with matching blouses. On special occasions, women frequently donned brightly colored [kbən]—similar to the Indian *dhoti*—arranged by wrapping, rolling, and tying a single piece of cloth such that it functions as a pair of trousers, with the hem falling between the knee and the ankle. After the service, the congregation often, if not always, joined together for an extended time of fellowship over a meal, or perhaps over dessert. Noodle soup known as [kuy tiev], similar to Vietnamese *pho*, was a crowd favorite in the United States, while *bo bun*, the French adaptation of *bún bò* noodle salad, also Vietnamese, was popular in Paris. My interlocutors in the diaspora likewise enjoyed sharing various Khmer curries and Southeast Asian fruits, such as rambutan, durian, and jackfruit, after a church service or Bible study. Rice cakes called [ʔansɑɑm], wrapped in banana leaves and filled with banana, jackfruit, or pork, frequently made appearances as postservice fare, as well.

At one church in Long Beach, a series of three large curtains adorned the wall behind the stage, with two royal blue curtains on either side of a red one. Viewed together, the three curtains evoked the Cambodian flag, rotated ninety degrees, and strikingly, without the image of Angkor Wat. Displaying the national flag in a place of prominence but without its crowning symbol enabled the congregation to celebrate their shared heritage while avoiding any controversy that might arise regarding the presence of the image of a non-Christian place of worship in the sanctuary of a Christian church.

For some of my older interlocutors who did not speak much English or French, belonging to a Cambodian church allowed them to participate there in ways that would have been difficult at other local churches. Others had previously belonged to multiethnic churches but had yearned for the chance to commune regularly with fellow Cambodians. Many of my interlocutors in the diaspora considered this opportunity a precious and, particularly in France, perhaps a temporary one. Before I left Paris, Lambert sent me an email in which he asked rhetorically, "Especially for the Cambodian churches in France (or in other countries outside of Cambodia): In fifteen or twenty years, will the Cambodian churches still give messages in Cambodian languages? In my opinion, I do not believe so." The Cambodian American congregations often approached the cultural preservation aspect of church life with more hope. With several strong cultural organizations—some of which involved Cambodian Christians in high levels of leadership—thriving in Long Beach and Philadelphia and actively working to teach the Khmer language and culture to younger generations, there seemed to be more jubilance and less anxiety surrounding matters of heritage preservation within the congregations I visited in the United States. Such celebration of cultural difference has historically constituted a point of contention in French society for ideological reasons. For example, the French government does not collect census data pertaining to its citizens' respective racial or ethnic backgrounds in the interest of promoting equality and perhaps at the risk of downplaying the important differences in various ethnic communities' experiences.[100]

Even at the time of my fieldwork, all the Cambodian churches I visited in Paris were bilingual. One church alternated, week by week, with a service in Khmer one week and a service in French the next. At another church in Paris, every service entailed certain elements that were to take place in French, and others, in Khmer. For example, the congregation always sang some hymns in Khmer and other hymns—in addition to contemporary praise songs—in French. Whenever the appointed preacher on a given day delivered a sermon in French, an interpreter stood onstage alongside him or her and rendered it in Khmer, and vice versa. Yet another church arranged for certain individuals to read Bible passages in French and for others to read different passages in Khmer. Each Sunday, a liturgist read the Old Testament passage in either Khmer or French, after which another liturgist delivered the New Testament reading in the other language. At this third church, the pastor delivered a sermon in French, after which the young people, most of whom did not understand as much Khmer as did their elders, relocated downstairs to continue worshiping in French. Meanwhile, the older parishioners remained upstairs in the sanctuary and listened to a version of the same sermon in Khmer. Despite this weekly bifurcation built into the program, the older, Khmer-speaking and younger, French-speaking members of the church remained acutely aware that they formed one community. Before the delivery of the sermon in Khmer translation, the older and younger members of the church sang together, with each congregant singing in the language in which he or she felt most comfortable. The voices of those singing in different languages overlapped, such that it was not always easy to make out the words either group was articulating at any point in time. The goal in these moments was not performance or intelligibility; rather, the goal was connection with God and with one another despite linguistic differences.

Similarly, in the United States, several of the churches I visited involved both English and Khmer components to each Sunday morning gathering. In one case, a church community began every service together, with a mixture of Khmer and English songs. After the offering, the so-called "youth"—the "youth" included anyone under approximately thirty years of age—left the sanctuary to have a lesson in English, while the "adults" remained together to listen to the sermon, delivered in Khmer. Several other churches scheduled entirely different services for English speakers and Khmer speakers. At one Cambodian American church, I witnessed the pastor's wife encourage a group of small children, ages ten and under, to learn the lyrics to a Khmer song. She conceded that it would not be easy for them, since most of them spoke English much better than they spoke Khmer, but she emphasized that it was important for them to try.

In Phnom Penh itself, my interlocutors evidently made little effort to preserve a particular understanding of Cambodian culture through dress, food, or decor. The first Sunday service I attended in Phnom Penh in April 2019 was at Descending Dove. I was surprised to see four or five young musicians wearing T-shirts and jeans while singing onstage. A young man enthusiastically strummed an acoustic guitar, while a young woman provided accompaniment on the keyboard. The vocalists held their microphones in one hand while lifting the other in praise, sometimes swaying, sometimes bouncing up and down. Colorful lights flashed exuberantly in the background. The songs, all in the upbeat style of contemporary Christian rock, represented original Khmer compositions. A small team of young people sat in a booth at the back of the sanctuary, monitoring the audiovisual experience, such that the slides displaying the song lyrics and the preacher's sermon points appeared in a timely manner. The young pastor, Matt, who typically wore a dress shirt and slacks, with or without a blazer, preached every other week. On the weeks he did not preach, it was Chaya, a young woman sporting a long, colorful blouse cinched with a decorative belt, fashionably ripped jeans, and high heels, who delivered the sermons. After the service, individual parishioners often scheduled appointments with one another to eat out at local restaurants, but there was no food served at the church itself.

At Knowledge of Christ, I encountered a calmer but nevertheless vivacious worship atmosphere. The instrumentation used in musical worship bore some similarity to Descending Dove's, with a single guitar and keyboard, along with two additional vocalists. Singers occasionally leaned gently into the music. Sometimes, all the musicians were male; at other times, male and female worship leaders sang in unison. The congregation, though smaller than Descending Dove, participated heartily in the boisterous singing. Pastor Samedy typically preached in a short-sleeved, button-down shirt and jeans. His parishioners, both male and female, often wore T-shirts and jeans, as well. Whenever he was out of town, other men preached in his place. A brief conversation with Pastor Samedy's wife, Jorani, clarified that the congregation's official position, based on their understanding of the Bible, precluded women from occupying the role of pastor.

At Life in the Spirit, the congregation quietly and reverently sang hymns from the combined Khmer hymnal. The singing was all a cappella, with the exception of a small hand drum, known as a [skɔɔ day]. Pastor Nimith often preached in a polo shirt and slacks. He shared the pulpit with a young woman named Sokha, who preached occasionally and also took on the brunt of the pastoral care of the community, as the leader of the nonprofit with which the church was associated. Following the service at Life in the Spirit, parishioners passed around a plate of dragon fruit or the pieces of a pastry.

Of course, Cambodian culture is not static or monolithic, and individual Cambodian communities around the world, both in Cambodia and in its diaspora, have found myriad ways to celebrate their culture over the years. Former refugees living in the United States and France, as tiny minorities living in societies very different from the one they remembered before the war, have struggled to preserve their culture and pass it on to their children. This danger is not present in the same way in Cambodia, especially for the younger generation—which accounts for the overwhelming majority of the population—who have no memories of war and genocide. While aware of cultural influences from Europe, the United States, and East Asia currently shaping Cambodian culture, the churches had not gone out of their way to defend a particular image of cultural purity. The wearing of traditional Cambodian formalwear, along with the communal consumption of Cambodian food, even if influenced by Thai and Vietnamese cuisine, allowed my interlocutors in Philadelphia, Long Beach, and Paris the ability to construct an image of a Cambodian church more consciously Khmer in a cultural sense, according to the norms and styles of the prewar era, than the congregations I visited in Cambodia.

Even while distinguished from one another along the lines of denomination, geography, language, and theological inclinations, the churches I visited demonstrated a connectedness identifying them as members of a single community founded on hope. Each congregation, in one way or another, was the product of the hope maintained by refugees who chose to lead, maintain, and propagate Christian communities within and beyond the camps in which they found themselves. With this awareness shaping the self-understanding of each community, members sought to carry forward the mission of hope by sharing with their friends and families about the forgiveness and sense of purpose they found through their relationships with the Christian God; by creating greater opportunities for education in Cambodia and for Khmer cultural preservation in the diaspora; and by demonstrating through their lives that survivor's guilt need not be the end of the story. Transnational Cambodian expressions of evangelicalism, marked by emphases on divine intervention in this world and the hope of restoration in the world to come, all bore the imprint of the genocide survivors who established ministries among their fellow refugees and propagated their understanding of the gospel of hope wherever they went.

Chapter 2

CONVERSION

According to the World Christian Database (WCD), Christianity in Cambodia has continued to spread with extraordinary alacrity. With an estimated growth rate of 6.05 percent per year between 2000 and 2020, Christianity increased more quickly in Cambodia than in any other country in Southeast Asia. Judging by these estimates, the growth rate of Christianity in Cambodia was nearly four times that of Southeast Asia as a whole (1.67 percent).[1] Of course, one must consider these numbers carefully. Individual Christian communities—and even individual Christians—will harbor distinct, if overlapping, ideas of how to define a "Christian," and the question remains as to how Christians are to be counted for the sake of social scientific or demographic research. In addition to the basic definitional question, the phenomenon of multiple religious belonging also complicates the matter of how, if at all, Christians can be counted. Categories of self-identifying religious adherents are not always mutually exclusive, and many Cambodian Christians simultaneously identify as Buddhists while also engaging in indigenous religious rituals that they do not consider separate from their practice of Buddhism. Keeping in mind these nuances, among others, the compilers of the WCD categorize and count practitioners of various religions based on individual practitioners' respective self-identifications. It is important to acknowledge that among those whose beliefs and practices borrow from more than one religious tradition, some do not feel comfortable identifying publicly with one or the other. Even so, the statistics provided offer a helpful framework for interpreting claims of Christianity's recent growth in Cambodia.

This chapter engages some of the stories behind this pattern of Christian expansion, exploring the concept of multistep conversion, in which individuals or families might initially identify with Christianity for reasons regarding this-worldly concerns, such as the need for food or friendship, and only later begin to integrate the religion's doctrines on an intellectual level. Despite the initial benefits conversion made available for some of my interlocutors, identifying with Christianity also often came with notable difficulties, such as social ostracism or, in certain cases, even physical danger. Some of my interlocutors pointed to forgiveness—an element of Christianity not found in Buddhism as they practiced it—as that which made conversion worthwhile, the risks and sacrifices notwithstanding. At various points along the way, many of my interlocutors spoke of relating to God—or of God's relating to them, sometimes through what they considered to be miraculous intervention—as the reason behind their decision to continue identifying as Christian. My interlocutors' conversion stories—involving multiple steps and often contrapuntal in nature—indicate that they have found in evangelicalism hope through a new sense of identity and purpose rooted in the idea that God intervened to save them both physically and spiritually.

Conversion in Multiple Steps

I want to honor the stories my interlocutors have entrusted to me while also taking a closer look, analytically. These stories are faith testimonies that were, in nearly every case, recounted many years, sometimes decades, after the featured events. It is with hindsight that the majority of my interlocutors currently consider themselves to have committed to Christianity only after experiencing cognitive reorganization—that is, a deliberate adaptation of beliefs—but most of these individuals also had gone through a period of association with an evangelical community before the period in which they now consider themselves to have internalized or committed themselves to it.

In France, Lambert recounted his faith testimony in such a way as to highlight the precise moment at which conversion took place. Here is an excerpt from his story:

The years of the Khmer Rouge regime—1975 to 1979—these were three years and nine months where there were no factories, no offices, and no recreation. In this very somber time, there was also no money. The Khmer Rouge forced everyone toward the countryside and the Organization, [ʔaŋkɔɔ], transformed all Cambodia into a concentration camp, one open camp.

I was gravely ill at this time, and the group of youth where I was assigned to work was a mobile group. I was required to get married. I married my wife in 1978.

In January 1979, the Vietnamese soldiers entered Cambodia to drive out the Khmer Rouge. The country was liberated but found itself very helpless. My wife had a sister in Thailand, so we—my wife and I—left towards Thailand, where we entered a refugee camp opened by the UNHCR [United Nations High Commissioner for Refugees]. By that time, I had heard the gospel, but it did not interest me.

A Chinese teacher born and raised in Cambodia who was in the same group at the camp said that she believed in God, and that she did not participate in the ceremonies in which offerings were made as part of the cult of the ancestors. This lady attended a course offered by the missionaries of the camp, but she did not understand the Khmer language enough to respond to the questions. To help her, I read the Bible and responded to the homework questions for her.

In 1979, I was in Thailand. In 1980, I arrived in Mulhouse, France. In Mulhouse, I lived in a hostel where I began to grow accustomed to life in France. A group of Christian young people came to evangelize in the hostel. I could not speak French at that time, but my wife could, since she had gone to school with the Catholic sisters in Cambodia.

The young evangelists invited me to their church in Alsace. I went and was full of questions. For example, I asked myself, "Why do the French believe in God?" I saw that there were many different people in this church, and they had different jobs. There were laborers, technicians, and people who had other jobs. I wanted to know, "What is the gospel?" Finally, I realized that their lives correspond to what they say. This was something important for me. I saw that they were a bit different from other French people.

I felt very attached to the church, going by moped before earning enough money to be able to buy a car. All the same, I had important questions—for example, concerning God, I wanted to know, "Why did he have to become a human being and die on the cross?" This

> was for me the most essential question, but it remained a cause of mental block.
>
> Even with this confusion, I stayed at the church until 1986 before becoming a Christian. Even at the time, I knew that [although] I went to church on Sundays, nothing [about my life] had changed during the week.
>
> One day, I prayed in my room and expressed my confusion to God. I asked in prayer my question with regard to why the humanity of Jesus and his death on the cross were the means of saving the world. Later, I understood that it was at this moment that I was converted, because I understood the Word more and more.

In some cases, this process of developing an intellectual understanding of Christianity only after having made a commitment to the religion is more explicit than in others. For example, one young woman, Sokha, explained that becoming a Christian is "a journey," and that over the years, she had drawn "close[r] and closer" to God. She told me that she had "made [a] decision" to identify as a Christian at the age of twelve, after having taken a course hosted by a mission agency. Years later, Sokha and her family went through a period of difficulty. Out of frustration, she "stopped believing [in] God for a while, but . . . still went to church," a clear example of the phenomenon known as "belonging without believing," proffered in response to Grace Davie's concept of "believing without belonging," to which I return in the next chapter.[2] Sokha's exit from her period of unbelief came through what she understands to have been a supernatural experience in which God spoke to her through the very words she herself was speaking to someone else. While working at an organization that served the victims of human trafficking, Sokha spoke to a little girl and, in that moment, felt that the words she communicated to the girl were precisely what God intended for her (Sokha) to apply to her own life. Reflecting on this moment, Sokha said, "It changed my life." This experience, perhaps due to its specifically personal and internal nature, was influential in convincing Sokha that Christian life was about "relation[ship] with God," rather than about receiving desired benefits from God. Sokha declared, "Before, [I used to] pray, ask, and I want[ed] to get [things]. Later, we see God's grace."

Without providing the same level of detail, two other interlocutors, Sokhanya and Chanvatey, told me in separate conversations that they had converted in their youth but quickly qualified these claims, indicating that their belief had deepened later in life. Sokhanya recounted having been invited to church by a Christian friend when she was seven years old, in 1995. She was baptized not long thereafter but added that she understood more about her faith as she grew older. Chanvatey told me that his family had begun going to church while refugees in Thailand, in hope of availing themselves of "donations" at the church. It was only when he was nineteen, in 1999, that he began his process of cognitive reorganization.

Nearly half of the individuals who shared with me about their decision to convert to Christianity mentioned the desire for some type of upward mobility, be it the hope of going back to school, learning English, or resettling in a Western country. The absence of any talk of upward mobility from an interlocutor's testimony does not mean that the search for this mobility was not a part of his or her conversion process or that the person was uninterested in advancing socioeconomically. I did not ask any direct questions about upward mobility, and any mention of it was in the context of the interlocutor's conversion account, either in a formal interview or in an informal conversation.

Some of my interlocutors reported having initially begun frequenting church-related events for the sake of their children's entertainment or well-being. In one instance, a Long Beach interlocutor named Lina shared with me that she first began attending church on a regular basis because her children enjoyed riding in the van the local church sent around the city to pick up would-be churchgoers who lacked cars or driver's licenses. Lina recalled the driver, one of the church's pastors, cheerfully singing "The Wheels on the Bus," to her children's utter delight. Riding to church became a form of free entertainment for them at a time when resources were scarce. It was only later that Lina developed an intellectual affinity with Christianity.

Mary, another Long Beach woman, also had her children in mind when she first began associating with Christians.

> *From 1979 to 1980, I didn't have awareness of months or days during this time. I had no watch, either. I was in a military prison and then was transferred to an old prison turned camp in Buriram, Thailand, once the people at the military prison realized the people from Cambodia were "refugees," rather than "illegal" immigrants. Now, in Buriram camp, one White couple came from Denmark, saying they were Christian missionaries. The chief—the refugee who oversees all the refugees—knew me and came with the missionaries to ask me if I could translate for the missionaries. I said "yes," even though*

> *I didn't like Christianity and felt it was a Western religion. When I went to Thailand, I'd left my kids on the other side of the border. This was my reason for helping the missionaries. I started to translate for the missionaries, hoping they might help me find my children. Every morning, at six in the morning, the missionaries were in the camp already. The missionaries spoke English. I spoke English and French. The missionary explained the gospel to me, but I thought to myself, "I don't want to be changed to a Western religion." He told me all these good things about Jesus, but I associated them all with Western religion. I thought about the principle of karma. When the preacher said you could be forgiven all your sins, I thought, "That's good." I heard God say at one point, "Child, don't be afraid to take me in. You do good. With me, you do even more good." In the morning, I told the missionary, "I'm ready. I'm ready to receive Christ." I climbed up the water tank together with him to speak to the people. Many hundreds of people gathered below. You don't know your fate one day to the next, so you just come out and listen, whether you believe or not. Every day, I translated for the missionaries. There was a series of lessons to complete before I was finally baptized, in the pond at the camp.*

Like several of my interlocutors, Mary was not initially inclined to be open to Christianity as a concept, due to its associations with Western dominance and oppression. Nevertheless, she made herself available to assist Danish missionaries with the hope that they might be able to provide her with much-needed practical assistance in her quest to locate her children. Although Mary only actually made the decision to identify as a Christian after becoming more familiar with the religion's primary teachings, it is worth remembering that she had become involved as a key part of their ministry well before that time. She began conversing with the missionaries and aiding them in their evangelistic endeavors for the children's well-being before she herself felt any affinity for the message that she was empowering them to convey through her translation services.

Contrapuntal Conversion

Scholars have debated the nature and conditions of conversion for decades within the academic study of religion. Robin Horton's "intellectualist" model puts forth a concept of conversion that emphasizes belief, in that converts choose their new religion because their view of the world now aligns better with the tenets of this religion than with those of the religion they had practiced previously. Referencing the situation of Aladura Christians in Nigeria, Horton writes, "the Aladuras have thrashed out their beliefs, often after much painful heart-searching, in response to radical changes in their own local experience of the world; and having come through this ordeal, they are consciously and profoundly 'doing their own African thing.'"[3] The "radical changes" Horton mentions refer to the Yoruba people's encounter with Western modernity. From his perspective, practitioners of Yoruba religion—which he believes to involve a cosmology featuring both a supreme being and lesser spiritual intermediaries who involve themselves more directly in human affairs—were already on track to dismiss the intermediary class upon encountering Western modernity and the "wider world" they understood it to represent.[4] In other words, Christianity acted merely as a "catalyst" for accelerated change that was going to happen anyway.[5] Horton argues that as they found themselves outside the "microcosms" of which the lesser spirits were considered the overseers, they ascertained that the intermediaries were fading into the background, while the supreme being was becoming more directly involved in daily affairs.[6]

Robert Hefner, in contrast to Horton's model, asserts instead an understanding of conversion that favors affective factors over intellectual assent with its doctrines. Introducing his "reference group" model, Hefner asserts that conversion requires, above all else, a change in "self-identification" rather than "a deeply systematic reorganization of personal meanings."[7] Hefner suggests that those in the process of conversion sometimes "go on to rationalize their experience" in accordance with the tenets of the new religion, but at other times, they do not, such as in cases where specific doctrinal knowledge is reserved for religious leaders or other experts. Hefner, borrowing the Weberian concept of "rationalization" and "rationality," warns his readers to avoid confusing the official systematization found in doctrine (rationalization) with an individual's own reordering of knowledge acquisition and action (rationality). He does not deny the possibility that public religious doctrines and individual experience can overlap; his main concern, rather, is to ensure that readers refrain from making assumptions that this connection exists in every case.[8]

One important aspect of Hefner's model is that it acknowledges that self-described converts to Christianity often have reasons other than attraction to a belief system for making the decision to identify as a member of a new religion, and that some identify simultaneously with Christianity and with one or more other religions. For the sake of methodological efficiency, I apply Hefner's definition of conversion and refer in this book to all self-identifying converts to Christianity as "Christians." This approach, while practical, is not without its downsides. From an anthropological perspective, Chris Hann takes issue with what he sees as an "anything goes" concept of Christianity.[9] This rebuttal is worthy of consideration. Commenting on instances in which individuals or communities choose to identify as Christian for the sake of interpersonal relationships, Jehu Hanciles remarks that it is "unclear why the change is considered conversion if the motive is primarily to maintain social relationships."[10] Hanciles cites historian Ramsay MacMullen, saying, conversion is "that change of belief by which a person accepted the reality and supreme power of God and determined to obey him."[11] I agree that relying solely on self-identification is less than ideal for numerous reasons, including that an emic understanding of conversion to Christianity—that is, one deemed acceptable by members of the community in question—would certainly be more limited than the one Hefner proffers. One church leader in Cambodia attributed the following word of pastoral caution to one of her ministry colleagues: *Many people are sitting in this church, but not all are Christians.* Nevertheless, in the context of social scientific research, I find it simplest to refrain at this time from entering into the theological debate about who can or cannot be called a Christian.

Richard Fox Young argues for a middle way between Horton's intellectualist model of "cognitive reorganization" and Hefner's reference group model in which the conversion process starts with converts' identification with a new religious community. Young asserts that while Horton is probably wrong in suggesting that "intellectualization precedes commitment," Horton offers something of value in acknowledging that "the main agents of religious change are usually or always indigenous," and that the transformations that take place often happen within a given community's own cosmology.[12] Even so, Young recognizes that on some occasions, conversions can involve intentional, theological considerations, especially among peoples possessing strong scriptural traditions. He makes the case for a fluid, "loss and gain" model of conversion, in which the motivations of converts to Christianity change over time.[13] Advocating the rehabilitation of Arthur Darby Nock's concept of "adhesion" and locating it on a "continuum" with conversion, Young argues that the two need not be seen as being in opposition to one another.[14] This has certainly rung true in the conversion testimonies of my interlocutors, and evidence to that effect will be adduced later in this chapter. Young sees an ally in Joel Robbins, who underscores the multiple steps almost always involved in an individual's process of converting to Christianity. Robbins notes that the concept of conversion at the cognitive level often fails to accurately capture the essence of "the very early stages of conversion," especially given that, in his view, "Christianity is unlikely to appear as fully coherent on people's first encounter with it." Instead, Robbins suggests, and Young agrees, that the beginning phases of conversion to Christianity are often quite pragmatic, while intellectual understandings of Christianity tend to develop later in the process. This deeper level of theological understanding, while not often the initial reason for an individual's decision to begin identifying with the new religion, often constitutes the reason behind a convert's decision to continue doing so and to eventually seek more profound religious engagement.[15]

I appreciate the space Young and Robbins both make for converts to identify as Christian initially for one reason, and then, over time, for another. Many of my interlocutors' conversion stories highlight theological reasons for their decisions to identify as Christians, suggesting a concept of conversion reminiscent of Horton's theory. Upon closer examination, however, one can see that these theological reasons oftentimes developed later in the process of conversion, whereas the primary decision to affiliate with Christianity might have been something much more this-worldly, such as the desire to worship with one's family or to avoid the obligation to offer money, food, or other goods to spiritual intermediaries. At other times, converts have reported inexplicable phenomena they consider to be supernatural interventions. In all these stories, interlocutors have indicated multiple phases in their spiritual journeys.

In sharing about their individual conversion processes, thirteen of my interlocutors who referred to phases corresponding to cognitive reorganization or commitment presented them in Horton's order. In each of their conversion accounts, cognitive reorganization preceded commitment, with utilitarian interests, in turn, often having inspired commitment in the first place. There were four in whose stories commitment preceded cognitive reorganization. An additional fifteen gave a basic outline of how they chose to become Christians but did not specify whether cognitive reorganization or commitment came first. Utilitarian, intellectual, and relational phases can overlap and even function contrapuntally. Sometimes, converts might cycle through the various phases multiple times and in different orders. In one case, a relational phase could pave the way for a deeper intellectual understanding. For the very same person, utilitarian interests could emerge and affect relational understanding even after significant cognitive reorganization has taken place.

Reckoning with Conversion's Concomitant Risks

Many of my interlocutors who converted and chose to remain Christians exposed themselves to considerable loss or risk thereof. It is worth noting that Christianity has been legal in Cambodia since 1990 and therefore conversion to the religion is not accompanied by the same type of discrimination, persecution, or danger as in certain other areas of Asia, as discussed in chapter 1. Even so, given the large degree to which Khmer identity is intertwined with Buddhism, Cambodian Christians frequently report feeling ostracized by relatives and friends who consider their conversion tantamount to a betrayal of their family, heritage, and identity. Several interlocutors shared about being taunted, publicly humiliated, threatened with violence, or expelled from their homes as a result of their newfound identity. In one intense example, an elderly woman shared with me that when she had first converted to Christianity, her son had threatened her with a gun, saying that if she dared to pray to Jesus again, that he would shoot. She continued praying to Jesus, and her son, acknowledging that she had called his bluff, dumped the bullets onto the floor. This particular anecdote was an outlier among those I heard during my fieldwork, but the risk involved in identifying as a Christian can take many forms. Even for those with less extreme experiences, loneliness and loss often stow away as unwanted guests along the journey of conversion.

Sorpheny, a woman I met in Phnom Penh in the spring of 2019, converted to Christianity from Buddhism a few years earlier as a young adult. Her brothers were both Buddhist monks, and although Sorpheny did not consider herself Buddhist, she shared about visiting the pagoda on occasion to spend time with her brothers, and also to dance. Despite these moments of connection, the religious difference between Sorpheny and her brothers had taken its toll on the family. During a lunch conversation after a service at her church one day, her face tightened with pain as she recalled how "close" her family had been, and how her brothers were "not okay" with her decision to convert. An unspoken rule developed in the family, she explained, such that whenever they gathered together, they "don't talk about religion" in order to avoid conflict. When I asked her who had established this rule, she simply responded, "We know." I took this to mean that she and her siblings implicitly understood what was needed to maintain the fragile peace among them.

Lina from Long Beach told me that after her conversion, she continued accepting her friends' invitations to participate in Buddhist community activities, but that eventually, she came to a turning point where she felt that she needed to make the decision for herself. "[Either] I'm scared of God, or I'm scared of people," she said. At that point, she began turning down invitations to attend religious events with her Buddhist friends. I asked her if she was still friends with the Buddhist individuals whose invitations she had begun to decline. She responded in the affirmative but also admitted, perhaps somewhat wistfully, that these relationships were no longer as intimate as they once were. She immediately qualified this statement, however, assuring me with a smile, "I don't mind."

The social strain that accompanied Lina's conversion affected not only her friendships but also her family relationships. In keeping with her new spiritual convictions as a Christian, Lina abstained from participating in the funeral rites for her mother. As extreme as such a decision might seem, Lina was not alone in her fervency. Toy, a friend of Lina's who also went to church with her, shared with me that she had forgone the funerals of both her parents, as well as that of an older cousin. Reflecting on her decision, as well as her friend's, Lina explained, "In the Bible, we cannot bow down" before an image of a divinity but instead must "trust only in God."

Lina remembered people in the community criticizing her, saying, "Your mom pass[ed] away, and [you have] no respect." Carol Mortland has written about how some of her Cambodian Christian interlocutors in the United States "were drawn back to Buddhism out of loyalty to their family," as "some worried that their neglect of ritual obligations might have consequences for [their family] if the ancestor spirits became angry with them."[16] Concerns related to retribution from the spiritual realm were well attested in my fieldwork, as well. Despite the undeniable pressure from those around her, Lina remained resolute. "I don't do [things] the same way [anymore]," she explained; "I change[d] my heart very completely."

The Difference Christianity Makes

Notwithstanding the numerous cases in which Cambodians, both in Cambodia and in the diaspora, began participating in Christian community and then eventually chose to cut ties with Christianity and return to

Buddhism, stories like Lina's and Toy's are quite common. What is it that these Cambodian Christians find so appealing about their new religion? What is so attractive about Christianity that they are willing to risk reputation and relationship to identify with the new religion? In other words, what is the difference that Christianity makes?

One potential factor is intellectualization. Whether before or—perhaps more frequently—after commitment, the vast majority of my interlocutors attested to a heartfelt belief in what they understood to be the Christian message. A key doctrinal point that came up with relative frequency was forgiveness from sin. Previous ethnographic research on Cambodian Christianity in the diaspora, also of an evangelical variety, has pointed to forgiveness as a driving factor in Cambodians' decisions to convert to Christianity. Nancy J. Smith-Hefner attributes the decisions of her Cambodian Christian interlocutors in the Boston metropolitan area in large part to "the impossibility of attaining forgiveness within Buddhism."[17] Elaborating, she locates this desire for forgiveness within a broader "preference for orthodoxy among Khmer evangelicals," which she views as "related to their attitude on Khmer identity as a whole and to what they perceive as the limited possibilities for change within Khmer Buddhism."[18] She explains further that many Khmer identifying as evangelical Christians find themselves drawn to their new religion out of "the desire 'to be reborn like a newborn baby' *(kaut cie menuh boriksot/kaut cie menuh songkruh)*."[19] Smith-Hefner's interlocutors saw rebirth in the Christian context as distinct from—although perhaps, through the eyes of some of them, overlapping with—rebirth in the Buddhist context. Whereas in their understanding of Buddhist soteriology, rebirth involved one's inescapable restitution for one's negative actions, rebirth in Christianity, they believed, rendered available "salvation through the forgiveness of sin and the establishment of a personalized relationship with Jesus Christ."[20]

It is important to note that not all who decided to identify with Christianity for practical reasons decided to retain this identity. Chean Rithy Men, drawing on research with Khmer communities in Providence, Rhode Island, and Lowell, Massachusetts, rejects the notion that Cambodians intentionally decided on Christianity as a means of explanation preferable to karma when seeking to make sense of the atrocities they had endured as a community. Instead, he counters, the choice to adopt Christianity as both "a belief system and social network" could be traced to the lack of temples in the refugee camps, as well as in the United States during the early years of Khmer resettlement in the country. Men explains that as more temples opened in the United States—there were approximately fifty by the 1990s, as well as about 150 monks—the urge to attend Christian gatherings waned significantly. He writes, "Many Cambodian families I knew who went to church in the 1980s have now stopped attending church and have returned to the practice of Buddhism."[21] Certainly, some apparent conversions proved merely temporary, having been initiated out of a time-bounded sense of desperation. Although these families likely would have preferred to participate in Buddhist religious practice at a temple, opportunities for such activity were scarce. Some measure of religious community involvement felt better than none, and until such time as they could access a Buddhist temple, they decided that church would have to suffice.

Often, however, Smith-Hefner's assessment from 1990s metropolitan Boston remains relevant among Cambodian evangelicals today and fits well with the understandings of most, if not all, of my interlocutors. While not all Cambodians believe that forgiveness is impossible within the Buddhist framework,[22] Smith-Hefner is not alone in her findings. Khatharya Um explains that in Buddhism, "the ultimate power to cleanse lies beyond any individual's power."[23] Since the time of the genocide, Cambodian Buddhists who do not believe that forgiveness is attainable have sought resolution and emotional healing through other means. In Cambodia, there was an unofficial but nevertheless potent annual commemorative event, the name of which can be rendered, "'Day of Hate' or 'Day to remain tied in anger,'" on which Cambodians annually showcased their rage vis-à-vis the Khmer Rouge on May 20.[24] In 2001, the name of this holiday was changed to "Day of Remembrance,"[25] but annual reenactments of Khmer Rouge violence continue to take place in Cambodia on this day. Caroline Bennett, an anthropologist studying mass graves in Cambodia, addresses the elephant in the room when it comes to discussions about emotional healing in post-genocide Cambodia: the ongoing Khmer Rouge Tribunal, which is intended to bring about closure for the survivors of the genocide, many of whom continue to struggle in the wake of the traumatic events of the 1970s.[26] Bennett claims that the impact of the Khmer Rouge Tribunal on the lives of everyday people is minimal, and that Cambodians therefore use alternate means to make sense of the period and its events, drawing heavily on Buddhism and indigenous religions. She reports that some Cambodian Buddhists believe that certain individuals who died under the Khmer Rouge have been reborn in the present generation. One of Bennett's interlocutors asserted that his own children fall into this category.[27] In an analogous vein, Eve Monique Zucker has called attention to the Khmer cultural reclaiming of the spiritual realm, which the Khmer Rouge had attempted to eliminate through its destruction of statues, temples, and stones that represented the guardian spirits. Zucker highlights a recent instance in Anlong Veng, the Khmer Rouge's final stronghold,[28] where locals had reformed a statue of a female Khmer Rouge soldier, adorning it in the colors of monks' attire, and considering it a spiritual guardian of the mountain. Thus, survivors of the Cambodian genocide have drawn on spiritual thought and practice found in both Buddhism and indigenous religions to overcome the traumatic memories of the Khmer Rouge period.[29]

Within the transnational Cambodian community, Christianity has functioned in an analogous manner. A Long Beach pastor named Joshua related the following story during his "testimony," which he emphasized was to be separate from his "interview":

> *My family was Buddhist when I was growing up. I went to the temple with my parents and brothers since I was born. I went to high school in the city. I got a job as a policeman first, and then as a soldier. I fought against the communists. I volunteered to serve my country, as there were not enough soldiers to help my country. I told my mom, and she kindly blessed me to go and serve in the army. I had 120 soldiers under my command. I set the guards and talked to them, asking, "Why do we kill each other?" I was with the Republic side. They said, "If we do not kill them, they come to kill us." But I thought at that time, "This is sin. How many good things can you do to cover the bad?"*
>
> *Then, in 1975, the Khmer Rouge took over. At that time, I said that I was a businessman, rather than a soldier. I lied. Otherwise, they would have killed me right away. They made me a fisherman, to fish in the Tonle Sap, a lake far away.*
>
> *They separated men and women into different camps. I was single, but my Khmer Rouge boss wanted me to get married. The Khmer Rouge boss found me a woman in another camp. The Khmer Rouge board decided, however, that the woman could not get married.*
>
> *The woman in charge of the women's side of the Khmer Rouge wrote three names on the board. Each girl lived in a different camp. I said that only the last woman had a beautiful name.*
>
> *They sent two cows to bring a cart to pick up the woman. They came back the next day around 6 p.m. When the lady came, she went straight to the meeting. There, they had to interview her.*
>
> *She said "No," because she didn't have enough time to cope with the communist rule yet. After two to three hours, she still had the same*

> *answer, so they left her. Eventually, she went to the place where people were cooking food. The old man who had driven the cart begged her, "Please, lady," and followed her and bothered her a lot. She started to talk to the cook lady about me. The cook lady knew me and vouched for me. She said, "I know him. He is a good man. He follows the communist rules." She said yes, and the old man jumped to the ceiling! I was cleaning fish while the lady was there. I knew who she was, but she didn't know that I was the man she had been sent to marry. The next day, we got married. This was in 1977. We are still married today, with eight kids and eleven grandchildren.*
>
> *Later, we ran away from the communists and went to the Khao-I-Dang camp in Thailand. At Khao-I-Dang, we received bamboo to build our own shelter. I had one friend who walked around the whole camp. He came back and said, "I have good news! You always ask me how to forgive sin. I heard they said only Jesus Christ can forgive your sin." The next day, Sunday, my whole family went to church. I believed during that time. I prayed only one thing during that time: "Help me study your word, so I can teach my people about the true God."*

The turning point in Pastor Joshua's testimony came after his friend announced to him, "only Jesus Christ can forgive your sin." Prior to that, Pastor Joshua had felt overwhelmed at the thought of "how many good things" he would need to accomplish within the karmic restitution system in order to "cover the bad."

Family ties undeniably stood out among the factors contributing to the conversion of my interlocutors and their loved ones. Of those interlocutors who shared with me about their conversion experiences, nearly half mentioned having initially attended church with a family member or an eventual spouse. Sokhanya told me that she was the first in her family to become a Christian and that now, all seven of her living siblings had converted.

Pastor Bona, the pastor of an evangelical church in Philadelphia, shared with me about how it was through friendship with a Catholic priest that he had first become acquainted with Christianity. Years later, after his marriage to an evangelical Protestant woman, he decided to join an evangelical church. He explained:

> *When I was in the refugee camp in 1980, I was a military officer, but I quit. I knew between three and five Catholic priests, including one, Father Michael, who met with me once a week. At five o'clock every*

evening, all the volunteers had to leave the camp, but Father Michael used to take me out to eat at really nice restaurants. He used to tell me, "Whatever you want to eat."

Father Michael started teaching me English, and one of my friends asked me to request that the priest teach us the gospel, so that we could learn more English. Father Michael taught the book of John. One day, I went to Mass with him.

When Father Michael asked me if I had family in the US, I said yes. He explained that most people didn't know how to sponsor their family. Father Michael gave me a prepaid envelope so that I could contact my uncle in Texas. Within a month, I got a resettlement petition. The people from the US embassy in Thailand came to interview me, but they couldn't find me.

Father Michael arranged my resettlement through a friend of mine. I moved to the US and met my wife, who was a Christian already. I began to accept Jesus in 1992 and joined the church that same year, after the wedding.

I stayed in touch with Father Michael, who came to visit with me in Reading, Pennsylvania after my son was born. I told him, "Now, it's my turn!" I insisted on treating Father Michael after having received from him so often before. I still want to find the place in Reading where Father Michael is buried.

Some people are drawn to God by worldly reasons. I was one of them, but now, things are different. I used to be more worldly, but it's different, now that I know God.

Pastor Bona's story demonstrates an awareness of the multistep nature of his conversion process. His testimony hinges not on attraction to Christian theology, whether Catholic or Protestant, but to more this-worldly benefits. Initially, he sought out further information about Christianity because of an interest in gaining additional knowledge of English and all the opportunities accompanying such language acquisition. He found himself moved by Father Michael's hospitality and practical assistance in resettling in the United States. Although Pastor Bona did recall having studied the book of John with Father Michael, Pastor Bona did not mention being drawn to anything in particular about the gospel itself or the tenets associated with it at that juncture. Eventually, it was Pastor Bona's marriage that sparked his decision to begin identifying as Christian, and particularly as a member of his wife's denomination rather than Catholicism, despite his longer history of interaction with the Catholic community. With hindsight, he mused that his initial association with Christianity had been motivated by "worldly" reasons, but now, after having lived in Christian community for nearly thirty years, he became confident that he had reached a new stage in his spiritual journey, after having the opportunity to "know God."

Of those who did not mention family as a factor in their own conversion, several of my interlocutors identified themselves as having shared with their relatives about Christianity—or in one case, having arranged for someone else to do so—with the result that at least one other family member now identifies as Christian. Samedy, a Phnom Penh–based pastor I met in Philadelphia during one of his ministry visits to the United States, invited me to carry out participant observation at his church in Cambodia. When I asked Pastor Samedy how he had become a Christian, he responded:

> *I became a Christian in 1996 in Ratanakiri, where I am from. I met an American missionary there from New Tribes Mission after a friend had invited me to a Christmas event.[30] My friend wasn't a Christian at the time, either—he was just going for entertainment. I don't remember who preached, but the message was about Romans. I got to know the missionary from that day onward. It had been the first time I heard about the wages of sin. The wages of sin is—*

Pastor Samedy paused here, waiting for me to finish the sentence, which I recognized immediately as having come from Romans 6:23. "Death," I responded, as though I were one of his Sunday School students. "Death," he repeated, with apparent satisfaction. Pastor Samedy continued:

> *Hearing about this made me scared about death. So, I decided to become a Christian. Three months later, my mother found out and kicked me out. I am from an ethnic Chinese family very strong in Buddhism. The missionary from New Tribes Mission invited me to stay with him and travel with him for two years. In 1998, I went to Phnom Penh Bible School, where I met my wife. It was my first time seeing the city. While at Bible school, I wrote a letter to my missionary friend, asking him to visit my house there and share the gospel with my family. As a result, my two sisters became Christians, as did my mother. By now, all four of my sisters and brothers are Christians. My whole family believed! God's working is for His kingdom, not for us. I am not special.*

Pastor Samedy's insistence that he is "not special" stood out as a pushback against what he perceived as a tendency toward a fixation on an individual's relationship with God in certain forms of Christianity, including in Cambodia. While many of my interlocutors shared and emphasized stories of what they experienced as personal interactions with the divine, to which I now turn, it is important to remember that the divine-human relationships they cherished almost always translated into an outwardly focused, mission-minded orientation, as is explored further in chapter 5.

Divine Intervention

For some of my interlocutors, especially among those who did not report having any Christian family members who played a role at the time of their conversion, what they understand to have been holy visitations offered a sense of hope that accompanied their conversion experiences. For example, after church one Sunday during my fieldwork in Long Beach, a middle-aged woman named Anne launched, unprompted, into a testimony of theophany—in this case, of what she believes to have been a visible manifestation of the Christian God—in the context of a labor camp during the Cambodian genocide. She recalled:

> *In 1979, near the end of the genocide, more than thirty members of my family had died at the hands of the Khmer Rouge. I was eighteen years old at the time. I had prayed to the Buddha, begging for death, but after waiting for a time and finding my prayer unanswered, I prayed to "the god of the sky," whom "no one can kill." Not long after that, I saw a man in white. The Khmer Rouge had made us wear all black, so I asked him, "Uncle, aren't you afraid to wear white?" He did not seem concerned. I called to him again, "Uncle, where [do] you work?" He told me, "Over there." I asked him, "What's your job?" He said, "I'm making a big road." Then, he told me that the next day, a man dressed in black, with a red scarf, with one paper and one pencil would come to me between one and two in the afternoon. The man in black would ask me if my mother had gone to a new city. Before that, I had been told that my mother had gone to a new city, but the man in white told me that she had actually been killed. He said I needed to say that I had no mother. The next day, a man in black matching the description given by the man in white arrived between one and two.*

> *The man in black asked me if my mother had gone on to a new city, and I said that I had no mother. Later, the man in black interrogated the other young people in my work group, asking them the same question about their parents. Each of them responded that their parents had gone on to other cities. Out of all the members of my work group, only I survived. Why do I believe in God? Because God saved me!*

In the weeks and months following that conversation with Anne, other interactions I had with members of that church and others in the area suggested that Anne's experience was far from unusual. One man, a leader at a local Cambodian community organization, without knowing what Anne had told me, offered the following story as a template for how Cambodian Christians, in general, converted to Christianity: they would call on "the god of the sky" when they were "under oppression" (that is, in labor camps), and then "a guy would show up." Only upon their arrival in the refugee camps, when they encountered others who practiced Christianity, did they begin to interpret these experiences through a Christian lens. I should also mention, testimonies of this sort are not exclusive to the Cambodian community in California. When I spoke with a young Cambodian American friend who grew up over two thousand miles from Long Beach, she shared with me that someone at her church had a similar story. At least within the United States, memories of live encounters with God are far from rare among Christian survivors of the Cambodian genocide.

When I have read other scholarly work addressing perceived divine appearances, the intrigue often has centered on assessing the details or quality of a given appearance, even if not attempting to determine its veracity. The late philosopher Phillip Wiebe, for example, has taken great care to capture such details as the criteria the "percipients" in each case used in identifying the figure in question; the presence of any witnesses to the event; and any "observable effects" of the figure's presence, such as the mysterious disappearance of snow around the figure's feet in one outdoor, winter encounter or, in another, of the figure having been caught on camera.[31] Wiebe continues to explore various possible causes for these experiences, splitting them up into categories of supernaturalistic, mentalistic and psychological, and neurophysiological explanations.

I would like to shift the attention away from the possible causes, at least for the moment, not because they do not matter—they certainly matter to Anne and to the other survivors who have similar memories—but because trying to evaluate "what really happened" can distract from the significance of the memory for those telling their stories. It might be tempting for some to dismiss or explain away testimonies like Anne's, suspecting that survivors experienced trauma-induced hallucination or simply fabricated the stories in the interest of acquiring greater spiritual authority within their respective communities.

Moreover, Bruce Hindmarsh, in agreement with Paul Ricoeur's theory of a "second naïvety,"[32] notes that one's awareness of a conversion narrative having been "produced and received under concrete historical conditions ought ideally to help us gain a more rounded picture of the religion of the converts."[33] Similarly, Allan Anderson, when writing about Pentecostal experiences attributed to "an encounter with God," suggests that researchers ought merely to interpret "the experiences recounted by others as they are," rather than to call into question or attempt to explain the stories their interlocutors tell.[34] Although many of my interlocutors were not Pentecostal—that is, belonging to a charismatic denomination or movement that identified as such—most nevertheless believed that encountering spiritual forces was simply part of human existence.

During my fieldwork, the recurrence of testimonies like Anne's caught my attention, and I began to wonder what they might tell us about evangelicalism as lived by survivors of the Cambodian genocide. Cultural anthropologist Carol Mortland explains that "while Khmer have for centuries utilized karmic theory to explain unusual or threatening events," attributing anomalies in life to "error in specific human action," many survivors found that "the Democratic Kampuchea years were of such extraordinary horror that usual explanations for the extraordinary did not always suffice."[35] Some have traced their feelings of guilt to activities in which they became involved under duress. Youk Chhang, executive director of the Documentation Center of Cambodia in Phnom Penh, explained, "To survive during the Khmer Rouge, you had to steal, cheat, lie, point fingers at others, even kill. And now you are ashamed."[36] In many cases, however, survivors of the Cambodian genocide, like survivors of many other tragedies, find themselves riddled with "survivor's guilt,"[37] rooted solely in the fact that they are alive when many of their friends and family members are not.

For a Cambodian evangelical like Anne, identifying God as responsible for one's survival represents a liberation from the sense of guilt over having lived when so many died. The idea of God's having come in person to arrange for one's rescue has brought about a sense of purpose for certain Christian survivors of the genocide, through the assurance that their survival was neither by accident nor somehow by their own agency, but by God's orchestration. The question now might well be, "Why would God save me, and not the others?" but the key actor in this case is now understood to be God, rather than one's own self.

For many Cambodian evangelicals, the idea of relating to God has arisen as an apparent reason for remaining Christian, even when it would be more convenient to return to Buddhism. Ricoeur has written of "close relations" as those who "approve of my existence and whose existence I approve of." While the birth and death of an ordinary individual are often deemed of little importance to the rest of society, except for the purposes of record keeping and statistics, the close relations are those for whom such moments hold special significance. Ricoeur writes, "Some of them will deplore my death. But before that, some rejoiced at my birth and celebrated on that occasion the miracle of natality, and the bestowal of the name by which I will call myself my entire life." Close relations, according to Ricoeur, are the people who "occupy the middle-ground between the self and the 'they,'" who compose—both in the sense of creating, and in the sense of constituting—key aspects of an individual's sense of self.[38]

In calling attention to this trope, I am not attempting to identify an "essence" of Cambodian evangelicalism, but rather to emphasize one important way in which Christianity has made a difference in postgenocide Cambodian experience. Shortly after explaining how her relationships with her Buddhist friends had weakened in the time following her conversion to Christianity, Lina told me, "Before, I used to pray like once a day," but now, even in the "middle of the night . . . [I] connect to God all the time . . . I have God as my father, my friend." Interactions like those recounted by Lina and Mary evoke those that figure prominently in the research of psychologically trained anthropologist Tanya Luhrmann, who spent years with members of the Vineyard Church community in Chicago. In the introduction to her popular ethnography exploring American evangelicals' claims of not only talking to God in prayer but also of hearing God's voice in return, Luhrmann explains, "We know that God is experienced in the brain as a social relationship. (Put someone in the scanner and ask them about God, and the same region of the brain lights up as when you ask them about a friend.)"[39] Commenting on the intimate character of the lyrics in the worship songs frequently sung at the congregation at which she was carrying out her fieldwork, Luhrmann noted that her interlocutors understood God as "a person: lover, father, of course, but more remarkably, friend. Best friend."³⁰

Conversations with Cambodian evangelicals throughout my fieldwork were peppered with language indicating their perception of God as an intimate friend or relation. Another lens through which to view this phenomenon is that of attachment theory. Developmental psychologist Pehr Granqvist writes that religious conversion can bring about a sense of security in an individual who had formerly been insecure. In the language of attachment theory, it could be said that converts might view "God as a safe haven during the distress precipitating the conversion" and thus form "an attachment-like relationship in which God functions as a secure base for the convert."³¹ For those Cambodian evangelicals of the generation who lived through the genocide, experienced betrayal at the hands of those they previously had trusted, lost loved ones, and barely escaped with their own lives, God served as one who affirmed their existence and met their emotional needs, even if those who normally would fill that role were gone. They perceived God as the one who heals painful memories in which they might otherwise question or even deny their own reason for living. Memories of what they believe to have been God's visible intervention in their lives bring hope in the wake of tragedy and despair.

Even for Cambodian evangelicals who do not have stories of having encountered God live and in person, conversion to Christianity often has provided a means of hope in the face of incomprehensible tragedy through a sense of relinquishing to God their anxieties about the uncertainties of life. Vicheka, a children's minister, explained to me that she felt that conversion is most likely to happen "when you notice there's something that is missing in yourself—especially hope." Having identified as a Christian now for over thirty-five years, she currently points to "the hope that I have" as the assurance "that God knows everything." She elaborated, saying that there are "a lot of things that we have questions about, but [we] don't hold it too long. God knows it. Just let it go. I remember that God is a God of hope."

Telling her conversion story, Vicheka explained that it took many years and multiple encounters with Christianity before she decided to convert. Initially, a young Cambodian boy had approached her with an evangelistic flier when they were both living in a refugee camp in Thailand after the genocide.

> *I remember when I used to live in the refugee camp, one boy came to me with a gospel tract. I didn't even look at it. I just knew it was some*

> sort of tract. He was probably younger than me. I knew him because we used to live in the same town before the communists took over. At that point, I didn't ask anything. He just introduced me to Jesus. I said, "Oh! I already believe in Buddha." I was all upset and got mad at him, and that was the end of that. And I used to pass by when I lived in the refugee camp. I'd see people meeting, and they'd be singing praises, but I didn't notice what they were doing.

After her arrival in Austin, Texas, where Vicheka had resettled as a refugee before her arrival in Philadelphia, she struggled with feelings of isolation. The idea of Christianity, especially expressed through involvement in church community, suddenly appeared more attractive from this vantage point, and she began to rethink her interaction with the young boy in the camp. She continued her story, saying of her early days in Austin,

> At that time, I felt emptiness. I lost hope, and I looked up to others, like, "Oh, that person, they are able to do this; they have this; they have that." And I look at myself and think, "Oh, I don't know what I'm going to end up with." So that's when I drove down the street and then, passing by one of the churches, saw that it was at the end of the service. And people came outside. They greeted each other. They talked, and they smiled, and it seemed like, "Oh, looks like a good place! Maybe I will go one day." So, I did make myself go there. I didn't understand English—I didn't understand a word. And that first time I got to the church, they were having the Lord's Supper! I thought, "What are they doing?" So, I just saw what they were doing. It was a Lutheran church. But one day, I remembered that that boy told me about Jesus and something about church. Then, I said, "Well, I guess I feel kind of lonely, actually—maybe hopeless and nobody to go to—so it might be a good place to go." I just wanted to say, "Hi." So, I just went one day. One Sunday, I went. I just passed by and thought, "Everybody looks happy! Maybe that's what I need." So, I went there! I did take the Lord's Supper, but I didn't understand what they were doing. I just know that I sat there and tried to listen, but I didn't get a word of what they were saying. I don't remember that I understood anything at all at that time. But at least God had placed me there. He had a plan for me. He knows my needs, and after that I realized God knows my name, so, yeah, that's what it is.

The themes of initially rejecting Christianity and later embracing it; of being drawn to Christianity originally in hope of meeting this-worldly needs, including friendship; and of finding assurance through the concept and experience of relationship with God were recurring throughout my conversations with Cambodian Christians.

Taking into consideration the multistep conversion process Robbins and Young envision and viewing it through the relational lens which draws on Luhrmann offers a reading of conversion that reflects many of my interlocutors' lived experiences, whether they first decided to commit and only later experienced cognitive reorganization or, perhaps less commonly, vice versa. Ricoeur points out that individuals have no memory of their own birth or death, but that it is their close relations who take note of such moments. In cultures in which names and dates of birth are important for participation in society, it is typically the close relations who communicate this information to a child, which form key components of the child's identity. In the perspectives of many of my interlocutors, God functioned as a close relation of this kind in that they viewed God as working behind the scenes to bring about orderly outcomes, even at times when they were unaware of such initiatives and did not understand what to make of their own circumstances. Pastor Samedy told me during an interview that

> *God prepares the ground, prepares the soil. He is in control of all things, even in the hard times. He's working. He tries to take us into relationship with him. He wants to take us into him. The people say that he isn't working, but he is working.*

One could say that many of my interlocutors viewed God as one who "rejoiced at [their] birth"—in the sense of their being "born again"[42]—because they believed that God sought to "take [them] into relationship with him" when they could not see that God was "in control" and "working." They viewed God also as the one who "deplore[d their] death"[43]—or the prospect of it—to the extent that God personally intervened and actively prevented them from dying at the hands of the Khmer Rouge. For many, a sense of hope could be found in the idea, expressed so clearly by Vicheka, that "God knows my name." Feeling known by God also often inspired an orientation toward mission, as a way of partnering with God in God's work in the world.

As we have seen in the faith testimonies above, a Cambodian evangelical way of life involves navigating interactions with a variety of spiritual beings, both visible and invisible. Some of these beings are believed to inhabit or act through human beings, and others, to operate independently. The next chapter explores Cambodian evangelicals' concepts about the spectrum of spiritual beings they believe impact their lives and communities, and the ways in which the felt presence of these beings represents rupture, continuity, or both as it pertains to preconversion belief and practice.

Chapter 3

COSMOLOGY

An awareness of which spirits could be associated with which actions and how these spirits tended to interact with human beings affected my interlocutors' understandings of how they were to carry out their mission in the world. This chapter, with its focus on cosmology, attempts to map out the religious world of Cambodian evangelicals—that is, to demonstrate how they typically delineate the dynamics of spiritual existence and, most especially, to explore the roster of spiritual beings that believers understand to inhabit the world alongside humans. Although God the Father and Jesus Christ were the figures most often mentioned in my interlocutors' stories concerning interactions with spiritual beings, it was not uncommon to hear of encounters with the Holy Spirit and other spirits clearly viewed as benevolent, such as angels; with spirits considered unquestionably malevolent, such as Satan or demons, sometimes identified by specific titles in Khmer; as well as with spirits whose identities and motivations appeared less clear to my interlocutors. Cambodian evangelical cosmology, which combines the overlapping influences of Protestant Christianity in the vein of the Keswick Movement, Theravada and Mahayana forms of Buddhism, early forms of Hinduism, and Khmer and Chinese indigenous religious traditions, exemplifies the ways in which Cambodian evangelicals have sought hope for themselves, and for their friends and families, in the prospect of freedom from karmic repercussions, protection from malevolent spirits, and comfort in interactions with the Christian God and other benevolent spirits.

Khmer Religious Cosmology

It is nearly impossible to talk about Cambodian evangelicalism without knowing at least a little about the multilayered cosmological system of Cambodian Buddhism. The Buddha himself, within the orthodox Theravada belief system, is not considered to be responsive to prayers or available to intervene in human affairs. For the most part, it is to a selection of Brahmanic deities and a variety of spirits that Cambodian Buddhists address their prayers for intervention in their daily lives. One broad category of spirits, the [neak taa], constitute a web of protector spirits who play a key role in popular religion despite their lack of connection to Theravada Buddhism, at least through the lens of doctrine.[1] One cannot comprehensively map out every type of [neak taa] given that new ones have been known to arise within Khmer cosmology, and those already known have been said to relocate and become associated with new geographical areas. Even so, the late Buddhism scholar Ian Harris divides the [neak taa] into three categories: nature spirits, ancestor spirits, and spirits whose identities draw on those of Brahmanical divinities and a variety of folk heroes.[2] According to Harris, the five Brahmanical gods traditionally linked to the rituals involving *bakus* (Hindu priests) at the Royal Palace in Cambodia's capital have been listed in a variety of ways, but the roster "always includes Īsūr (Śiva), Nārāy (Visnu), and Umā/Candī." Interestingly enough, neither Indra nor Brahma ever appears on this list. In Cambodia, these two Hindu deities are typically categorized as Buddhist gods because neither one had been considered particularly prominent within Cambodian cosmology prior to the arrival of Buddhism in the area.[3]

Indra, typically revered among Cambodian Buddhists as the god of the sky,[4] appeared to receive several mentions during my fieldwork, although never by name. For example, Anne, whose testimony of theophany appears in chapter 2, mentioned near the beginning of her account that after calling on the Buddha, she then cried out to "the god of the sky." I found it particularly interesting that "the man in white," whom she identifies with the Christian God, claimed in this story that his "job" was "building a big road." According to the Cambodian myth "The Foundation of Angkor Wat," the god Indra had "built roads" in a "previous life" in which his name was Māghamānab.[5] One wonders if Anne might have imagined the "man in white" as having dropped this subtle hint to indicate that he was indeed answering her direct call, intended originally for Indra.

Brahma, the other main Indic deity regarded as a Buddhist god in Cambodia, might have received mention in my fieldwork, as well—although, like Indra, never by name. As in Anne's story, in which she felt that the Christian God had appeared as the man in white after she had called out to Indra, the god of the sky, another Long Beach woman, a pastor named Sarah, had an analogous experience in which Brahma could well have been the god with whom she intended to communicate. Here is an excerpt from Pastor Sarah's faith testimony:

> In 1977, I was pregnant with a baby boy. I remembered that when I was a little girl, my mother had taught me about the Big God, who created the world. I called out to the Big God, and I told the Big God that I was in a jail, that this jail had no walls. I said I wanted to live long enough to see what my baby would look like, and whether it would be a boy or a girl.
>
> At Site II, a refugee camp in Thailand, I was invited to attend a camp church, where I heard people talking about the "good news." I asked them, "What's that?" They said to me, "Do you know who created the world? God has a son, Jesus Christ, who died on the cross, rose from the dead, washed our sins with his blood"—and I was confused. "God forgives us of sins?" I thought. This confused me.
>
> Every day, I always prayed. I said, "God who created the world, I want to see you." Then, in front of the big moon, I saw him. He called me and said, "Here I am, Daughter." He had a big stick and long hair. He was wearing white clothing. I tried to wake my husband, but when I looked again, the one I saw was gone. From that time, I believed. I always prayed from that point onward, "Please bring me out of this camp. I want to be resettled in a third country."

Pastor Sarah recalled having learned from her mother who, she informed me, was not a Christian, that "the Big God" was the one who had "created the world." Although cosmogonic myths tend to be de-emphasized in Cambodian Buddhism, it is likely that Brahma is the god Pastor Sarah's mother had in mind. In canonical Theravada Buddhism, there is no creation story, as the Buddha did not believe the universe had a beginning. Departing from Hinduism, in which Brahma is credited with having created the world, Buddhist teaching asserts that deities, like humans, are caught within the cycle of death and rebirth, and that it is natural laws, and not any particular being or beings, that are responsible for the world's existence. Buddhaghosa, one of Theravada's most influential philosophers, explicitly rejects the idea of Brahma or any other creator. Nevertheless, Brahma remains essential within Cambodian Buddhist cosmology.[6]

Interestingly, both Anne and Pastor Sarah found hope upon seeing figures dressed in white, likely after having prayed to gods of Hindu origin. When anthropologists studying Cambodian Christianity have come across testimonies in which an individual recounts having encountered the inexplicable presence of mysterious figures—often, although not always, wearing white—the mysterious figures sometimes have been identified as "angels." For example, Janet McLellan, working with Cambodian refugees in the Canadian province of Ontario, recalls the testimony of one of her interlocutors, a pastor living in the city of Hamilton. His story features a semiotically illustrative segment in which his wife had been struck with a "severe sickness." In the story, the man had prayed for his wife, and afterward, "She said to [him], 'I saw a boat filled with people dressed in white, with a fire in the middle of the boat.'" In his interpretation of his wife's vision, the pastor identified "the people in white" with "the angels of God," and the "fire," with "the Holy Spirit," whom the man credited with having healed his wife.[7]

Given this trend, some readers might be confused as to whether Anne believed she had seen the Christian God, an angel, or some other supernatural being. It seems that the distinction between deity and angel is not always as critical in Cambodian religious cosmology as it is in much of Western cosmology. As Nancy J. Smith-Hefner points out, "Among the spirits figuring in Khmer descriptions of heaven, for example, are gods of Hindu origin, who are alternately referred to as 'angels' (tévoda), such as *Preah An* (Indra in Hinduism) and *Preah Prŭm* (Brahma in Hinduism)."[8] Classified in the Cambodian Buddhist pantheon as [teevea?daa], a word of Sanskrit origin, Indra and Brahma could be described either as gods or as angels.

This kind of ambiguity, while perhaps surprising to some readers, ought not to come across as completely unfamiliar to those acquainted with the Hebrew Bible—although it is of course important to acknowledge the lack of a one-to-one correspondence with the Cambodian setting, given the differences between ancient Hebrew religion and modern Cambodian Theravada, influenced by Brahmanism and by Khmer and Chinese indigenous religions. In Genesis 16, Hagar interacts with one referred to as "the angel of the Lord" in verses 7, 9, 10, and 11; in verse 13, however, it is said that Hagar "named the Lord who spoke to her, 'You are El-roi'; for she said,

'Have I really seen God and remained alive after seeing him?'" Similarly, in Judges 13, after "Manoah realized that it was the angel of the Lord" with whom he and his wife had been speaking, Manoah laments to his wife, "We shall surely die, for we have seen God" (vv. 21, 22). While the earliest Christian teachings did not condone of "the worship of angels" (Colossians 2:18) and acknowledged that even an "angel from heaven" should be "cursed" if it were to preach a false gospel (Galatians 1:8), the fact that Christian religious heritage includes a misty boundary between "the angel of the Lord" and "the Lord" (YHWH) in moments of supernatural revelation to humans could be seen as an indication that the insistence on attempting to identify an absolute distinction between the divine and the angelic in such circumstances represents more of a Western cultural fixation than a biblical one per se.

Some scholars who have written about Theravada Buddhism have noted that practitioners within what is known as the "great tradition"—typically monks and others educated in the Buddhist scriptures—tend to be more committed to Theravada doctrine as laid out in the Pali Canon, while those within the "little tradition" tend to incorporate a significant portion of beliefs and practices from indigenous religions into their expression of Buddhism.[9] Gananath Obeyesekere, drawing from his expertise on the Sinhalese Buddhist tradition of present-day Sri Lanka, refers to "the Buddhist monk [as] the representative of the great tradition."[10] This pattern is evident in Cambodia too, although, naturally, there are exceptions to the general application of the categories "great tradition" and "little tradition." For example, spirit houses, constituting one nearly ubiquitous vestige of pre-Indic religion in Cambodia, can be found on the grounds of Buddhist temples.[11] Many Cambodian spirit priests, known as [kruu]—a word literally meaning, "teacher," from the Sanskrit and Pali term *guru*—have previously been Buddhist monks, and "others claim to have learned their healing techniques from Buddhist ascetics."[12] One spirit priest specialized in "invoking the previous incarnations of the Buddha."[13] Furthermore, the spirit priest's "ritual space has a cosmological significance" which involves an intermixing of indigenous religiosity and Buddhism. Harris describes the indigenous healing ritual, in which the spirit priest's "patient kneels on a wooden board balanced on a central bell representing Mount Meru, the central world mountain" in Buddhist cosmology.[14]

The layering of religious traditions within Cambodian Buddhism reveals itself to be more complex than a situation in which Buddhist practice builds upon Brahmanist practice, which in turn builds upon Khmer indigenous religious practice. Indeed, although "some of these tutelary spirits probably predate the arrival of Indic influences, . . . it is also clear that Brahmanical deities have themselves sometimes been assimilated into the folk level,"[15] as evidenced by the presence of such [neak taa] as "Ganeś, better known as Siddhi-Suost," and "Me Sa, the white mother of Ba Phnom."[16] Anthropologist Jean M. Langford notes that there exists a social pressure in certain cases for Cambodians to reject the [neak taa] as a "superstition,"[17] while Penny Edwards calls attention to the fact "that oaths in Cambodian courts are still sworn not in the presence of either Buddha or the state, but in the presence of neak ta."[18]

In addition to [neak taa], Cambodian Buddhist cosmology includes an entire spectrum of other spirits, particularly in rural areas.[19] Ancestral spirits, even if not associated with particular ancestors, are believed to provide protection for individual families and therefore constitute one important category.[20] There is also a category of "exclusively female and highly dangerous spirits of virgins or of women who have died in childbirth," known as [priey]. Many Cambodians believe that these spirits, though "malevolent by nature, . . . may be domesticated" individually.[21] As for the spiritual makeup of the human body, Cambodian Buddhists typically conceive of each body as possessing nineteen [prɔliŋ]—that is, souls, or spirits—which are believed to wander away from their designated location inside the body on occasion. In such cases, a ritual known as [hav prɔliŋ], a "calling of the souls," can be held in order to invite their return or reintegration.[22] Harris notes that since nineteen is "a number difficult to harmonize with any of the customary categories of orthodox Theravada metaphysics," it is clear that the "Indianization of the Khmer self was never entirely completed."[23]

At least on occasion, certain spirits are said to occupy physical space. For example, the one hundred [priey] said to guard Wat Vihear Thom in Cambodia's Kratie Province, sometimes called "the pagoda of one hundred columns," are said always to travel with the chief monk whenever he leaves for a journey. For this reason, the chief monk "cannot travel by car but must ride in a truck."[24] My interlocutors' stories point to a similiar understanding. In a meeting with multiple evangelical leaders at Word Made Flesh Church in Cambodia, Pastor Somlain and his ministry partner Rith laughed jovially as they recalled an event in which a woman was said to be delivered from an evil spirit. According to their story, ten people surrounded her to pray for her. Toward the end of the period of prayerful intervention, the spirit believed to be possessing the woman reportedly cried out, "How can I leave if you all surround me?" Rith and Pastor Somlain explained that the people praying stepped aside so as to create a space through which the spirit might exit, and as the story goes, the spirit proceeded to do so.

Vicheka, whose story appears in chapter 2, described her understanding of spiritual beings, which combined Buddhist and Christian cosmologies. She told me:

> *At one point, I used to listen to people talk about ghosts. Older people loved to talk about ghosts! When I was still young, I liked to listen to them. And I sat really close to them when they talked about that. And I said, "Oh, oh!" One time, I remember, I wondered if it was real or not, but I was real young. But I feel like I saw. In Cambodia, we didn't have our own bedroom; we all slept on one flat, wooden bed. We slept next to each other. So then, at that time, I think I had covered myself with a blanket, and we shared the blanket. And then I felt that someone kept pulling my blanket. I kept pulling it back, but I didn't see anybody pulling it! The blanket kept pulling away from me. And that's when I remembered that they talked about ghosts. I thought that maybe the ghosts had come around, and I got so scared. I slept close to whoever I slept with that night! I don't know if someone else tried to move and pulled the blanket, but it didn't seem like that. But I don't know if that was real. But some people said you could see ghosts—white with long hair. I never saw them. Some people said they saw them under the trees. There are certain trees where the ghosts stay and live. So, when they pass by the trees, people start to run. But I think I know, if you believe in them, they will harm you. Because I know before I became a Christian, I used to be so scared whenever I was going somewhere, or when I was at home when nobody else was around. I used to think that a ghost would come around. But when you become a Christian, you say, "Oh, don't let them come near you." If you feel that you are kind of afraid, you can be thankful that God is with you all the time, so you can let go of all that.*

Vicheka's understanding of certain spirits, such as ghosts, was such that they were able to manipulate objects in physical space, like the blanket under which she was trying to sleep. Following her conversion to Christianity, she started to doubt at least some of the ways she used to believe the spirits of the dead could affect the physical world. When describing the practice of leaving food offerings for the ancestors during her growing up years, she explained:

> At home, we had a jar. After you burned incense, you said something. You talked to the spirits—like your great-grandparents who died—and you talked, saying things like, "Please help us," or, "Watch over us!" without knowing that they cannot do anything for you. We didn't know that! People still do it today. And that's how we did it. We didn't recognize where we had come from. We just knew that we came from our parents, so we showed respect to them. Even when they died, we still respected them. We were still hoping that they would be with us and help us. I don't know how, but we believed that. We used to put out the offerings, expecting that they would probably come up and eat them, but it never went empty. The food is still there. We didn't realize that. We just knew that we did what our father did. But people deeply believe in that. So, they call on the spirits of the dead, not knowing that nothing can be done. It's a way of respecting the family.

While Vicheka no longer believed that spirits of the ancestors possessed the ability to consume food offerings, she nevertheless retained her conviction that they had the power to "harm" those who believed in them. She indicated that Christians, too, could be at risk of harm brought about by ill-intentioned spirits, but that God's presence provided peace of mind for those who asked for God's protection.

Given the complex layering of religious traditions in Cambodia, evangelicals have wrestled for years with how to render the name of the God of the Bible in the Khmer language. Jean Clavaud explains that the word [preah], used to indicate an individual or object's superiority, sacredness, or divinity, likely comes from the Sankrit word *vara*, meaning "'noble,' 'elevated,' 'excellent.'" Clavaud explains that the word "God" comes from the root "*Dev* or *Dep*, found in Cambodian in the form *Tevoda*," and that within "the polytheistic context of Brahmanism obviously *Tevoda* should not be translated by God but by divinity."[25]

When addressing or referring to the Christian God, my interlocutors typically used the terms [preah ʔaŋ] or [preah ʔaŋ mcah]. The term [preah] can mean "sacred, divine, holy" and "often serv[es] as an honorific/elevated form, particularly before words pertaining to members of the royal family, priests, the Buddha, God, and certain deified elements: land, fire," or the sun. It can stand alone and refer to the Buddha, God, or other holy beings. On its own, the term [ʔaŋ] is a classifier used when speaking about members of the royal family, monks, and statues of a religious nature. It can also refer to the Shivalinga, an abstract image of the Hindu deity Siva.[26] The word [ʔaŋ] has a number of other meanings, including "body" or "virtue." The combined term [preah ʔaŋ] is used when addressing or referencing a person considered sacred. The longest form, [preah ʔaŋ mcah], is used when addressing royalty.

Identifying Malevolent Spirits

One Long Beach pastor, Pastor Joshua, told me the following story:

> *There was a boy, about seventeen, eighteen, years old, and a girl, and they loved each other. But in Cambodia, if you love each other but don't let the parents know, the spirit of the grandfather can come to get you. The girl in love with the boy lived in the same house as a baby who was sick. But no one knew about the girl and her interest in the boy, nor about the boy's interest in her. The man and the girl were supposed to get married or engaged, and also to offer something to the ancestors. Otherwise, the ancestors would get mad. It's like you try to sneak, to lie, to cover. The boy and girl talked to each other and tried to see, "Should we tell them?" They decided, "No, don't tell them." The baby girl died.*

Dramatically, Pastor Joshua declared at this point, "That [was] me," identifying himself as the young man in the story. Shortly after sharing this memory, he asserted confidently, "It wasn't the ancestors . . . it was Satan" who had taken the life of the baby girl who had lived in the home of his early love interest. Pastor Joshua was speaking English here, but when he referred to "the spirit of the grandfather," he had in mind a specific type of ancestral spirit, known as a [mee baa].[27]

Within traditional Cambodian cosmology, [mee baa] are to be kept abreast of every significant event in the lives of their descendants, who are expected to make offerings to them on major holidays. Although [mee baa] are typically considered innocuous, they have been thought to harm the relatives of individuals whom they consider to be guilty of wrongdoing, including child abuse or extramarital sexual relations.[28] When the relationship between the living and the [mee baa] has gone awry, retribution from the spiritual realm—for example, the onset of sickness—is not expected to directly impact the person who committed the offensive act, but rather a child or another member of the offender's family.[29] Pastor Joshua rejected this framework and identified the cause of the child's death not as retaliation by the [mee baa], but as an attack of Satan. It is not at all uncommon for Cambodian evangelicals to begin to identify as "Satan" those spirits they had previously categorized as spirits of the dead, especially when they feel that these spirits are demanding a kind of attention or deference that belongs only to God. "You cannot worship God and Satan at the same time," Pastor Joshua told me later in this same interview.

Along similar lines, Ponleu, a young Cambodian woman living in France, recounted the story of a friend of hers who had attended a church that met in a woman's home. Eventually, the church hostess died. Ponleu's friend told her that one day, the "soul" of the hostess came to her. The friend said to the apparition, "I know this soul does not come from my owner [that is, the owner of the house that doubled as a church]. It is from Satan." Ponleu's friend continued, rebuking the apparent "soul" of the church hostess, saying, "Satan, go away from me, in Jesus's name." According to Ponleu, her friend "called Jesus's name three times," and the "soul" left. Not yet a Christian at the time she had this conversation with her friend, Ponleu found herself impressed by the story and hoped someday to be able to pray in this same manner. It is possible that Ponleu's friend imagined that the figure that appeared in the likeness of the church hostess was inviting a kind of reverential act—as one who had been influential and benevolent during her life on earth—that she felt was due only to God. These stories notwithstanding, it would be inaccurate to say that Cambodian evangelicals automatically categorize every encounter with spirits other than the Christian God as an experience of Satan. Many of my interlocutors recognized a broad variety of categories of spiritual beings—some malevolent, some benevolent, and all submitted to the authority of the Christian God.

Sokha, part of whose story appears in chapter 2, told me that her mother had served the Cambodian Christian community in their area by responding to new converts' requests that she remove spirit altars from their homes. Sokha's mother made it part of her ministry to pick up old altars and other trappings of preconversion life from her friends' homes and then to destroy these items at her own house. Sokha explained that ever since her mother began destroying spirit shrines, her family started witnessing unwanted spiritual incursions at home. Sokha mused aloud, "I think the spirits are not happy with her," because on occasion, "we see ghosts. But we know that God who is in us is greater than that."

Sokha then launched into a story, impeded ever so slightly by her own lighthearted laughter. "This is funny," she put forth as preface. One night, when she and her siblings were attempting to sleep in their room, she "saw an elephant flying." Assuming it to be an evil spirit, she called out to rebuke it, "In the name of Jesus!" and, "In the blood of Jesus!" To her horror, the elephant remained in the room, apparently not at all perturbed by her invocations of the name of Jesus. Finally, her brother turned on the light, and the siblings suddenly realized, with great relief, that "the only spirit" they were unable to "chase out" was nothing but an elephant-shaped balloon. Sokha recalled that on every other occasion on which she and her family had found themselves interrupted by the unwelcome presence of ghostly apparitions, these figures responded to the name of Jesus by promptly vacating the premises. Based on her experience, Sokha believed that God had demonstrated loyalty to her family by defending them from the spirits that sought revenge for her mother's disruptions within the spiritual realm.

Spiritual Encounters in Dreams

The spiritual advice given by the Cambodian evangelical leaders I met during my fieldwork, including Pastor Joshua, often involved dreams. In one case, Pastor Joshua shared with me about incorporating dreams into his evangelistic strategy. In his own telling of it, he often recommends to older Cambodians who are in the process of discerning their own thoughts about God, "If you want to know which one is the true God, you ask him to show himself when you sleep. One lady, she called me and said, 'Pastor Joshua, I had a dream, and God told me, "I am the true God." And she believed! She still believes.'"

Pastor Joshua continued his story, telling me that this woman's daughter once dreamed that her (the daughter's) deceased father called out to her, saying, "I am hungry." After awakening, the daughter asked her mother if she should give her father some food, to which the mother responded, "It's not your daddy. It's Satan." In this case, it appears that the mother identified the figure in the dream as Satan due to an inference that the figure wanted to convince her daughter to return to a preconversion understanding of the relationship between the living and the ancestors—an understanding that seemed, to the mother, to jeopardize fidelity to God.

Some of my interlocutors spoke of similar situations while using other terminology. Samen, an elder-care worker in Philadelphia, never mentioned the name "Satan" in her conversations with me, but she did speak of having dreamed of "ghosts." To clarify, she spoke of "dream[ing] sometimes about my relatives" who had died. While these moments were distressing to her, she asserted, "[God] protects me," and "the bad angels cannot come and make me scared" anymore. Samen's pastor, Pastor Bona, also used the language of "good and bad spirits" or "bad angel[s]." Pastor Bona explained to me one afternoon, "The angel is used by God, and the bad angel is trying to get you away from God. God uses angels to keep us from the bad guy."

Carol Mortland recounts the story of an interlocutor she calls Bounthan, who recalls the pivotal role a single dream played in her decision to convert to Christianity. Mortland describes the dream as being "about a church," although the description of the dream involves not a church but a "lady with long white clothes," in Bounthan's words. Bounthan notes in her explanation of the dream, "I didn't know about church. I saw the lady with long white clothes. I asked her, 'Can I go across the river?' She talked to me, but I don't remember what she said. After that I woke up. I wanted to go to church, but I didn't know where to go.'"[30] Mortland adds that following the dream, Bounthan had shared the story with "a foreigner," who brought her to a church. From that moment onward, Mortland explains that her interlocutor "decided 'to believe in Jesus.'"[31]

When I asked Pastor Joshua if he knew of many people who had dreamed of God, he answered quickly that he did. Hoping to gauge an estimate, I asked him if he knew of more than five people who had had this experience. Apparently finding this to be an absurdly low number, Pastor Joshua waved his hand in the air and responded in the affirmative. When I asked him if the number were more than twenty people, he admitted that he was unsure, because he "did not count" the number of such testimonies he had come to hear. Regardless of the specific number of stories Pastor Joshua had heard about divine encounters in dreams, he envisioned dreams as a space particularly conducive to interaction between the occupants of the physical and spiritual realms. However, conversations occurring in the dream space were still subject to scrutiny.

Despite the conception of dreams as zones in which the spiritual and physical worlds overlapped with unusual clarity, supernatural interventions believed to have taken place outside the dream space nevertheless garnered even greater credibility. For example, after sharing with me about the prevalence of spiritually relevant dreams within his community, Pastor Joshua noted that his wife, Prachna, had had an experience in which a supernatural occurrence had taken place during her waking hours. According to Pastor

Joshua, Prachna had been tending to one of their children, who was sick with a fever, when Prachna "saw a light and a cloth." At this moment, the child's temperature dropped, and Prachna cried tears of joy and relief. When I asked Pastor Joshua what type of cloth his wife had seen, he responded that it was "a bright, silver robe." It was apparently of great importance to Pastor Joshua that this experience did not take place when Prachna was asleep. "She did not dream. She *saw*," he declared emphatically. For Pastor Joshua and others, the perceived reality of what they considered to be supernatural irruptions or visitations contributed to the events' significance.

To add nuance to this dialectic, I should note that despite the privileged position of spiritual encounters believed to have taken place within an individual's waking hours, versus within the dream space, events occurring within dreams typically sufficed to impact my interlocutors' personal understandings of the spiritual world. When I interviewed Raksmey, a former Cambodian refugee living in Philadelphia, I asked her, "Do you believe in the existence of spirits?" She paused a moment, apparently out of self-consciousness, and then softly admitted:

> *I do. Is that weird? There's evil out there. I heard that when you drink alcohol, spirits go in you. I've never had any experience with spirits, except maybe in dreams. I had a dream where the Holy Spirit touched me, shocked me, and lifted me. I was cradled by the Holy Spirit. It was awesome. I'm pretty sure it was a dream because I woke up.*

Although Raksmey remained fairly confident that her experience with the Holy Spirit took place while she was sleeping, she nevertheless brought up the dream as evidence to support her belief in the existence of spirits—even though she feared that such a belief could be interpreted as "weird."

Spiritual Encounters through Interpersonal Interactions

Sometimes, the encounters my interlocutors classified as spiritual did not involve spirits either disembodied or confined to the realm of dreams, but rather they involved spirits thought to be resident within or otherwise acting through living human beings. Over the course of his conversion testimony, Kham, a Chinese Cambodian former refugee living in Long Beach, recounted a series of interactions he and his family members had experienced with supernatural beings connected to people they knew personally. Near the beginning of his story, Kham shared about special powers possessed by his aunt's husband, a monk who had been forced by the Khmer Rouge to marry. According to Harris, "reports of monks, either individually or en masse, being coerced into taking partners are extraordinarily frequent, and the practice may have been more widespread than evidence suggests." Many of the monks who were reinstated during the People's Republic of Kampuchea period were reticent concerning "any diminution of celibacy during the Democratic Kampuchea period," as information of this kind would have jeopardized their "spiritual prestige and their future career prospects" within the community of monks, known by the Pali term *sangha* throughout the Buddhist world.[32]

The monk in question, Kham's uncle by marriage, was said to have been endowed with certain powers, including the ability to become invisible. As shocking as this claim might seem to those of us accustomed to Western cosmologies, the power of invisibility is not considered a strange concept within esoteric Buddhism, in which access to a variety of powers, known as *siddhi*, characterizes a successful "sorcerer." Among these powers, invisibility has been categorized as a *nidhi*, or "ability to find treasures in the earth."[33] Some scholars suggest that the Southeast Asian expression of Theravada Buddhism contains some esoteric elements, and Kham's story appears to support this perspective.[34] When I asked Kham if he himself had ever seen the monk become invisible, he indicated that he had not, but that he had heard the stories and knew that the monk was able somehow to travel frequently across the Cambodian-Thai border to acquire medicine for his stepdaughter, Kham's cousin, at a time when such a journey posed grave danger.

On one such cross-border trip in 1979, the monk paid a visit to Kham's family in the Thai refugee camp to which they had fled following the genocide. Kham told me, with tears in his eyes, that the monk had prophesied that the family would endure many troubles, but that they would not die. Shortly after this encounter with the monk, the Thai government expelled thousands of Khmer refugees to the Thai border and forced them to reenter Cambodia by walking down a mountain and making their way through mine-strewn territory. This event took place at the historic Preah Vihear temple, located near the border between Cambodia and Thailand. Thai soldiers forced more than 45,000 refugees back into Cambodia in June 1979, "apparently . . . in reaction to what it perceived as a lack of response on the part of the international community to the refugee problem in Thailand."³⁵ Before Kham's family's perilous journey back to Cambodia, Kham's father left his other son, who had polio, back at the refugee camp, certain that the boy would be unable to make the trip. Kham remembers that his father trained his brother before their separation, telling the boy to identify himself as an "orphan," so that people would not assume that his family had left him behind for being "a bad kid."

Kham told me that his family, with the exception of his brother, walked for three months and finally ended up back in their hometown in Phnom Thom. Determined to venture back to the Thai border, the family began their return journey only a few months later. Upon arrival Kham's father searched frantically for the son he had left at the camp, hoping to find someone who might have seen the boy. One person claimed that yes, the son had been seen but added, to the father's dismay, "but he's dead."

Kham told me that the Thai officers at the refugee camp had been under orders to kill every former inhabitant of the camp who did not return to Cambodia. This presented an impossible dilemma, since Buddhism forbids the killing of a disabled person. Kham's brother heard them debating amongst themselves concerning what to do about him—to kill him or not. As they were arguing, a monk approached, announcing that he had sensed that he ought to come to check in on one of the officers working at the camp. The monk—not the same monk who had become Kham's uncle by marriage—explained that he had recently dreamed that the officer in question, who had at some prior time received a protective waistband from him, had been in a car accident.³⁶ It turns out that the dream was inaccurate, as this particular officer had not been in any automobile collision. Even so, the monk's visit was not in vain. When the monk became aware of the topic of the officers' debate, he commanded them not to kill the disabled boy and instead offered to take him to a Buddhist temple. This is what the monk did, and Kham's brother found shelter in the temple until he was able to contact extended family in France. When I asked Kham about his interpretation of the monk's intervention, he indicated that there was a spirit that had influenced the monk's decision, but that it was "not the Holy Spirit." Kham seemed rather certain of this but nevertheless included this story in his own faith testimony. He considered this vignette to be an example of the Christian God having worked through another spirit—not a spirit typically consulted within Christian practice—to rescue his brother, who had since been reunited with Kham and the rest of their family.

Multiple Religious Belonging

More than tolerating spirits associated with Cambodian Buddhism, some self-identifying Cambodian evangelicals also identify simultaneously as Buddhist. This might not come across as particularly surprising, given the already hybrid or syncretic nature of the Cambodian religious landscape prior to Christianity's entry into the mix. The overlapping practice of two or more religions is known as "multiple religious belonging" or "double religious belonging." I use the term "multiple religious belonging," rather than "double religious belonging," to refer to the experience of Cambodians who self-identify both with Buddhism and with an evangelical form of Christianity. I find the former more accurate, given the aforementioned religious hybridity that has constituted much of Cambodian Theravada belief and practice, even dating back to the time before Christianity entered Cambodia.

Among those who practice both Buddhism and Christianity, some identify fully with two or more religions, while others identify primarily with one religion while supplementing their practice of that religion by drawing on a second, including, in certain instances, for enhanced faithfulness in the first. McLellan cites one of her interlocutors, who shared about deciding to identify as Christian with an eye toward living according to the Buddhist value of honoring one's hosts. This woman, a refugee living in the city of Kingston, Ontario, spoke of feeling especially indebted to church members who had shown great hospitality toward her, including by welcoming her after her plane had landed in Canada. The woman elaborated, "Because we are good Buddhists, we become Christians here. Inside we still hold many Buddhist ideals, but we don't tell them or say anything because this would make them sad. Buddhism teaches us that we must be flexible."[37] As Peter Phan has noted, "multiple religious belonging emerges as a theological problem only in religions that demand an absolute and exclusive commitment on the part of their adherents to their founders and/or faiths," such as in the three Abrahamic faiths, but this is "not so with most other religions, particularly in Asia."[38]

Thus, we have seen in the multilayered nature of Cambodian religiosity, even apart from the practice of Christianity, that there tends to be a great deal of flexibility within Cambodian Buddhism. Smith-Hefner recounts an episode revolving around a woman who arranged for "an exorcism" for her husband—unbeknownst to him—and "invited an *achaa* (a Khmer ritual specialist) and several [Buddhist] monks."[39] Although this ritual was rooted in Khmer indigenous religion, rather than in Buddhist tradition, the woman sought to include the monks, as she considered herself unquestionably Buddhist. Smith-Hefner emphasizes that the "exorcism was clearly unorthodox," but that this mattered little to those sponsoring the intervention. She notes that the Buddhist monks, who "were not directly involved in the exorcism," stayed present for its duration with full knowledge of what it entailed, making no effort to stop the [ʔaacaa] from proceeding.[40]

The type of religious mixing Smith-Hefner observed in this instance, though technically syncretic, is widespread within Cambodian Buddhism, and analogous forms exist throughout the Buddhist world, with indigenous religions intermingling with the practice of Theravada or Mahayana. The latter tradition, practiced primarily in East Asia, features a concept known as "skillful means" as its key principle. According to this principle, Mahayana Buddhism allows space for temporary engagement in practices that might not be wholly aligned with Buddhist doctrine but that would be expedient in eventually propelling them toward nirvana. Michael Pye, a scholar of East Asian Buddhism, describes skillful means, or "skill in means," as the concept within Mahayana thought that "Buddhist teaching and practice are declared to be provisional means, all skilfully set up by the Buddha for the benefit of the unenlightened."[41] While the skillful means principle is primarily associated with Mahayana, Pye notes, importantly, that the "call to the discernment of real meaning was already at home in pre-Mahayana Buddhism."[42] The Pali Canon, the collection of Buddhist scriptures generally seen as determining the boundaries of orthodoxy in Theravada Buddhism, employs the term only rarely, but according to Pye, these ancient texts nevertheless contain the concept of skillful means. Elaborating, Pye points to the Pali Canon's "parable of the raft," in which a man crosses a body of water via a makeshift raft composed of a "miscellany of materials" to which he has access at the moment—namely, grass, leaves, sticks, and tree branches. In the story, the Buddha explains that the most appropriate course of action for the man is to leave the raft "at the beach" after accomplishing his mission of arriving on the far shore.[43] Pye notes that the concept of skillful means has enabled Buddhists "to acclimatize their religion in diverse societies," such that there simultaneously exists "patience in accepting heterodox and even contradictory tendencies in their surroundings" and persistence in "the eventual recoupment of Buddhist meaning."[44] In brief, Cambodian Buddhism is capacious in its ability to accommodate a variety of indigenous, Hindu, Christian, or other religious practices theoretically incompatible with Buddhist doctrine.

Some practitioners might be unaware of the different cosmological strains in their religious thought and expression, while others intentionally choose to identify with a secondary religion with the hope of earning greater merit within the Buddhist system.

I encountered some Cambodian evangelicals who shared how they had also practiced multiple religious belonging on a temporary basis, before making a commitment to the singular practice of Christianity. There were various reasons behind this decision-making process, including to keep peace within a spousal relationship. Just as marriage could be a reason for choosing to leave one religion for another, as explored in chapter 2, marriage could also be a reason to enter the practice of multiple religious belonging. One of my interlocutors related an anecdote in this vein:

> *When I came to the US, my sponsor was Cambodian, and to this day, she practices both Buddhism and Christianity. I didn't want to become a member of my sponsor's sister's Buddhist group, but my husband asked me to do it to honor my sponsor. I said, "God, forgive me." When I moved to another city within the same state, I did not use the Buddha statue or incense. I kept them tucked away in my car. Later, we moved again, and I still went to Cambodian cultural events with monks. My husband wanted to do this, because he thought it was part of what it meant to be connected to the culture. Eventually, I decided not to give food to the monks anymore.*

Such accounts were not uncommon, especially in descriptions of past behavior, but the vast majority of my interlocutors eventually declared an exclusive allegiance to Christianity. Choosing to leave behind the religion of their family and culture came, for many, at great cost; the idea of being labeled as Buddhist, despite the relational sacrifices entailed in their conversion, would surely be felt as a wounding insult. Pastor Joshua bluntly remarked, *Some people go to church one day and to the Buddhist temple the next day. God created everything. God saved your life. God forgave you of your sin. Then you go to worship Satan.* Pastor Bona expressed a similar opinion: *You cannot worship two gods. You cannot worship idols and God.* Samen, also living in Philadelphia, appealed to practical reasoning in her explanation of why one should avoid practicing both Buddhism and Christianity at the same time. She explained, *When you go to the pagoda and go to the church, you are like a cake that is not cooked. You're going to be confused.*

Multiple Religious Believing without Multiple Religious Belonging?

In my own ethnographic research, I encountered fewer Cambodian evangelicals who openly self-identified as both Buddhist and Christian than who exhibited signs of what I would regard as multiple religious believing without multiple religious belonging. This admittedly cumbersome turn of phrase combines the concept of multiple religious belonging with that of "believing without belonging," which sociologist Grace Davie introduced to describe the "relatively high levels of belief" accompanied by "low levels of practice" among those of Christian heritage in Britain during the second half of the twentieth century.[45] In a similar vein, Cambodian converts to Christianity sometimes retain certain central aspects of Buddhist doctrine following their conversion to Christianity, but according to the very nature of the incorporation of these doctrines into their new Christian worldview—or, perhaps the incorporation of Christian doctrines into their original Buddhist worldview—those who fall into the category of multiple religious believing without multiple religious belonging are adamant about their lack of belonging vis-à-vis Buddhism.

Despite my interlocutors' rejection of Buddhism, this persistent remnant of Buddhist-inspired thought contributes significantly to the cosmology of those who experience multiple religious believing without multiple religious belonging. One interlocutor who endured the Cambodian genocide confided in me that she had "lied [her] whole life about [her] identity" in order to "surviv[e]" under the Khmer Rouge, and that she had felt burdened during and after those horrific years at the thought of having to undergo multiple rebirths within the karma system. She recalled wondering "how many lives" she would have to endure before she could be free from her "sin." Although she had initially been opposed to Christianity, thinking of it as a Western religion, she became more open to the idea of conversion when she heard a preacher in her refugee camp mention that through Jesus, one could receive forgiveness from sins. Not long thereafter, she decided to become a Christian. When I asked her when she had stopped believing in karma, she stared at me blankly. I suddenly realized that I had been too hasty, perhaps, in concluding that she had ever stopped believing in karma at all. What if she had, rather than replacing a Buddhist soteriology with a Christian one, merely figured that converting to Christianity provided an escape from bearing the weight of karmic justice and that those who remained Buddhist would continue to transmigrate through the cycle of deaths and rebirths for lives to come?

Thomas Douglas recalls an interlocutor having told him that if "a person lived a good life," the religion he or she chose to practice was of little consequence, but that "Buddhism was the 'express route.'"[46] Similarly, Carol Mortland notes that one of her interlocutors told her, "It would be a lot easier just to become a Christian and get saved . . . and then I know I will be okay after I die."[47] As I have noted elsewhere, the point at issue in these situations "is not whether Buddhism or Christianity is the correct means to salvation, or even what that salvation would entail in either case, but rather, which option would be 'easier.'"[48]

It is possible that the Khmer translations of the Bible contribute to some Cambodian evangelicals' continued belief in the karmic restitution system, even if they believe themselves to be exempt from it through the forgiveness made possible by Jesus Christ. The Khmer Old Version (KHOV) of the Bible, published in 1954 and then again with minor corrections in 1962, is the version that most of my interlocutors faithfully use and passionately support, over and against newer versions that have attempted to provide translations more firmly rooted in Khmer culture. I encountered this phenomenon most strongly in the diaspora. In France, for example, Ponleu patted her KHOV lovingly and asserted, "I know that Jesus takes care of this one."

While much of the discontent concerning the newer Khmer Standard Version (KSV) has to do with its perceived ties to Buddhism, the KHOV also employs certain vocabulary that lends itself to a Buddhist interpretation. One simple example is the word for "die" used to refer to Jesus's death. In Khmer, the term used when a common person dies is [slap],[49] while the corresponding term used for the deaths of "high persons" excluding the king, is [soʔkɔət].[50] New Testament references to Jesus's dying, such as 1 Corinthians 15:3, use [soʔkɔət].[51] A Buddhist term derived from the Pali word *sugata*, [soʔkɔət] not only means "to die" but can also imply that after death, the person is "reincarnated in a good environment" or has "attained the realm of bliss"[52] or nirvana. The KSV, published in 1997 and 2005, uses [tiʔvʊəŋkʊət][53]—the regal word for "die"—which indicates the translators' envisioning of Jesus as king, but which can also connote that the person who has died has "go[ne] to heaven (and be[en] reborn as a god)."[54] Each of these more respectful words for "die" comes with its own associations rooted in Buddhist cosmology and has likely affected the lens through which Cambodian Christians have understood Jesus's death—a central aspect of their faith—and perhaps their own existence after this life, as well.

Reflecting on the values of the communities with whom he worked in Thailand, Edwin Zehner asserts that they identify with a typical "orthodox[y]," which renders it reasonable for them "to stand in for evangelical Christianity in general."[55] On the whole, my interlocutors demonstrated assent to the overlapping visions of evangelicalism that Zehner describes. Lambert, a Cambodian church leader I met in France, expressed the opinion that an "evangelical" is "someone who believes principally in the word of God, salvation by grace alone, and the Trinity." In his analysis of Thai evangelicalism, Zehner identifies two types of "hybridities" that appear within his focus community, which are helpful in illuminating Cambodian evangelical cosmology. The first category of hybridity he introduces is the concept of "hybridities of extension and elaboration," in which recent converts borrow details from Buddhist cosmology to fill in the blanks, as it were, within their new, evangelical cosmology. For example, while most evangelicals, even in the West, retain an understanding of a spiritual realm, they rarely have a detailed demonology. Zehner's interlocutors believe the biblical category of demons applies to a variety of specific spirits with which they had been familiar within their Thai Buddhist context, prior to conversion. In his own words, Zehner explains, "The notion of supernatural power gets elaborated in terms of a local panoply of spirits that is unique to Thailand yet provides concrete elaboration of an evangelical cosmology that would otherwise remain vague."[56] The second category, that of "transitional hybridities," involve competing cosmological frames that "become congruent" because of symbols perceived to have "roughly the same meanings and resonances in both frames."[57]

One example Zehner proposes is that of the notions of heaven and hell within the Theravada Buddhist and evangelical cosmological frames, respectively. As is often the case, confusion arises here through language. In Thai, as in Khmer, there is no grammatical distinction between singular and plural nouns. Unless a speaker names a specific number or uses the word for "many," it is not always possible to determine from context whether he or she means to refer to one, two, or multiple items. When a Thai evangelical who has converted from Buddhism speaks about heaven, he or she may have in mind the Buddhist idea of multiple heavens, under the impression that this belief is in line with evangelical theology. Commenting on "the overlap between popular Buddhist and Christian notions of heaven and hell and of the consequences of this-worldly action," Zehner helpfully draws a distinction between the views of "philosophically oriented" and "traditionally oriented" Buddhists in the Theravada context of Thailand. The former category, which includes monks and others who take into consideration the texts of the Pali Canon, would view Buddhism and Christianity as quite disparate. The latter, who constitute the majority in both Thailand and Cambodia, tend to be less concerned with nirvana as an end goal and more concerned with karma and its effects on their rebirths in the relatively near future, including whether or when they might land in one of Buddhism's numerous heavens and hells.[58] When Zehner speaks of "philosophically oriented Buddhists," he is referring to those whom Obeyesekere classifies as members of the "great tradition," who base their beliefs and practices on the texts of the Theravada scriptures; on the other hand, the category of "traditionally oriented Buddhists" refers those within Obeyesekere's "little tradition,"[59] to which many of my own interlocutors belonged before converting to Christianity. Many lay Buddhists do not believe themselves to be in a position to strive toward nirvana—at least, not anytime in the foreseeable future—and turn instead to working toward more attainable goals, such as being reborn in a better position in the next life, and perhaps, at some point, into one of the heavens, although none of the heavens constitutes a final or eternal destination. Eternity, as a concept, does not exist within Buddhism.

Kham, whose testimony appears in part earlier in this chapter, has incorporated into his personal Christian cosmology the first type of hybridity Zehner introduces—that of extension and elaboration. While Kham's family was in the refugee camp the second time, before they had been reunited with his brother, Kham's father had encountered Christianity after hearing the song "Oh Happy Day" emanating from a church operated by Bangkok-based Chinese missionaries. Kham's father soon converted to Christianity and eventually became a leader in the camp church. Before long, Kham's whole family began attending the church. Shortly thereafter, his family's next-door neighbor, a new convert to Christianity and former "palm reader," asked Kham for a Bible, hoping that Kham's father, as a church leader, might be in a position to acquire one on his behalf. Kham learned through conversations with his neighbor that ever since converting to Christianity, the man had lost his powers, which he believed he had received from a spirit that enabled him to watch others' lives "like a movie." Kham explained to me how difficult it was for people to convince such a spirit to live within them. Apparently, parting ways with this particular spirit came with difficulties of its own. Kham said that after his neighbor's conversion, the spirit tormented the man, including by making his child sick and threatening to kill the child. The spirit reportedly asked the man, "I took care of you and fed you all these years—are you really going to leave me?" Kham's neighbor nevertheless remained resolute in his newfound Christian faith. The church community prayed for the man, and although the spirit threatened to come back, it did not. Kham considered this episode, albeit one in which he was not the protagonist, as one that solidified his own Christian faith. He, like many of my other interlocutors, found himself drawn to the power of the Christian God, which he believed he had witnessed in the defeat of spirits that had revealed themselves as agents of suffering. In continuing to acknowledge the existence of a specific type of spirit known within Cambodian Buddhist cosmology and incorporating his assessment of its characteristics into his current Christian understanding of the world, Kham elaborated upon the category of demonology, which typically remains, as Zehner notes, rather unspecific in Western expressions of evangelicalism.

On the other hand, my interlocutor, whose fear of having to endure multiple lives, and perhaps torturous ones at that, led her to convert to Christianity, has a conversion story characterized by what Zehner would call a transitional hybridity. She saw the forgiveness she believed to be available through Jesus as an opportunity to attain freedom from the punishment she feared awaited her within the karmic restitution system. The concepts of sin and punishment, and heaven and hell, appeared familiar enough to her, based on her understanding of Buddhist cosmology, that she apparently viewed the Buddhist and Christian frames as overlapping, such that converting to Christianity would provide an escape route, while remaining Buddhist would require her to suffer on account of her sins through the long cycle of deaths and rebirths.

According to Zehner, his Thai evangelical interlocutors tended to be more tolerant of the first type of hybridity than of the second. The bottom line for them, whenever they found themselves in a position of having to choose whether a certain belief or practice qualified as properly "orthodox," was "loyalty." Certain types of hybridity, perhaps especially those falling within the category of transitional hybridity, came across to Thai evangelical pastors as signaling "divided loyalty," as their understanding of faithful Christianity necessitated "a mono-centric loyalty to Christ at the expense of other sources of spiritual power and authority."[60] The next chapter, building upon the Cambodian evangelical conceptions of cosmology discussed here, explores in greater detail questions of my interlocutors' understandings of the ideal pattern of interactions with God and with the other beings inhabiting the spiritual realm. As with Zehner's Thai evangelical community, loyalty lay at the foundation of my interlocutors' decisions concerning holy living.

Chapter 4

SPIRITUALITY

Whereas cosmology refers to the roster of spiritual beings believed to inhabit the world, spirituality has to do with beliefs surrounding how one ideally ought to interact with such beings. In the Cambodian evangelical context, individuals often make decisions about how to interact with various spiritual beings based on the concept of loyalty to the Christian God. To be sure, the intimacy my interlocutors described feeling in their relationships with God did not take place in the context of mere affirmation and freedom of expression. In response to the magnanimous love and loyalty they received from God, my interlocutors demonstrated an understanding of loyalty to God in return. This loyalty came with rules—some that were quite costly to keep to. Viewing their own spirituality through the lens of relationship with a present and responsive God, many Cambodian evangelicals have drawn on their faith to overcome the experience of loneliness and destitution associated with their traumatic collective past. The sense of hope that my Cambodian evangelical interlocutors derived from their belief in God's relational availability and generosity often manifested as a tendency to interact with God with relative ease and informality, as well as to place a high value on exclusive loyalty to God over against other potential sources of spiritual and material security, and to anticipate resultant life transformations for themselves and for those in their communities.

Relational Ease

The spiritual practices that occupy Cambodian Christians' lives demonstrate the freedom they see in accessing and relating to God spontaneously. Let us return for a moment to Vicheka, the children's minister whose story appears in chapter 2. In describing her own pattern of interacting with God, Vicheka told me:

> *I pray many times throughout the day. When I get up, I know that in the morning, we are all rushing and all. I'm not in the form of sitting—quiet time—but I pray in my heart. Sometimes, I pray, silently pray, when I go to work, at break time or mealtime, and in between. If there is something that is hindering you or disturbing you, then I pray and remember God is there. I just continue to focus on what is the right thing to do, instead of focusing on the circumstances around me. So, God is my hope and strength right there, and I know that he is there.*

Like Vicheka, many of my interlocutors from each fieldwork location viewed God's constant availability as a hallmark of Christian spirituality. Some identified the ease with which they could pray to the Christian God as an important difference from their experiences of Buddhist prayer prior to conversion. Pastor Somlain in Phnom Penh said of his and his friends' preconversion practice, "We used to go to the temple every Buddhist day... but [this did] not [involve] relationship." By contrast, Pastor Somlain spoke of their current spirituality in the emotional terms of intimacy, saying, "We love God." Along the same lines, a pastor named Pastor Nimith told me, "We believe that our father is living. He hears us." To illustrate his confidence in the immediacy of God's availability, Pastor Nimith added, "I can stop and pray now." Samen, a Philadelphia laywoman with two children, explained to me that within Buddhism, people looking to pray needed to go to the temple or another designated location in order to do so. For Christians, however, "You can pray [on the] toilet, [in] the bathroom," she said with a smile. "[God] doesn't mind about you."

Exclusive Loyalty

For most of my interlocutors, relationship with God was bounded by an expectation of exclusive loyalty to God. As can be seen in both the Khmer

Old Version (KHOV) and Khmer Standard Version (KSV) translations of 2 Chronicles 16:9,[1] the Khmer word for "loyal," [smɑh],[2] can have the connotation of complete reliance on God, over against other potential protectors. Multiple religious belonging and exclusive loyalty often coexist within individual families, with parents and children finding themselves at variance concerning what it means to demonstrate Christian faithfulness while honoring one's Khmer cultural identity. For many of the Cambodian evangelicals I encountered during my fieldwork, loyalty to God, or to Jesus Christ, constituted a highly emotional matter. Chanvatey, whose story also appears in chapter 2, grew teary-eyed as he shared about his parents who, in his words, continue to "worship the Buddh[a]"[3] after having become involved with a Christian church in Thailand during his youth. He expressed the hope that one day, they would worship Jesus only.

Mary, first mentioned in chapter 2, passionately exclaimed during a prayer meeting that she felt uncomfortable even pronouncing the names of any deities other than that of the Christian God—an act she condemned as a violation of Exodus 23:13, which contains the command, "Do not invoke the names of other gods; do not let them be heard on your lips."[4] In Khmer culture, the refusal to mention the name of something or someone whom one desires to reject is known as [kat kal caol], which Khatharya Um defines as "disowning." In this context, the term [kat kal], meaning "to disown," "renounce," or "cut ties with" a person, combines with [caol], meaning "to abandon" or "to discard." Um identifies [kat kal caol] as a custom by which "moral transgressions are punished," by way of "a form of *damnatio memoriae*," such that "what is not articulated . . . does not exist." In other words, "to speak of evil is to give it life and to invite its presence." Khmer people have lived out this concept of [kat kal chaol] by refusing to mention the names of "dangerous jungle animals," and Um believes that denying the "actualization" of "political evils . . . through their banishment from speech" represents an analogous situation. Um calls attention to the story of an elderly Cambodian refugee who found excessive the media attention focused on Pol Pot after his death. It struck Um's interlocutor as simply inappropriate to give "so much attention" to Pol Pot. "Speaking about him, writing about him, is like honoring his existence, his evil. In so doing, we perpetuate the memory of him. Why would we want to memorialize such evil in our nation's consciousness?"[5]

Narin, a Philadelphia man, appeared to hold a similar perspective in his approach to navigating the spiritual. When I asked Narin if he believed in the existence of spirits, he replied, saying, *Yes, before I believed in Christ,*

I believed in ghosts, Satan, and people who pray to make other people sick, but after I started believing in God, I realized that there is no such thing. There are other spirits, but I chose to believe in the Holy Spirit.[6] Interestingly, Narin holds together the apparently paradoxical claims that "there are other spirits" and "there is no such thing." The two claims can coexist for Narin only because of his decision "to believe in the Holy Spirit." He believes that spirits other than the Holy Spirit are real in some way, but he feels that they are of no consequence to him now that he has "believed in Christ," "in God," and "in the Holy Spirit." Narin disowning the other spirits by refusing to acknowledge them forms a critical part of his expression of loyalty to Christianity's triune God.

There is some debate within Cambodian evangelicalism as to precisely which types of interactions with the Christian God and other spiritual beings are appropriate to seek within this framework of loyalty. For example, in Cambodia and in the diaspora, many of my interlocutors shared about the complex, and sometimes emotionally exhausting, process of negotiating interreligious friendships and family relationships. In the previous chapter, two elderly Long Beach women, Lina and Toy, strikingly decided to refrain from attending their own parents' funerals in order to avoid participating in Buddhist ritual. However, not all my interlocutors, even among those adamant about their exclusive commitment to Jesus Christ, felt that it was necessary to avoid attending all Buddhist ceremonies. Madeleine, a middle-aged woman who had resettled in Long Beach with her family as a teenager in the early 1980s, explained that although she no longer frequented the temple for her own spiritual needs, she had no qualms about visiting merely for the sake of supporting friends and family. She elaborated:

> When I was younger, I went to the temple with my parents, even as I went to church with my sponsor. But when I got to know Jesus, I stopped going to the temple. Now, I go to the temple just to meet friends or for family gatherings—like, if they have a funeral, I just go to respect the family. I don't sit down and worship with them completely. "I'm Christian. I cannot worship with you guys," I say. I'm not afraid to tell them that. I tell them, "I can pray if you need something, but I can't worship with you. God is jealous."

Madeleine felt comfortable with a more nuanced approach in which she could be present for a Buddhist ceremony as long as she communicated that she was not at liberty to participate to the fullest extent. Evidently,

Cambodian evangelicals' approaches to the question of attending Buddhist rituals, especially for the sake of maintaining relationships, exist along a continuum. The bottom line for many came down to demonstrating loyalty to God, whether by attempting to avoid spiritually ambiguous situations altogether, or by engaging in potentially uncomfortable conversations to clarify what one could and could not do while remaining within the bounds of one's own spiritual convictions.

Spiritual ambiguity posed a concern not only in social settings but also in the context of private devotional life and, particularly, when individuals hoped to hear from God. Pastor Samedy in Phnom Penh encouraged the members of his congregation, Knowledge of Christ Church, to listen for God's voice exclusively through the Bible, and specifically not through silent meditation. "Prayer is one-sided communication," he reiterated during an interview. Importantly, Pastor Samedy assured me that he did indeed believe that God possessed both the capability and the desire to communicate with humans. Nevertheless, he asserted, "Prayer is not the place where God talks to you." Pastor Samedy elaborated, "God wants to talk to us through the Bible, and through the other people around [us]." Pastor Samedy spoke disapprovingly of cases in which people added "yoga into the prayer." He was concerned that his parishioners would confuse the process of listening silently for God's voice, as is popular in more charismatic circles within the Cambodian evangelical community, with the meditation practices in which some might have engaged as Buddhists prior to conversion to Christianity.

In sharing this vignette, I do not intend to communicate that Pastor Samedy categorically opposed all activities with roots in non-Christian religions. In fact, the reality could not be further from the truth. Shortly after I arrived in Phnom Penh in April 2019, Pastor Samedy introduced me to the staff at one of the Christian schools his family operated, and the teachers—many of whom also attended Knowledge of Christ Church—invited me to join them for a Khmer New Year celebration with them and their families. Approximately fifty of us, including Pastor Samedy and his family, gathered in the school courtyard for an elaborate feast, during which guests separated into clusters and grilled meat and vegetables together at our individual tables. Lively Khmer pop music emanated from the speakers, and the dance floor remained open throughout the night. The young teachers, eager to show off the latest dance moves, leapt and twirled gracefully while circling a large, festive fruit display set up for the occasion. The evening climaxed with a giant talcum powder fight, a Khmer New Year tradition similar to that practiced as part of the Hindu festival Holi. Adults and children alike chased after one another, hurling powder through the air, smearing it on each other's faces, and dusting one another's hair in the spirit of celebration. No one was spared! When I returned to my apartment that night with my hair, face, and clothing completely daubed in white, my neighbors grinned knowingly as they wished me a happy new year.

Pastor Samedy's willingness, even enthusiasm, to engage with his family and parishioners in the celebration of the Khmer New Year, a holiday stemming from both Buddhism and indigenous Khmer religion, distinguished him from others of my interlocutors, particularly in the diaspora. In France, one Cambodian evangelical woman told me that as Christians, she and the other members of her church did not celebrate the Khmer New Year.[7] Although I was not in the United States during Khmer New Year during my fieldwork year, I remember that it constituted a notable omission on the list of annual gatherings for the interdenominational organization for Cambodian Christians in Long Beach. In explaining to me about the operations of this organization, Pastor Joshua informed me that the group hosted three large events: Thanksgiving in November, Christmas in December, and a three-day revival meeting in the spring. I never heard anyone in the Cambodian American setting openly disparage the celebration of Khmer New Year, although Quentin, a pastor in Long Beach, did make an effort to put the holiday in its proper place. In response to a friend who had asked him why Christians wanted to celebrate Easter so close to Khmer New Year, he pointed out that the date for Easter is tied to the date for Passover and made sure to note that Moses lived before the Buddha.

Thus, for Pastor Samedy, the calculus involved in ascertaining which Khmer cultural activities constituted acceptable Christian behavior proved more complex than merely whether a given custom had originated within Buddhist or indigenous Khmer religious practice. In rejecting the practice of listening for God's voice during Christian prayer—on the grounds that it evoked Buddhist meditation to the point of probable confusion on the part of his parishioners—Pastor Samedy's concern was apparently that his parishioners could end up interacting with spirits other than God, which then would constitute disloyalty. Pastor Samedy asserted that he himself had never gotten mixed up with other spirits, and that he hoped to keep it that way. "If you don't play around with them," he said, "they don't play with you."

Meanwhile, certain others of my interlocutors depended and thrived on direct, personal communication from God. Martine, a Vietnamese woman who had been raised in Cambodia from the age of twelve or thirteen and decided to convert to Christianity through the ministry of the Phnom Penh–based Life in the Spirit Church, where she served in lay leadership at the time of our meeting, cited hearing directly from God as an important component of her journey toward conversion.

> *I was raised in a Vietnamese Buddhist family. After I had moved to Cambodia with my family, I got to know a missionary couple, and I was taking English classes. Later, I made a commitment. I asked the couple if Christians liked eating dogs because I had heard this. I also asked if Christians liked to eat other kinds of meat. The missionary couple responded, "Do Buddhists also eat meat?" This was true for my family, and this was a key question on the part of the missionary couple. I have been involved with the church since 2002 and made my decision to become a Christian in 2003, when I was nineteen years old.*
>
> *I grew up in a very strict Buddhist household, and I used to chant every night. It took a while to make a decision. In 2002, I went to Life in the Spirit Church for Bible study, even though I was not yet a Christian.*
>
> *After a while, I stopped going, but it seemed like God called me back. It took me a while to accept finally. When baptism classes were offered, I attended all the classes, but the day before the baptism, I wasn't ready. So, I delayed for one year.*[8]

When I asked Martine to explain more about what she meant by "God called [her] back," and how it was that she knew that God was calling her, she responded thus:

> *My family would not allow me to change religion. But I heard a voice talking to me: "Go. Go back." I felt all the chains holding me back. I told my family, "I don't care; I will go back." I wasn't afraid anymore. I felt a boldness. No matter what happened, I knew that I should go.*
>
> *Since no one in my family was a Christian at the time, I had no role model. Every day, I had two different worlds. When my family talked about church, they said, "Oh, this is a Western thing." But I couldn't ignore the differences between what I saw at church and what I saw at home. At church, each person has value. We are made in the image of God. This kind of mutual respect for people didn't exist at home.*

After almost ten years, my life was lukewarm. I tried to compromise. On death anniversaries, my sister made me burn the paper. I didn't know how serious I was being. So, I continued to participate in Buddhist rituals, even after having made the decision to become a Christian.

I have lived in Cambodia for twenty-two years. For most of that time, I was living here with my family, including my extended family, although now, my mom has gone back to Vietnam.

In 2014, I was running a business: a guest house. For the first two years, business was going all right, but by the third year, it was bad. I didn't know what to do, so I just read the Bible. Normally, I didn't enjoy reading, and especially not the Bible, because it was boring to me. But this time, I read 1 Samuel, 2 Samuel, and it was like a movie to me. A voice told me, "Do this; do this," and then it worked! And within five days, I got all my problems solved. I ended up selling my business.

Something told me to fast, and after twenty-four hours, I heard the voice again, and I knew it was God. I said, "God, I know you are real."

Previously, in my life as a young Christian, I had encouraged my mother to go to the Buddhist temple. "Buddhism is also good," I used to think, even though I believed in God. But in 2014, after I heard the voice, everything changed. I said to God at that time, "I know you are the real God, 100 percent." And then I started to pray for my mom, because I wanted her to receive Jesus also.

I prayed for my mom for two weeks. Eventually, I wanted to go to visit Vietnam to see how my people worshiped. On the bus ride to Vietnam, the woman sitting next to me was on the phone with her pastor, and I realized that this woman was also a Christian. I eventually got to connect with her, and the woman invited me to her church. My mom had come to pick me up at the bus station, and since I didn't know my way around, my mom also ended up responding positively to the woman's invitation for her to come to church. At this church, there were different small groups for people according to their age. So, my mom and I were separated. I told the woman to be gentle with my mom because it was my mom's first time ever in a church. When we got back together after the group times, I learned that my mom had made a commitment.

I wasn't happy. I was worried that the people had taken advantage of my mom. But when I asked my mom about it, I learned that she had *been passing by a Catholic church for some time, seeing it all packed out, with people crowded around outside, parked on motorbikes. My mom had been wondering what it was all about. After hearing this, I was able to be happy for my mom.*

When I told my mentors, they asked me, "Why are you surprised? We've already been praying for your mom ten years."

I was humbled when I heard this. In some ways, I had rejected God, but within two weeks after I started praying for my mom, she became a Christian. Now, I will never leave Jesus. Before, I was lukewarm because nothing had been proven to me yet.

For Martine, hearing from God in the form of a "voice" provided hope through clear discernment at various important junctures during her conversion process. The first time, she felt that the voice had called her to return to the church after she had stopped attending. Next, the voice offered specific, detailed advice about how to sell her business and obviate her money problems. The final time she heard the voice in the story was after she had been fasting for twenty-four hours. It was after this incident that she felt moved to pray for her mother to convert to Christianity. The mother's eventual conversion served to solidify Martine's own faith, prompting her to declare, "I will never leave Jesus."

Ponleu also listened for specific instructions from God with respect to various details of her life, including her lengthy times of personal prayer and Bible reading. When I asked Ponleu how she chose which chapters of the Bible to read each day, she told me that she had two methods. The first involved reading the entire Bible from start to finish at the pace of ten to thirty chapters per day. The second required listening for a spiritual prompting from God concerning any additional passages God might desire for her to read on any given day. Ponleu kept a Khmer-language journal of meticulous notes, recorded daily in vivid, sunset-colored gel ink, to record what she believed to be God's words for her.

Even as Ponleu prioritized two-way spiritual communication through prayer, however, she rejected the notion of seeking guidance from spirits other than the God of the Bible. Ponleu was overcome with dismay when her mother, a new Christian, began visiting a spirit medium after having fallen ill. Recalling the Bible story in which Saul enlists the help of a spirit medium in conjuring the spirit of Samuel,[9] Ponleu rued her mother's decision, declaring that God would not approve of such behavior. Ponleu explained that whenever she herself was sick, she simply drank a glass of water and declared it to be medicine from Jesus. By her own account, she had received healing in this manner on more than one occasion. "I drink water [from] the glass," she told me, "and I pray and say, 'This water is medicine from you,' and I'm finished [with my] sickness." From Ponleu's perspective, all Christians ought to put their trust in God alone, rather than looking to other spirits for aid.

One point of contention concerning spiritual loyalty within the Cambodian evangelical community was the Khmer hymnal—particularly, the indigenous segment, *Tomnuk Khmer Borisot*. Despite its near ubiquity, the hymnal was not uncontroversial. Barnabas Mam writes in his memoir that certain people accused his songs of "bringing the Satanic culture to the church."[10] In Paris, Ponleu expressed deep concern about the hymnal, in keeping with the suspicion Mam had encountered while preparing his contributions for *Tomnuk Khmer Borisot*. I remember visiting Ponleu at her apartment one day, having asked if she might be willing to teach me how to sing a hymn in Khmer. When she pulled out her copy of the combined hymnal, I found myself transfixed. Lying face-up, her hymnal slanted downward from the spine, the way an empty binder would. I took a closer look and realized that approximately three-quarters of the pages were missing. When I asked her what had happened, Ponleu proudly acknowledged that she had torn out pages featuring what she understood to be "music from Satan." In response to my query about how she had come to know that these songs involved music from Satan, she said, of a woman she knew, "[when] she sings [those songs], she sees Satan."

In Long Beach, one woman excused herself from joining her peers onstage to lead the women's song at an interdenominational Christmas service. I had been sitting next to her during the service, and when I saw most of the other women of her generation ascending the stage, I asked if she planned to sing with them. She seemed appalled at the idea and explained that no, she had already told them that she had no intention of doing so, and that she had a "conviction" about "secondhand" songs. The problem, as she saw it, was that the songs had been set to tunes customarily played in bars and clubs. She felt that a better way to do things would be to use new tunes created specifically for worshiping God, or to take songs from other cultures, if these tunes had been composed for God, rather than taking tunes from "the culture."

In the Cambodian evangelical context, the most common instances of music being borrowed from other cultures involved Khmer lyrics, often direct translations of existing Western hymns, set to tunes of European origin. Notable exceptions include the popular "I Have Decided to Follow Jesus," likely written by Simon Kara Marak, an ethnic A·chik (Garo) pastor, teacher, and missionary from Jorhat, Assam, in northeast India. It is possible that the song could fall into the category of a Christian bhajan, a type of Hindustani hymn associated with the bhakti movement, which aims for unity between devotees and the divine. The C major scale, employed in "I Have Decided to Follow Jesus," corresponds to the Bilāwal rāga, a North Indian or Hindustani scale associated with the morning hours and a profound emotional sense of devotion. Given the association of this scale with spiritual songs within the Hindu context, it is quite likely that the hymn's melody, as well as its lyrics, were intended to evoke religious devotion.[11]

In the charismatic evangelical context, translations of songs of African American origin sometimes made their way into Cambodian settings. Ting Xiu shared with me during an interview that before she left Cambodia for the United States, she had joined and, eventually, become ordained in a church led by a well-known Cambodian charismatic church founder. Partway through her interview, Ting Xiu burst into song, belting out the Khmer lyrics to "When the Spirit of the Lord" by gospel rhythm and blues artist Fred Hammond, dancing gleefully in a traditional Khmer style.

While many of my interlocutors, particularly in the diaspora, were interested in the preservation of Khmer culture, they often experienced a tension between cultural interests and Christian faithfulness. Many of the Cambodian evangelicals I met in the field attributed great loyalty to God as they spoke of God's characteristic availability for relationship with humanity. Samen, mentioned earlier in this chapter, told me, "Sometimes we forget [God], but he never forgets us." My interlocutors' general response to God's loyalty toward them has been to commit to maintaining a loyalty to God that precludes relationships with any other spirits, including transactional relationships into which one might enter in order to acquire protection or material favors. Edwin Zehner describes Thai evangelicals as believing that certain "practices—such as the possession of charms and amulets, the veneration of ancestors and local spirits, leaving offerings at others' shrines, and celebrating the holidays of others"—indicate "divided religious loyalties" and uncertainty about whether the power of God is truly adequate.[12] Zehner's interlocutors, in their approach to determining which of their preconversion practices were acceptable to retain postconversion, tended to be less concerned about "cultural mixing" and more so "about ambiguous religious loyalties and competing sources of spiritual power."[13] For my interlocutors, identifying the difference between cultural mixing and ambiguous loyalties regularly presented a theological quandary. Conversations I witnessed at prayer meetings and other church-related gatherings often centered on weighing and reflecting on different perspectives on how to ascertain this distinction.

Martin Lindhardt notes that "little light has been shed on the ways spiritual warfare is fought through the handling of physical objects."[14] Building his claims on ethnographic fieldwork among Pentecostal and charismatic Christians in Iringa, Tanzania, Lindhardt calls attention to the way in which "Pentecostals/charismatics . . . insist that praying over a glass of water will actually turn it into the blood of Jesus (even if it still looks and tastes like water) and that drinking it will therefore have healing and empowering effects." In giving this example, Lindhardt hopes "to establish the point that spiritual warfare involves a specific stance to materiality and is fought through the religious engagement with places and objects."[15] For Ponleu, water could serve as a weapon against the spiritual powers behind a given illness if she had first declared it to be medicine from Jesus. Ponleu, like Lindhardt's Tanzanian interlocutors, believed that Jesus could mediate healing power through a material object—in this case, water.

Malevolent spirits, as well as benevolent ones, can be associated with material objects, both in the Tanzanian and Cambodian Christian contexts. Within both communities, in cases where Christians have determined malevolent spirits to be associated with certain objects, the Christians have often sought to destroy the affected objects. In chapter 3, Sokha's mother's motivation for assisting others in removing and destroying spirit shrines they no longer want was that a Christian had done this removal for her after she had complained of feeling "scared of the altars" that a spirit medium had encouraged her to set up at home. Lindhardt details an analogous phenomenon in Tanzania, saying, "At open-air revival meetings [in Iringa], new converts are asked to bring all their . . . medicines and protective amulets provided by traditional healers, which are then burnt during a ritual where the power of God is also invoked through praying."[16] Presented with the anecdote in which Sokha sees what she believes to be a flying elephant and immediately invokes "the name of Jesus" and "the blood of Jesus," some scholars, including Lindhardt, might argue that Sokha is also engaging in a form of materially grounded spiritual warfare.[17] Such a claim would articulate with "linguistic theories that emphasize the material, acoustic qualities of words and sounds."[18] It is unclear to me, however, whether Sokha held the conviction that the actual pronunciation of Jesus's name aloud constituted a crucial element in ridding her home of spiritual intruders, or whether the same effect could have been achieved through silent prayer, without uttering a word at all. Without more clarity on the matter, I hesitate to classify Sokha's invocations as examples of material religion, but there is no doubt that her mother's destruction of ritual objects associated with malevolent spirits and Ponleu's use of water-turned-medicine fall squarely into this category.

Another example of the role of material objects in the struggle surrounding questions of loyalty in Cambodian evangelicalism has to do with the cutting of waistbands and wristbands traditionally worn for spiritual protection. Alexander Laban Hinton has pointed to "the ability of monks to make magical strings" as evidence of Cambodian Buddhists' belief in "the protective force of dhamma."[19] Hinton's ethnographic interlocutors in an anonymous Cambodian village saw such strings as a way to defend themselves against potential attacks by "an unknown adversary" who might "enlist the services of a sorcerer *(krou tmuap)* to afflict them with magic."[20] In reference to the Cambodian American context, Carol Mortland has written, "A monk may bless string to be tied around a child's wrist, neck, or waist to prevent illness or death."[21] Pastor Somlain, who appears earlier in this chapter, practices a charismatic form of evangelicalism and frequently prays for physical healing for people to whom he is ministering. If the prayer for healing does not appear immediately effective, his next step is to ask permission to sever the bands around their waists or wrists. This strategy is compatible with the concept of destroying material objects believed to be linked to malevolent spiritual forces, in order to break the relationship between the person possessing the objects—in this case, waistbands and wristbands—and the spirits with whom the objects are associated.

Stephen Selka, who has worked primarily with Afro-Brazilian evangelicals, as well as with *povo de santo*, practitioners of Candomblé in Brazil's Rêconcavo region, notes that *povo de santo* who have converted to evangelicalism often feel spiritual pressure to return to Candomblé.[22] As *povo de santo*, these individuals believed they had entered relationships of reciprocal, moral responsibility with *orixás*, a category of spirit found in Yoruba religion. Some *povo de santo* converted to Christianity in hopes of escaping what they had come to perceive as burdensome responsibilities concomitant with their relationships with their *orixás*.[23] To commemorate the breaking of such relationships, some converts engaged in the "breaking of ritual objects."[24] To their dismay, however, it was not uncommon within the community for *orixás* to "appear in the middle of [Christian] worship services," an interruption frequently interpreted as "a summoning back to Candomblé."[25] Many of these converts do in fact return to Candomblé in response to these demands for renewed loyalty. According to Selka's *povo de santo* interlocutors, even among former *povo de santo* who never again step foot in a Candomblé *terreiro* after their conversion to Christianity,[26] some "continue to make secret offerings—burning candles or paying to have an animal sacrificed—out of fear of the *orixás*."[27] One might consider this a type of reluctant multiple religious belonging. Many believe that "a Candomblé initiate does not have the choice to simply sever his or her relationship with the spirits" and must therefore continue interacting with them despite any feelings of fear or disinclination.[28] This belief is based on experiences in which former *povo de santo* have encountered angry *orixás* who threaten violence in response to the broken relationship, in a manner evocative of Kham's story of the former palm reader who reported receiving threats from a spirit on account of his disloyalty toward it.[29] For example, one of Selka's evangelical interlocutors claimed that "her *orixá* threatened to kill or cause an accident for her family members if she did not return to Candomblé."[30]

My interlocutors shared similar stories relating to the Cambodian context. Similar to Sokha's mother's experience, Pastor Somlain recounted that in his ministry, the breaking of ritual objects—representative of the severing of ties with the spirits associated with them—could initiate jealous responses on the part of the spirits whom the converts sought to abandon. In this vein, he shared a story about a woman he identified in English as "a witch doctor." In all likelihood, the woman would have been called, in the multilayered context of Cambodian religious practice, a *"rup arak,"*[31] which is a type of female spirit medium through whom "*arak*, a class of benign and malevolent spirits," express themselves verbally "during possession ceremonies *(cuen arak)* that usually take place in January and February."[32] According to Harris, "A *rup arak* has no training but is regarded as a woman with particularly good character and a natural tendency to fall into a trance."[33] Having spent all her earnings on offerings to the spirits, the woman in Pastor Somlain's story approached a friend to borrow money. Her friend told her, "I don't have money," but offered instead to take her to a "[kruu]" which—as I mentioned previously—literally means "teacher," but which can also be used to refer to religious leaders in various traditions. The woman was disappointed to learn that in this case, the individual described as a [kruu] happened to be a Christian minister. Pastor

Somlain told me that while with the minister, the woman "jumped" out of the house and landed on the ground. She was uninjured, and before they parted ways, the minister cut the waistband she had been wearing. The woman complained of being tormented by spirits after this incident, and remembering the minister, she ran to a local church, where she reportedly received prayer for her deliverance. In cutting ties—sometimes quite literally—with the spirits whose appeasement they used to seek, Cambodian converts demonstrate an intention to begin depending on the Christian God instead of other sources of power.

Living Differently

For my interlocutors, adopting a Christian spirituality centered on exclusive loyalty to God was supposed to involve a transformation of one's life. Differences in opinion sometimes arose within various communities I visited—particularly between pastors and parishioners, but also between parishioners—as to what specifically was required to live a properly changed life. Across my field sites, my interlocutors tended to agree that in general, changes expected to accompany conversion included those concerning one's relationship with one's family, as well as with one's own personal resources, in response to the fatherly loyalty and generosity of God.

Narin, mentioned earlier in this chapter, recalled the transformation he had undergone after converting to Christianity, especially with respect to his attitude toward his children. Narin elaborated during an interview:

> *I have lived in Philadelphia since 1987. I came to church with a friend who first shared with my wife about Jesus. I started coming irregularly, and when I heard the pastor preach, I realized that this was something I didn't know. I thought I had done nothing wrong. In fact, I was doing a lot wrong without knowing it. I knew I'd better start to learn from God and follow him. I started to teach my children. Once I started following God, I saw that he wanted us to be his good children. I changed. I no longer yell at my children. The words that really kicked me were Galatians 5:22–23. I memorized those verses. That's what I teach my children. You have to forgive.*

Earlier in this book, I addressed the ways in which many converts to Cambodian evangelicalism have listed the promise of forgiveness as a point of attraction within Christianity. Narin's story illustrates the ways in which evangelicalism's emphasis on forgiveness dovetails with the concept of God as father in a way that resulted in a change in Narin's relationship with his children. After coming to church, Narin adopted the viewpoint that he had not lived up to God's standard of what a "good" child should be, based on his failure to exhibit the aspects of the "fruit of the spirit" listed in the Galatians passage to which he alluded during his interview: "love, joy, peace, patience, kindness, generosity, faithfulness, gentleness, and self-control."[34] In response to this developing sense of his own moral frailty, Narin looked upon his own children with greater compassion. In this way, conversion to Christianity was seen by Narin and other interlocutors as offering the opportunity not only to receive forgiveness from their own sins but also to enjoy improved relationships with family members by choosing to extend forgiveness to them, as well.

One of conversion's concomitant changes that came up frequently in conversations with my interlocutors was the question of what it looked like to depend on God for one's financial well-being, including by giving of one's material resources or, just as significantly, of the time required to produce such resources. This, too, is rooted in the concept of God as father within Christianity. Pastor Quentin in Long Beach chided members of his church one Sunday morning for having taken back the fruit they had given for the offering after the previous service. Fruit as an offering is not unusual in Cambodian congregations, whether in Cambodia or in the diaspora, particularly on special occasions. This is widespread throughout many parts of Asia, including India, where it is common for "Hindus and Christians [both to] offer fruit . . . at temple or church."[35] As often happens throughout the world of Christianity, however, pastor and parishioners in this case viewed the situation quite differently. From Pastor Quentin's perspective, taking back the offering was wrong-headed. From the pulpit, he called attention to the incident, saying,

> *I saw some mistakes. The offering is supposed to be put in a bag and given to everyone that needs it. The richest person in the universe, who owns every planet, had only one son. His son died. He wants to adopt me and adopt you. May you give without expecting anything in return, as an expression of loving God.*

To hit the point home, Pastor Quentin told a story—a parable, perhaps—about a wealthy man living in a Thai village. The man's son had died, and he began searching for someone else on whom to bestow all his property. In the end, the man decided upon his hired dishwasher.

This simple story, though brief, is illustrative on multiple levels. First, Pastor Quentin calls for a generosity driven by the freedom that comes from knowing that one will always have enough. This spirituality of abundance, in turn, stems from one's having been adopted by the one who "owns every planet," whose infinite wealth eliminates the fear of scarcity. Finally, the adoption itself is born of a situation in which the one who becomes the adoptive father has first lost a son.

Few of my interlocutors were able to identify with the experience of significant wealth, either before or after the Khmer Rouge regime, but many, especially in that latter period, knew all too well the devastation of having lost a child. When sharing about the number of children in their family of origin, my interlocutors often provided two numbers: first, the total number of children to whom their mother had given birth, and then, the number of these children currently living. In homing in not only on God's generosity but also on God's bereavement, Pastor Quentin painted a picture for his parishioners of a God intimately relatable to those in grief. Adoption was another concept with which many of my interlocutors were familiar. Some were adopted themselves. Others grew up among adopted siblings. Still others had adopted children of their own. While the adoption trope within Christianity is nothing new—with the early church's practice of adopting infants whose parents had abandoned them in the Roman Empire[36]—it is not ubiquitous within Christian communities around the world.

It will come as no surprise to most readers that the concept of God as father, embedded in the Bible and in the ancient Christian creeds, is far from peculiar to Cambodian expressions of the religion. Even so, the particular underscoring of the fatherhood of God has figured into Cambodian evangelicalism since the early days of the Christian and Missionary Alliance (CMA) mission to Cambodia. As I have written elsewhere, Arthur Hammond and his ministry colleagues struggled to explain the "love" ([srɑlɑɲ]) of God in a way that Khmer listeners did not find offensive, due to the word's usage in erotic contexts. The chosen solution was to explicitly note God's love as a fatherly love.[37]

Bearing all this in mind, I found Pastor Quentin's emphasis not merely on the concept of God as father but also as adoptive father to be rather striking, as it once again called attention to God's relatability within the Cambodian context. Pastor Quentin here envisions God as profoundly familiar with Cambodian experiences, both as one who has experienced bereavement and as one who has chosen to adopt. The emphasis on areas of overlap in the Cambodian perception of what the death of Jesus would have been like for God the Father points to a life of emulating what they understand of their God's behavior—in this case, with respect to giving. In short, by telling this story, Pastor Quentin invites his congregation to relate simultaneously with the grief of God as a bereaved father, and with the awe-filled gratitude of the dishwasher at having received such a lavish and unexpected gift.

Pastor Quentin's parishioners clearly held a different understanding of the significance of the church offering and its relationship to Christian spirituality than he himself did. It is not unusual for various parties within a given community to attribute disparate values to the same ritual objects. James Egge, calling attention to "sacrifice" in Vedic tradition, identifies the sacrificial ritual as consisting of "acts of making offerings, especially of food, to a worthy recipient." After the offering of the food to the deities, it "may be abandoned or destroyed, such as by being burnt by fire or eaten by priests, or the worshipers may consume part or all of it, but in either case sacrifice serves as a point of communion between worshiper and recipient."[38] Some of the members of Pastor Quentin's church, especially those raised in homes where their families made food offerings to various spirits and then joined together to consume these offerings together, likely became confused at no longer being able to enjoy that which they had brought for the offering.

According to Lindhardt, "Even within the same society, the meaning of objects is often underdetermined, allowing them to move in and out of distinct spheres of value."[39] Moreover, Lindhardt argues, "It is exactly by being both money (cash value) and at the same time something more than just money that donated coins and bills can serve as a point of transfer of spiritual powers into everyday economic affairs."[40] Indeed, at Pastor Quentin's church, he and his parishioners both considered the fruit given as part of the offering to be simultaneously fruit and something more than fruit. Pastor Quentin viewed the fruit, by virtue of its status as an offering to the church, as a consecrated means of expressing love to God through care for those in need.

For Pastor Quentin, as well as for the Christians in Iringa, the inalienability of ritual objects held critical importance. Mama Jimy, one of Lindhardt's interlocutors, believed that through prayer, she had the ability "to invest . . . bills [i.e., currency bills] with divine power," but only when these bills were given as a gift. "If they had been a loan," then the imbuement of power "would not have been possible."[41] Lindhardt infers that the distinction between gift and loan is significant in this case because "divine power" within Mama Jimy's community is thought to be able to "reside only in personalized money." A loan, on the other hand, while "still a personal favor," nevertheless needs to "be repaid at a later point," which therefore renders it "an impersonal transaction" that is by definition ineligible to host divine power.[42] Although Pastor Quentin never indicated that he believed God to be physically present in the fruit set apart for the offering, his assumption of the offering's inalienability is apparent. The case Pastor Quentin was making was for a kind of giving unencumbered by a fear of lack and based in the knowledge that God, as wealthy adoptive father, would provide for the needs of all his adopted children.

Along the lines of Marcel Mauss's theory of the gift, Pastor Quentin could also have figured that "by giving one is giving oneself."[43] In this case, the parishioners contributing fruit to the church offering—intended to be simultaneously a way to give to God and to the poor—would constitute not only giving the fruit but also giving of their own selves. The donation of fruit therefore represented a commitment of one's life to God, to the church community, and to the well-being of the poor. Taking back that which one had given, therefore, would have been to falter in one's commitment of one's own self to God and to those whom God loves. This would be seen as a type of spiritual disloyalty, not in the sense of trafficking with other spirits, but in the sense of abandoning God.

For the parishioners, on the other hand, the fruit's status as offering also instilled it with special significance in that it enabled them to earn social credit within the community. Fellow church members who saw them giving fruit would perhaps view them as more faithful Christians. In Cambodian society, Didier Bertrand notes, gift giving is a primary contributor to social identity in a setting in which giving, rather than possessing, contributes more to individual prestige. "To give is to show power,"[44] Bertrand asserts. To be recognized for one's giving is important within Cambodian culture. With respect to the Cambodian American context, Carol Mortland recalls an elderly Khmer Buddhist's incredulous reaction to the envelopes made available in some Christian churches for the purpose of anonymous giving: "What is the point of giving if no one knows how much you gave?"[45] Similarly, for Pastor Quentin's parishioners, the ritual act of giving, and of being seen giving, was perhaps more important than whether the giving was permanent.

This scenario could be viewed through the lens of the cultural aspect of religious capital, as opposed to its emotional aspect. Rodney Stark and

Roger Finke define religious capital as "the degree of mastery and attachment to a particular religious culture." They identify the "mastery" piece with culture and the "attachment" piece with emotion. They explain, "To participate fully in any religion requires mastery of a lot of culture: how and when to make the sign of the cross, whether and when to say Amen, the words to liturgies and prayers, passages of scripture, stories and history, music, even jokes."[46] Pastor Quentin's parishioners appear to demonstrate concern with the cultural aspect here, as their actions are in keeping with a commitment to exemplifying visibly praiseworthy action in a religious context.

As it turns out, temporary giving occupies a special place in Buddhism as practiced in Cambodia with respect to the building of both social status and karmic merit. Elizabeth Guthrie comments on "Cambodian women['s] ... generous and enthusiastic [support] of Theravada Buddhism," demonstrated, among other ways, through the tradition of "freely giving their ... sons to the Buddhist sangha."[47] This giving, however, need not last a lifetime, and in fact, novice monks often only receive a temporary ordination. Frequently, this brief novitiate lasts only for the "Buddhist Lent," which takes place between the full moons in the months of July and October.[48] According to Ian Harris, "One of the distinctive features of Theravada Buddhism in Cambodia and Thailand, as opposed to that in Sri Lanka, is the ease with which one can enter and leave the monastic life."[49] This practice is so common that the late comparative religion scholar Hans Penner asserted that in South Asia and Southeast Asia, "to become a monk is a rite of passage required of almost every young Buddhist boy, the equivalent of confirmation in Christianity or a bar mitzvah in Judaism."[50] If a novice chooses to return to his family even before the end of Buddhist Lent, he is permitted to do so, and "there is absolutely no stigma attached to leaving" the novitiate.[51] In living as a novice monk, even for a short period of time, a boy brings honor to his mother.[52]

The acceptability of temporary giving in Cambodian culture can be perceived in the popularity of the *Vessantara Jataka*, one of 547 *Jataka* tales featuring the lives of the Buddha. The *Vessantara Jataka* is the story featuring the Buddha's penultimate birth, with the final birth being that of the historical Buddha, Gotama. In Southeast Asia, the *Vessantara Jataka* is the best known of all the *Jataka*.[53] In the story, Prince Vessantara, notable for generosity so expansive that he was willing to give away even his wife, Maddī, and his children, Jāli and Kaṇhājinā, is recognized within Cambodian Buddhism as the very "embodiment of generosity."[54]

While relatively unknown in India, the *Vessantara Jataka* has held a place of honor within Southeast Asia, including Cambodia.[55] According to Katherine Bowie, a Khmer inscription dating back to the eighteenth century mentions the popularity of this tale's recitation among Angkor laity.[56] Adhémard Leclère claimed in 1902 that the *Vessantara Jataka* was "certainly the most important, the most beautiful and the best known" of the *Jataka* tales.[57] At the end of the story, Vessantara and his family find themselves reunited after Sakka, a deity, returns Maddī to him, and Vessantara's father pays the ransom to retrieve Jāli and Kaṇhājinā. Penner explains that by giving Maddī back to Vessantara, "Sakka violates the rule of gift giving," but that "Sakka had no real choice in the matter." According to Penner, Sakka needed to return Maddī in order to prevent Vessantara from "enter[ing] the life of the renouncer," which would have obstructed Vessantara from receiving the eight wishes Sakka had granted him earlier in the story.[58] In other words, the *Vessantara Jataka* itself does not teach that gifts are to be temporary, and Vessantara's situation represents an anomaly within Buddhist ethics. Even so, the reasoning behind Sakka's decision in this case might not be well-known among adherents of the little tradition of Cambodian Buddhism, and it is not out of the question that some, including those of Pastor Quentin's parishioners who grew up hearing this story, might have developed an understanding that giving need not be permanent to be spiritually efficacious.

On another note, Pastor Quentin and his parishioners apparently viewed the fruit offering in different ways with respect to the importance—or unimportance—of its practical, this-worldly utility. Similar to the cash given in Lindhardt's study that still functioned as legal tender, in addition to its sacredness qua church offering, Pastor Quentin saw the fruit donated at his church as special in part because it could be used as food for the poor. For his parishioners, however, preserving the fruit's value as an offering did not require it to be of any particular use beyond the act of giving itself. Within this context, they did not find it necessary to forgo personal consumption or regifting of the fruit. Part of this likely has to do with the religious culture in which they had been immersed prior to their conversion to Christianity. In defense of her and her fellow parishioners' decision to take back the fruit they had offered, one woman in the congregation protested that "it's expensive" to buy fruit to bring to the church, especially when attending more than one service in a single week. Buying enough fruit to make separate offerings for each gathering would have presented a financial hardship for some of the parishioners. One might wonder whether some of Pastor Quentin's congregants also might have believed that the ritual act of giving, regardless of the usefulness of the gift in this life, would enable them to earn spiritual credit akin to karmic merit, just as Vessantara was able to reach perfection while also receiving back the most precious of the gifts he had given. A decision to identify as Christian does not necessarily entail a discontinuity of belief in the karma system. As discussed in the previous chapter, Christian and Buddhist cosmologies often overlapped in the spiritual imaginings of converts—or, as Richard Fox Young and Chad Bauman have said, "those who, more properly, are engaged in the process of converting (conversion, as such, is never finally over in any aoristic sense)."[59]

As with the matters of conversion and multiple religious belonging, marriage played a significant role in conversations surrounding giving and finances, as well. Over lunch one Sunday, a young, single woman named Sorpheny told me that she had come from a poor family, and that she sometimes struggled with envy when she encountered people possessing more material resources than she did. Later in the conversation, she shared with me that if she were to get married, she would need to marry a Christian man, because this would be the only way to ensure her ability to tithe freely. Sorpheny anticipated that a Buddhist or otherwise non-Christian husband would never agree to part with 10 percent of the household income. She noted that young people from her village did not always have a choice in whom they married, although she expected her parents would allow her to decide for herself, since she was already twenty-six and had not been promised to anyone. For context, the median age for women to marry in Cambodia was 20.5 years in 2014, as compared to 23.0 years for men.[60] Sorpheny suggested at one point that regardless of her eventual husband's faith, she was still committed to tithing. Her primary fear in this matter was that if she were to marry a non-Christian, he surely would notice the money disappearing, which would cause her to feel that she was being "unfaithful."

Sorpheny's attitude toward tithing in the context of marriage corresponds with the discussion earlier in this chapter surrounding religious or spiritual capital. Sorpheny's actual finances constituted a tangible example of her spiritual capital, particularly with respect to the "attachment" element. She briefly contemplated tithing in secret but quickly decided that this would not be right. Ultimately, she could not bear the prospect of not giving at all, which led her to resolve not to marry a non-Christian man if she had any choice in the matter. The investment of her money reflected her emotional investment in her religion, and she did not want either to be threatened by a potential marriage to someone who did not share her religious convictions.

Fleeing Financial Temptation

In my conversations with Cambodian evangelicals in Cambodia and in the diaspora, I heard a number of my interlocutors expound on the importance not only of giving in particular but also of entrusting one's financial situation to God more broadly. Pastor Quentin warned members of a weekly Bible study he led that sometimes, becoming a Christian would require a change in employment. Crime scene cleanup, as well as involvement in the sex industry, were among those occupations that fell into Pastor Quentin's category of work inappropriate for those identifying as Christians. He matter-of-factly noted that if a person were "a prostitute" or "a cleaner," then the person would need to pursue a different line of work. Expressing loyalty to God through finances included not only giving to the church but also ensuring that one's means of acquiring money was acceptable to God.

One woman in the diaspora talked about falling into a habit of being dishonest about her work situation in an attempt to qualify for financial assistance. During this time, she had an experience where she felt that God had assured her that she was *not alone*. She recalled that she had been at work one day and murmured aloud, upon receiving her paycheck, that it was not enough to cover her rent. Her boss overheard her lament and asked how much she would need to pay for her housing for the month. In an unforeseen turn of events, the boss added an additional hundred dollars to her paycheck every month, not as a temporary advance payment to be taken out later, as she had initially supposed, but as a permanent raise. In response, my interlocutor burst into spontaneous praise, exclaiming, "God, you are so amazing!"

Around the same time, this same interlocutor's pastor had been preaching about the necessity of honesty in Christian life. She began to experience inner turmoil as she remembered her dishonesty concerning her work situation. While still enduring distressing financial difficulties, she suddenly felt uncomfortable lying to those who were providing her with help. Thus, she eventually mustered the courage to tell the truth. Her decision resulted in a loss of a notable amount of financial assistance, as she had feared. To her great joy, however, she found out not long thereafter that she was eligible for inexpensive government medical care for her son. This surprise made a significant difference in her household budget. Overwhelmed with gratitude, she declared, "God takes care of me!"

Remembering the Sabbath Day

One way that the Cambodian evangelicals I encountered entrusted their finances to God was through the practice of refraining from working during certain times of the week, perhaps several hours or even an entire day, in order to dedicate that time to interacting with God. Most often, my interlocutors who referred to setting aside time for God had in mind a Sunday Sabbath day, a discipline which some but by no means all evangelicals practice today, and for which the CMA mission in Cambodia in the early to mid-twentieth century likely laid the foundation.[61]

For my interlocutors, refraining from work for even part of what otherwise could have been a workday often came at great financial cost. Pastor Sarah, like several of my other interlocutors in Long Beach, operated a donut business. During the 1980s, a proliferation of donut shops owned by Cambodian refugees expanded throughout California, due to the initiative and support of donut pioneer Bun Tek "Ted" Ngoy. Ngoy, a former Cambodian refugee himself, started as a trainee at a Winchell's franchise and eventually bought his own shop, Christy's (the first of many). As Ngoy expanded his reach, he and his family supported other Cambodians interested in joining the donut industry, including by sponsoring visas and starting new shops before renting them to other Cambodians as turnkey businesses.[62] Ngoy's efforts were enhanced by those of his cousin, Bun H. Tao, who opened a donut supply business, offering instant credit and lending out coffee machines.[63] As of 2014, there were 1,500 Cambodian-owned donut shops in California. Pastor Sarah was one of those who had been in the business over the long haul, having operated her shop for twenty years. As I chatted with Pastor Sarah and a handful of other Long Beach interlocutors in a booth at her donut shop one day, she acknowledged that the parishioners at the church she served sometimes expressed concern over her decision to work at the shop on Sundays before the church service. She eventually sought solace in the gospel story in which Jesus heals the man with the withered hand on the Sabbath. In this story, Jesus defends his decision to heal—that is, to work—on the Jewish day of rest by indicating that it is lawful to "do good" on the Sabbath.[64] Pastor Sarah likewise supported her choice as a Christian to work on the Sabbath, especially since she viewed her donut shop as something of an outpost for neighborhood evangelism.

Others were stricter in their keeping of the Sunday Sabbath and in their desire for others to do so, as well. Pastor Joshua, part of whose story appears in chapters 2 and 3, explained that before he entered pastoral ministry, he worked seasonally in a Christmas tree lot. His supervisor made an impression on him, because the man "open[ed] the Bible and read a chapter and then pray[ed]" before work every day. Pastor Joshua remarked, apparently with gratitude, that the supervisor did not stay to monitor the workers or pressure them to work faster. On Sundays, the supervisor did not schedule any shifts, thereby creating space for the workers to "go to worship God." As a Christian leader, Pastor Joshua retained his firm belief in the importance of Sabbath rest and began exhorting his parishioners to abstain from work on Sundays. When a woman from his congregation asked him to pray for her as she prepared to launch a sewing business, he assured her, "If you do open the business, don't do [business] on Sunday. God will bless you." Initially, the woman followed Pastor Joshua's advice but, he shared with a tinge of disappointment, as demand for her services grew, she started working on Sundays in an effort to fulfill the influx of orders for clothes to alter.

Ruth, a rideshare driver, explained that previously, she had been caught up in alcohol and drug abuse, but that after she became a Christian nine years prior, she felt empowered to adopt a different lifestyle. As part of her new spiritual practice, she joined a morning prayer group and a Bible study that Pastor Quentin hosted once a week. During these gatherings, Pastor Quentin and the other participants brought food to share, took turns selecting and expounding on a Bible passage for the week, and prayed together for any concerns that arose during the gathering. Ruth prioritized her attendance at these meetings and noted the sacrifice implicit in her involvement. If she were not at the meeting, she would have used those hours to work and make money. Ruth used to wake up at four in the morning to start work, but after her conversion, she spent her early morning moments in prayer. The morning I first met Ruth, she intimated that God had brought to mind the passage Lamentations 3:24–25. This experience was salient for Ruth because before that day, she explained, she had never known these verses, which read: "'The LORD is my portion,' says my soul, 'therefore I will hope in him.' The LORD is good to those who wait for him, to the soul that seeks him. It is good that one should wait quietly for the salvation of the LORD." Ruth interpreted the passage, and the experience of the reference coming to mind without her having read the verses previously, as encouragement from God that her time in prayer and Bible was well spent, even though she had been accustomed to using that time to drive passengers. She felt it was worth it to dedicate this time to God and, in so doing, entrust her financial situation to God.

For many Cambodian converts to evangelicalism, Christian spirituality is characterized by an informal relationship with a God they see as ultimately accessible, by a commitment of exclusive loyalty to God, and by an expectation that their pattern of interactions with God will result in visible changes in their lives, including with respect to how they manage their finances and other material resources. Within Cambodian evangelicalism, there is a concept of God not only as father but specifically as a bounteous, generous, adoptive father who understands and relates to the experience of genocide survivors and their descendants. Confidence in this relationship with a God that they believe to be alive and available to them equips many to overcome long-held feelings of isolation.

In this chapter, I investigated a system of spiritual practices and values that typically accompanied the expressed religious ideals of my interlocutors, both in Cambodia and in the diaspora. These ideals resulted from the cosmological remapping that occurred alongside Cambodian conversion to evangelicalism. In the book thus far, we have considered stories affecting individuals and local communities—for example, a single church or community group. I would like to take a step back in the next chapter and acknowledge the nuances characterizing the connections and distinctions within Cambodian evangelicalism as a transnational phenomenon.

Chapter 5

TRANSNATIONAL MINISTRY
AND MUTUAL MISSION

Thus far, this book has explored aspects of Cambodian evangelical spirituality involving the interactions between humans and spiritual beings. Lest I inadvertently give the impression that my interlocutors practiced a solely individual form of Christian piety, I emphasize in this chapter the fervency for mission that formed a key part of most of my interlocutors' approaches to spirituality. My interlocutors conceived of mission as going out beyond one's immediate surroundings to evangelize, that is, to communicate to others one's understanding of Jesus's message. This mission took place in the context of transnational ministry, including ministry within an interconnected community of ethnic Cambodian evangelicals in Cambodia and throughout its diaspora. One important theme arising in the midst of mission to other Cambodians was the emphasis on honoring one's parents, especially as Christians have had a reputation among Cambodian Buddhists of abandoning their parents after conversion. Another common, mission-related concern that my interlocutors harbored revolved around the improvement of American society, including, in many cases, through staunch support for then president Donald Trump. To my surprise, Cambodians both inside and outside of the United States often championed Trump's cause.

With respect to method, much of the mission within transnational Cambodian evangelicalism occurred with the aid of the internet. This was the case even before COVID-19, but given the recent shifts that have taken place in global communication in the wake of the pandemic, it is worth considering the potential long-term impact of the pandemic on Cambodian evangelicals' approaches to transnational ministry. This chapter makes the case that Cambodian evangelicals tend to practice an outwardly oriented form of Christianity characterized by connections between different communities within the Cambodian world, toward the goal of individual and societal restoration both in Cambodia and in the West by means of frequent international travel and, increasingly, digital media.

Outward Orientation

With a few exceptions, each of my interlocutors exhibited an ardent yearning to see other Cambodians—and, in the diaspora, Westerners, as well—develop a deeper understanding of Christian faith. One of my Phnom Penh–based interlocutors, Pastor Samedy, whose story appears earlier in this book, upheld mission—through his understanding of "discipleship"— as a Christian's highest priority. While acknowledging the importance of prayer, Pastor Samedy voiced dismay over what he saw as a tendency among some Christians to focus so heavily on prayer that there was no time or energy left for discipleship (the inviting and guiding of new disciples of Jesus Christ). He opined:

> So many Christians in Cambodia only pray, and they don't make disciples. We are in the spiritual war, fighting, but we need to go out. What we pray shows us who we are to God. For myself, I focus on missions. The word discipleship is the most important thing in my life and my ministry. God is the Father. He knows before we pray. The way we talk to him shows us who we are. Discipleship is my heart. I want to help people to understand what discipleship is.

When I followed up with Pastor Samedy and asked, "What is good discipleship?" he answered by way of a short sermon, beginning with the rhetorical question, "What did Jesus tell us about discipleship?" Starting to answer his own question, he continued, "Come and follow me; I will make you—"

Pastor Samedy paused here, perhaps testing my knowledge of the gospel story by inviting me to finish the sentence. Caught slightly off-guard, I gathered my thoughts and slipped back into Sunday School mode, responding, "Fishers of men."

"Fishers of men," he repeated with the approving nod of a teacher. "Come and follow Jesus. Disciples are the ones who want to come and follow Jesus. They follow Jesus every day. Disciples are the persons who change their life through Jesus—making disciples of Jesus, with Jesus."

Pastor Samedy appealed to scriptural authority at this point, saying that the definition was "not from my definition, but from the Bible." He elaborated, saying,

> *The way to be disciples is through relationship. We need to help others to grow, so that they can progress from being spiritual infants and become children, teenagers, and adults. We need someone to help them grow from infants into parents who can make disciples—someone who will go and step in to share their problems, and not only their happiness, to go deep into their lives. That is discipleship. It's not only Sundays. We need someone to coach or to walk together with others.*

Pastor Samedy's ministry proved effective in accentuating the importance of discipleship in evangelical life. Marshall, a young educational administrator who attended Pastor Samedy's church, shared similar thoughts on discipleship when I met him for lunch one afternoon at a vegetarian restaurant popular with students in Phnom Penh. Sharing his own views on discipleship, Marshall explained,

> *Jesus spoke not just to the leaders, not just to the pastors. We are all supposed to spread the gospel. We need to believe, but if you don't also change, how can the people see your life as a good example? Your belief should change, and so should your behavior. The process of changing is not that easy. We need mature Christians who can help us.*
>
> *The mission of Christ is to be fishers of men: to make disciples and to baptize people. The teaching process is better in a small group. Jesus had twelve disciples, but he spent most of his time with Peter and John. Jesus said that his mission is complete. Jesus trained the people he was supposed to train, and now, we are supposed to train up new people.*

Marshall's views on mission through disciple-making evoked those of his pastor, exemplifying the kind of intergenerational spiritual mentoring—discipleship—for which certain expressions of evangelicalism have become known.

In Long Beach, I met with a young Cambodian American professional named Teresa, who was involved in leadership at her church on a volunteer basis. She also spoke of this kind of personal, relational discipleship, particularly in the intergenerational context. In the diaspora, where Cambodian churches often included many elderly members, churches often developed a familial atmosphere. Teresa considered the Cambodian American understanding of church relationships as tantamount to family relationships to be an aspect of Christian life from which Western Christians could learn. Indeed, I noticed in my Long Beach fieldwork the ways in which older and younger evangelicals of the same gender, although not always of the same congregation, sometimes met informally, one-on-one, for the purpose of spiritual encouragement, cultural education, and practical assistance.

Mission from the Global South

The conversation about how to speak about transnational ministry originating from the Global South has been ongoing in World Christianity circles for decades, with various scholars employing such terms as "reverse mission" or "reverse flow of mission"[1] to refer to mission from the Global South to the Global North; "South-South mission,"[2] to indicate mission from one part of the Global South to another; and mission from "everywhere to everywhere"[3] as an umbrella term which emphasizes the increasingly multidirectional quality of Christian mission, and which calls attention to the global nature of both the sending and receiving of mission in Christianity worldwide.

In their conversion stories and informal conversations with me, some of my interlocutors shared that at one point in their experience, they had thought of Christianity primarily, if not exclusively, as a Western religion, but eventually overcame the distrust they felt toward the religion prior to converting. Others, however, shared about having become acquainted with Christianity through other Cambodians or through individuals or groups from elsewhere in the Global South.

Nimith, a Cambodian pastor and development worker I met in Phnom Penh, initially encountered Christianity through a combination of mutual mission and South-South mission. Sitting across from me at a café owned by a Christian woman, with the tunes of instrumental Western hymns gently playing in the background over the loudspeaker, Pastor Nimith shared his conversion story with me:

I became a Christian in 1998, when I was a young man—twenty-four or twenty-five years old. I came to Phnom Penh that year from my hometown of Battambang, where I was a hopeless man. I had been smoking, drinking, and gambling. I came to Christ through a poor lady.

I came from a poor family and decided to come to Phnom Penh to look for a job and an opportunity to continue my studies. I didn't have friends or family in Phnom Penh, but I borrowed money from people back in Battambang, so I was able to stay at a guest house.

I asked a [mootoo dup] [motorcycle taxi] driver if he knew of any orphan centers where I might be able to work and get vocational training. I found one and lived there and taught the children and some of the teachers English, since I knew a bit.

One woman came from Pursat Province to visit her son, who was also living at the orphan center. She talked to me about Jesus and showed me the love of Jesus. I thought that if I believed in Jesus, I might have a job and proper place to stay.

The woman told me that if I believed in Jesus, then God would do miracles. She said that she could not promise, but that God could send me to study anywhere. Just because I needed a job, I believed in Jesus.

The lady from Pursat was Khmer, but she saw the sign for a Korean church here in Phnom Penh and introduced me to the pastor. I gave my life to Jesus at that church, hoping I might be able to attend an English class, only to find out that they used to offer such classes but had stopped a while earlier. I was disappointed to hear this, but I was impressed by the welcoming atmosphere of the community. It seemed like they knew me long ago.

One day, at church, one of my cigarettes fell out of my pocket. The pastor asked me, "You are smoking?" I admitted that I was, but I was surprised that the other people at the church were not smoking.

I told the pastor that I wanted to stop smoking and asked him to write out some words I could pray at home to help me. The pastor did not agree to this and said, "Tell your Father what you need."

So, I went home and prayed, "If you are really God, help me to stop smoking."

Not long after that, I felt that something inside me told me that I needed to have a high commitment to stop smoking, rather than only praying about it, if I truly wanted to stop. Helping me to stop smoking

> was the first miracle I believe Jesus really [accomplished for me]. I went from smoking a full pack of twenty cigarettes a day, to fifteen, to two, to one, to zero.
>
> After that, I started praying more and reading the Bible. When the director of the orphan center asked me to get ready to leave, the center provided an opportunity for me to take a course on how to fix television sets and other electronic devices, and to open up my own shop. But I was afraid that if I went to this vocational training course, I would be far away from the church and then would not be able to follow my dream, which was to become a pastor. But if I gave up the vocational training opportunity, then I would lose my place to stay.
>
> I shared about this concern with the pastor, who recommended that I continue praying. Eventually, the church offered me the chance to live on-site. The church paid me thirty dollars a month for food. I worked at the church by cleaning and arranging chairs.

Pastor Nimith would eventually encounter Western missionaries—in fact, the development organization that currently employs him is American. However, his first understanding of Christianity came through the Khmer woman from Pursat and the Korean church to which she introduced him. It was through this church that he experienced belonging, the encouragement that came with overcoming his smoking habit, and the opportunity to pursue his ministerial vocation. During his time in Bible school, Pastor Nimith lived on campus throughout the week and then came back to stay at the Korean church on the weekends. It had become for him a home away from home. Although he was working at a Khmer church when I met him, rather than the Korean church, he remembers the impact that community and, particularly, its pastor had on his development as a Christian and as a spiritual leader.

Matt, the young pastor of Descending Dove Church, also described himself as hopeless prior to his conversion, which came about through an encounter with a church planted by Christians from the Philippines. When his parents divorced, Matt mourned the essential loss of his family's home as he and his siblings scattered. While a university student living far from his village, the grief soon became too much for him to bear, and he became suicidal. A classmate invited Matt to church not long thereafter, and he remembers being impressed with the way the young people at the church were "so good at encouraging people." In the following years, however, his despair deepened. "Buddha said when you have life, you have suffering," he explained. "In order to kill suffering, you kill self." Remembering a turning point that took place during this difficult time in his life, Matt shared the following story:

> One day, I was on the university campus, and I called out to God and said, "If you are real, God, do you see what I am going through? If you are real, come and help me." After five minutes, a mission team from the church came up to me. They asked me how I was doing, and I explained my struggles. They said to me, "Don't worry. There is a God who can help you with your situation." I told them, "I know who. My friend already told me. I just asked for his help."

Matt recalls that the church members inspired him to "be hopeful in life," and their ministry to him inspired him to adopt a spirituality characterized by a desire to encourage others. He thought to himself, *If I believe in God, I might be full of wisdom and able to comfort other people like they do.*

For Pastor Nimith, Matt, and others who were nurtured in their faith through the evangelistic work of Christians from East or Southeast Asia, the concept of mission was not conflated with Western culture the way it has been for so many others, both in the Global North and in the Global South. Within this context, there was nothing strange for them about the idea of Cambodian evangelicals ministering to other Cambodians, to Westerners, or to anyone else. Of course, I do not mean to be simplistic about this by implying somehow that this subset of Cambodian Christians is free from Western influence. It must be noted that Cambodian Christians of this younger generation, who encountered Christianity after the refugee camp period through the ministry of non-Western Christians, are still impacted, even if indirectly, by the work of early Christian and Missionary Alliance (CMA) missionaries from the United States, Canada, and France, as well as by the Cambodian Christian refugees who led ministries along the Thai border during and after the genocide. One prime example of CMA influence on essentially all Christians in Cambodia and its diaspora is the translation of the Khmer Old Version (KHOV) Bible. Many of my interlocutors, as I have mentioned already, showed undying loyalty to this particular version, believing it to be more accurate than the easier-to-understand Khmer Standard Version (KSV) Bible. Even those who use the KSV, however, are not beyond the ambit of early CMA influence, including through the impact of the KHOV on the team of translators who produced the KSV. For example, Barnabas Mam, who served on this translation team, used the KHOV as a new Christian, as it was the only Khmer Bible in existence at the time. In his memoir, *Church Behind the Wire*, Mam writes about working for the Bible Society in order to earn enough money to buy Bibles in English, French, and Khmer.[4]

To be sure, as I have emphasized throughout this book, Cambodian evangelicals have not been merely recipients of mission, but also initiators of it. To the list of categories of mission enumerated at the beginning of this subsection, I add the category of "mutual mission," a multidirectional pattern of ministerial itinerancy and communication among various nodes of a diaspora and its original homeland. Mutual mission is evinced in Cambodian evangelicals' commitment to spreading their vision of Christian hope throughout the Cambodian world.

Mutual Mission

It is not uncommon for members of an ethnic group to minister among members of their own group. What I find especially noteworthy about mutual mission within transnational Cambodian evangelicalism has to do with how converts strive to navigate the nuances of ethnic and national belonging while seeking to live their faith in public. During this often-fraught process, Cambodian evangelicals frequently go to great lengths to relate to their friends and family their understanding of what it means to have hope after having endured intense, collective suffering in the wake of the Khmer Rouge regime.

Kathryn Poethig has written about the sense of vocation that former Cambodian refugees identifying as evangelicals have felt toward their country of origin, calling attention to how they have believed themselves called by God to return to Cambodia in order to take part in the nation's restoration. Drawing on her research with Cambodian Christians based in the United States who joined their Buddhist counterparts in making their way back to their homeland during the 1990s, Poethig explains that rather than involving themselves explicitly in the world of politics in Cambodia, such Christians "chose instead to 'share Christ' with government officials." Poethig recalls that one of her interlocutors prayed that Cambodian political leaders would receive wisdom and salvation from God. They believed that if Cambodia were to exemplify what they deemed the best of Christian values, the country would be strengthened through the power of God. Former refugees returning to Cambodia from the United States, which they imagined as "a Christian nation," enjoyed a certain level of respect for having lived in "a democracy with a Christian majority." With firsthand experience of this kind, returnees could identify aspects of American culture and society that they found properly Christian and therefore worthy of emulation, such as "honesty" and "faithfulness," while rejecting those that fell short of Christian holiness, like "decadence" and "materialism." Poethig suggests that Cambodian Christians who prayed for the conversion of government leaders did so due to the notion that Christianization, in addition to democratization, was crucial to full entry into modernity.[5]

My own interlocutors, like Poethig's, generally maintained a desire to work toward the transformation of transnational Cambodian society. I observed during my fieldwork a multidirectional flow of mission in the Cambodian evangelical community around the world, in which Cambodian Christians crossed international boundaries, whether physically or digitally, with the purpose of ministering to other Cambodian communities. Often, the work of transnational ministry needed to take place over the phone, videoconferencing, or social media, as finances and visa acquisition often proved prohibitive. Even so, there were many among my interlocutors who managed to find ways to travel in person, even at great personal cost.

This phenomenon of multidirectional, transnational ministry was apparent in the lives of many of my interlocutors, whose frequent mobility sometimes directly impacted the nature of my research. For example, I met Pastor Samedy in Philadelphia, at Pastor Bona's church, when Pastor Samedy was visiting from Phnom Penh to teach for three days on basic theology. I was surprised to learn that it was not, in fact, a three-day intensive course, as I had initially assumed, but rather a face-to-face continuation of a course he had already been teaching for quite some time via Google Hangouts. When Pastor Samedy heard about my research, he gave me his business card and informed me that when I arrived in Phnom Penh the following spring, there would be people at his church whom I could interview. He pulled out his phone, took a picture of me to send to his parishioners, and assured me I would be warmly received within his community.

Eight months later, after my arrival in Cambodia, I called Pastor Samedy to remind him of when and how we had first met. When I asked him if it would still be permissible for me to visit his congregation, he responded with enthusiastic recognition, ready to make good on the promises he had made in Philadelphia. The very next morning, he arrived at my apartment building and eagerly invited me to settle onto the seat behind him on his motorcycle. Before long, we arrived at one of the Christian schools that he and his family operated, and eventually, he introduced me to his entire congregation. He later arranged for me to accompany a small team from the church out to a daughter congregation in the nearby province of Takeo. Pastor Samedy's parishioners in Phnom Penh readily accepted me as one of their own, even when he left for three weeks for ministry-related events in the United States. He later told me that he had been to forty-five states on his many visits combined.

Larry, a minister to whom I had been connected through friends of friends, first spoke with me over the phone before I left for fieldwork. He and I met in person shortly after my arrival in his hometown of Long Beach, where he provided a helpful orientation to important sites for the Cambodian evangelical community. I was unable to formally interview Larry during my time in California, so I carried out my interview with him over Skype, after I had begun research in Paris. Somewhat uncannily, Larry and his wife moved to Phnom Penh within the same forty-eight-hour period during which I myself landed in Cambodia's capital. The interconnectedness of the Cambodian diaspora has primed it for a circular pattern of mission from the diaspora to the homeland and from the homeland to the diaspora.

In this network of mutual mission, neither the churches in Cambodia nor those in the diaspora fell into the category of mere recipients of mission; rather, churches in Cambodia, France, and the United States were all, in different ways and at different times, both senders and recipients of Cambodian Christian missionaries and itinerant pastors. Despite the significant cost involved in international travel, the Cambodian evangelicals I encountered in my fieldwork prioritized visiting Cambodia as often as they could afford, frequently with ministry in mind. This type of travel was not limited to the wealthiest among the refugee population. Ting Xiu relocated from Cambodia to Long Beach, where she lived on a few hundred dollars a month. Fervent in her desire to engage in volunteer ministry in Cambodia, she saved aggressively, resided with a friend with the aim of decreasing her living costs, and set aside enough money to make the journey.

Pastor Sarah, part of whose story appears in chapters 3 and 4, shared the following story about evangelizing among Cambodian communities in Long Beach and in Cambodia:

> *By 1990, I was attending [a multiethnic church with a large Khmer service]. I joined with the church in an evangelistic outreach event*

where we were knocking on doors and sharing the gospel. I spoke to one woman on this day, and the woman spoke Khmer. I prayed to ask God to show me which passage to share, and Psalm 23 came to mind.

In 1995, the pastor's wife asked me to go to Cambodia just to pray, but while I was there, I ended up teaching the Bible and teaching songs. When I got back to Long Beach, I went through Khmer Bible training for three years. I graduated in 1998 and was ordained that same year. In 2006, I started working at Neighborhood Light Church, where I pastor today.

Within Cambodian evangelicalism around the world, this impetus toward making disciples took on a multidirectional, as well as transnational, quality. As I was traveling for my fieldwork, some of my interlocutors were also on the move. Kalyann, a member of Pastor Bona's church in Philadelphia, was preparing to leave for Cambodia late in the summer of 2018, around the same time that I was saying my goodbyes to the community in advance of my departure for Long Beach. Indeed, the first time I visited Pastor Quentin's Bible study, he had appointed another minister to lead in his place, because he himself had just returned from Cambodia.

As is the case for many Cambodians living outside their homeland, my interlocutors typically found themselves connected to a broad network of friends and family members throughout their transnational ethnic community. This has long been the experience of Cambodians in the United States, France, and elsewhere. Khatharya Um has noted that the Cambodian community is a globally connected one, making it difficult to draw a hard line between the experiences of Cambodians from Cambodia and those based in the diaspora.[6] She therefore rejects the Asia-America divide in cultural studies and points to the multiple ways Cambodian refugees defy this binary.[7] This pattern of transnational communication, support, and travel between the diaspora and the homeland has continued for decades, with some individuals and families opting to live part of the year in one country and part of the year in another. I also encountered several Christian leaders during my fieldwork who lived on a different continent from close members of their immediate family. Decisions regarding the frequency of such travel may also be impacted by the desire to nurture relationships with parents, siblings, and children who live in other parts of the transnational Cambodian community.

Former Cambodian refugees who have become Christians tend not to identify primarily as citizens of Cambodia or of the United States—although many of them possess dual citizenship—but rather as citizens of "the heavenly kingdom."[8] For Cambodians who came to the United States as refugees, social rejection has come from multiple directions. Cambodians remaining in the homeland have sometimes refused to acknowledge as true Cambodians those returning from the United States or elsewhere in the diaspora.[9] East Asian Americans whose families have been in the United States for multiple generations, though caught in the struggle against the unwanted label of "perpetual foreigner" themselves, have not always viewed Cambodians as among their own. Leakthina Chau-Pech Ollier depicts the ways in which a segment of young Cambodian refugees living in the United States responded to the frequent sense of exclusion from the Asian American category, explaining that this experience of marginalization has caused even those among them who are US citizens, whether by birth or by naturalization, to associate the category "Cambodian American" with a certain kind of discomfort. In this vein, she notes that some, notably including the Khmer rapper Prach Ly (styled praCh) more readily identify as "Cambodians in America," thereby acknowledging the distance they already feel from each community contributing to their aggregated cultural experience. As "strangers to Cambodia while they are not yet made to feel part of America," they are also "Asian and yet disavowed by Asian America." For this reason, many of Ollier's interlocutors have sought solace in rap music as a means of expressing themselves in a context in which being heard is easier said than done.[10]

While there were no rappers among my interlocutors, the experience of rejection from multiple communities was widespread. For Cambodian evangelicals in the United States, it was often an uphill battle to be taken seriously by other, non-Cambodian members of the Christian community. Teresa lamented that when she was growing up, the other congregations within her denomination always thought of her church as "the church to help," rather than as a full partner in Christian community and ministry. She expressed frustration and fatigue regarding the ways in which she felt that the rest of the American church had overlooked her congregation, dismissed them, and characterized them solely according to their apparent need.

Pastor Sarah pulled me aside after a Bible study meeting in Long Beach and pointed in her Khmer Bible to the following passage:

> On the contrary, the members of the body that seem to be weaker are indispensable, and those members of the body that we think

less honorable we clothe with greater honor, and our less respectable members are treated with greater respect; whereas our more respectable members do not need this. But God has so arranged the body, giving the greater honor to the inferior member, that there may be no dissension within the body, but the members may have the same care for one another.[11]

I gathered from this encounter that Pastor Sarah intended this passage as a charge for me as an ethnographer. In pointing it out to me, she hoped to remind me of my accountability to my interlocutors who had been refugees and whose contributions to the broader Christian community often had been overlooked.

In Paris, Ponleu also emphasized her role as a contributor to what she saw as the mission of Jesus. One afternoon, Ponleu and I met for refreshments at her apartment, as we were wont to do during my time in France. I waited for her at the table as she used a manual orange squeezer to make juice for us to share. She proceeded to pour the orange juice into the two halves of one of the oranges she had just juiced: one orange peel cup for me, and one for her. As we chatted about family, her French language studies, and a wide variety of spiritual topics, Ponleu reached for her Khmer Bible and turned to John 17:4, in which Jesus tells God the Father, "I glorified you on earth by finishing the work that you gave me to do."[12] She emphasized after reading this verse aloud that Jesus had tasked his followers with participating in the work he had begun, that they would complete it while he was physically absent from the earth. Ponleu then flipped back a few pages in her Bible and pointed to John 14:1–3, in which Jesus reassures his disciples, telling them that although he will soon leave them, he "will come again" and "take [them] to [himself], so that where [he is], there [they] may be also."[13] Ponleu, interpreting this as a passage about heaven, declared repeatedly, "I don't want to go to heaven alone." Taking this passage as something of a foundational text for her personal mission, she stressed that it was important for Christians to evangelize to friends and family, so that they would be able to be together in heaven.

Honor Thy Father and Thy Mother

Several of my interlocutors spoke of the necessity of striving to overcome misconceptions about their new religion when speaking about Christianity with Buddhist friends, colleagues, and relatives. Chief among them was the idea that converting to Christianity required one to abandon one's parents. Pastor Nimith told me that the Buddhists at his place of work believed not only that Christians lacked respect for their own parents but also that Christians taught others "not [to] cry when [their] parents die." In conversations with his Buddhist colleagues, Pastor Nimith attempted to disabuse them of this notion. Larry told me that when he encountered young people considering converting to Christianity, he recommended that they first approach their parents and talk to them about "the decision [they are] about to make." He encouraged them to explain to their parents, "I'm not leaving you," and to ensure the parents understand that Christianity tells children to "honor" their parents. The conception in Cambodia of Christians as unfilial likely has its roots in the tendency of some Cambodian Christians to avoid participating in ancestor rites due to concerns of the spiritual implications and repercussions of such activities.

Some of my interlocutors underscored how the commitment to filial piety needed to be more than an ideal to be defended verbally, but also an observable aspect of a Christian's comportment. Marshall pointed to an increase in enthusiasm with respect to honoring one's parents as a form of life transformation that would confirm an authentic conversion to Christianity. He explained, *Some adult people do not really obey their parents. The change should start in your house. At home, young people need to do more housework.* In Marshall's view, therefore, honoring one's parents through obedience, even into adulthood, and making oneself useful around the house were ways in which both male and female converts could produce recognizable evidence of Christian faithfulness.

Reverse Mission: Toward a Greater America?

Another key theme within the context of mission from Cambodia relates to commitment to the improvement of American society, even by Cambodian evangelicals living outside the United States. As World Christianity scholars have noted for over twenty years, Christians from the Global South have begun feeling called to carry out mission in the Global North—and sometimes, within the very countries that had initially sent their own missionaries in previous generations. Cambodia is no exception to this rule.

While those who witnessed refugee camp revivals, led to a significant extent by Cambodian evangelicals themselves, knew that Christianity was not merely a Western religion, many remained of the mind that the West was invariably Christian. My interlocutor Lina chuckled slightly while relating the story of her and her husband's initial exploration of Christianity while they were refugees in Thailand:

> *I became a Christian in the Thai camp in 1979. I had never heard about Jesus in Cambodia. My husband accepted Jesus first. He told me, "You have to believe in Jesus." His point was not really to go to heaven, but maybe to be able to go to the US or somewhere else.*

This part of Lina's story is so common among Southeast Asian refugees who converted to Christianity during this period it has become expected in certain scholarly circles. Members of the refugee community in Thailand understood that their means of leaving the camps rested at least in part on the favor of a sponsoring organization based abroad. As the majority of the voluntary organizations present in the refugee camps expressed Christian beliefs,[14] many refugees were under the impression that becoming Christians would land them the opportunity to resettle in a wealthy Western nation.[15] Cambodian refugees thought of the United States as an ideal country for resettlement, and they also thought of it as a Christian country. However, following their arrival in the country, it did not always live up to their vision of a "Christian" nation.

By the time I began my fieldwork in 2018, it was no secret that the vision of America that my interlocutors initially had held was not at all accurate. They were by then cognizant of an array of social problems affecting American society, including, in many cases, in the very neighborhoods in which they lived. My interlocutors maintained an acute awareness of their vulnerability to robbery, theft, and other crimes, for example. In Philadelphia, Pastor Bona declared during an adult Sunday School class one morning, *If everyone is a Christian, then no one has to lock their door or their car.* In Long Beach, Pastor Quentin advised me not to park my car, a thirteen-year-old Hyundai Elantra, on the street, but rather inside the church parking lot, which was protected by a chain link fence about ten feet high. A prominent bullet hole in the window of one of many Long Beach donut shops at which I liked to sit sometimes and enjoy a chocolate old-fashioned reminded me to keep my wits about me. While speaking with Frank, the White American pastor of a multiethnic Long Beach church comprising several congregations, including one that met in Khmer, I learned about the suffering the community had endured in the midst of the gang wars of the 1990s. During that time, three young Khmer men from the church were killed, and another was shot four times but survived. In her essay on Cambodian rap music, Ollier calls attention to the difficult lives Cambodian refugees led after arriving in the United States. Analyzing themes figuring into Cambodian rap music in the American context, Ollier poignantly notes that despite the initial welcome refugees received through public assistance and literacy courses, once they arrived "on the streets of Long Beach, Oakland, Stockton, or Lowell, they would have to fend for themselves, walking to the corner grocery stores with food stamps in hand while dodging one of the few indiscriminations: bullets."[16]

The disparity between the image of the Christian nation that many of my interlocutors initially had envisioned and the stark reality of poverty, addiction, gang violence, and other dangers, combined with the sense of purpose they found in the idea of having experienced God's rescue during the Khmer Rouge period, gave rise to the concept of the United States as a new mission field for Cambodian evangelicals. Robert Wuthnow takes a somewhat dismissive tone when responding to the prospect of "a kind of reverse missionary movement from South to North," saying that such a concept "is certainly worthy of consideration, but its current scope should not be exaggerated." To support his call to caution in this matter, he suggests that "the 33,000 foreign missionaries said to be working the United States could well describe nothing more than immigrant pastors ministering to immigrant congregations."[17] One might infer from such a statement the assumption that "immigrant congregations," led by "immigrant pastors," are too concerned about their own affairs to be seen as agents of what properly would qualify as mission.

On the topic of being an ethnic specific church, one Cambodian church leader in the United States recalled with no small tinge of sadness the weariness with which she had entered discussions with Americans leveling the accusation of insularity against her and her congregation, located in a primarily non-Cambodian neighborhood.

> When we first moved to the new church, we met in the building of an African American church. They asked us if, when we're there in the neighborhood, if we were planning to serve the community—because I know the area around there, there are no Cambodians. So, to me, when someone asks you that question, "Is your church only going to serve Khmer people, or also the community?" I think, we are no different than Americans. It's just that we have limits because of our language

barrier. We don't want to introduce Jesus or speak about Jesus and then not explain it in the right way. We definitely have no separation when we think about which people we like to tell about Jesus. That's why the last year and the year before, we tried to be more involved in the community, but there are only certain things we can do. For some things, because of the different culture, people didn't feel comfortable to be involved with us, how we worship and all.

My interlocutor shared in this conversation about wanting to serve the community across ethnic and cultural lines but experiencing practical difficulties, such as anxiety surrounding inaccurate preaching due to linguistic limitations, as well as of rejection, or fear of it, by those to whom she and the other Cambodian evangelicals in her church hoped to minister.

In addition to this expectation of insularity, applied by many in the United States to immigrant churches more broadly, refugees find themselves facing another level of suspicion when it comes to thoughts concerning their agency or impact beyond their own community. Thomas Pearson specifically critiques the typical depiction of refugees, even among scholars. He joins Liisa Malkki in lamenting the portrayal of "refugees as victims, reduced to a faceless mass of displaced humanity and subject to . . . healing intervention."[18] Referencing Malkki, Pearson explains that through this stereotyping and "silencing of refugees,"[19] they "are reduced to . . . passive objects."[20] Through his ethnographic study of a Vietnamese Montagnard-Dega community in North Carolina, Pearson paints a different picture of refugee life, highlighting their general success as "well-integrated and self-sufficient citizens." The title of his book, *Missions and Conversions*, relates not only to the conversion of his interlocutors from their indigenous religion to Christianity—or from refugee to their "new 'Dega selves'"[21]—but also to the Montagnards' conversion of certain American Special Forces soldiers who were stationed in their midst during the Vietnam War.[22] Pearson makes a point throughout the book to depict his interlocutors not only as recipients of change but also, and perhaps primarily, as agents of it; in so doing, he could be seen as attempting to mitigate against symbolic violence or to restitute a stolen history.

Within the diaspora, it often happened that the communities in which my interlocutors sought to spread their understanding of the Christian message were made up of Westerners in addition to Cambodians. The desire among many Cambodian evangelicals for mission to the West—"reverse mission,"[23] as Afe Adogame and others have called it—serves to overturn the false narrative of refugees and immigrants as too helpless or insular to be concerned about anything beyond the ambit of their own ethnic communities.[24] For many of my interlocutors, Christian mission offered a sense of purpose in the midst of a communal search for meaning after enduring tragedy on a national scale. As we have seen in the stories of many of my interlocutors in Cambodia and its diaspora, Christian survivors of Cambodia's civil war and its aftermath often have come to view God as responsible for their survival. Such individuals, many of whom fled Cambodia hoping for a better life abroad, have resettled as refugees in the West. Andrew Walls, one of the founders of the field of World Christianity, calls attention to the distinction between what he calls Adamic migration, characterized by "disaster, deprivation, and loss," and Abrahamic migration, which involves "a superlatively better future," even while acknowledging that the two "models overlap."[25] In the case of most refugees, including those whose stories appear in this book, the Adamic aspect is that which tends to be most visible to outsiders. For many of my interlocutors, however, the Abrahamic aspect imbues the pain of loss with profound, spiritual significance. In addition to commemorating their rescue from danger, they also tend to find affirmation and validation of their survival by living into what they perceive to be a specific purpose in this life.

The nuances characterizing this conviction of purpose vary from community to community, and even from person to person, but for most of my interlocutors, it relates in some way to what they understand to be both a responsibility to demonstrate the ideal Christian life to others, and also to teach those who have already converted how to honor their respective relationships with God more fully. The transnational nature of the Cambodian evangelical community provides a global opportunity for survivors to affirm and embody the Abrahamic aspect of their migration experience, celebrating the purpose they believe God to have infused into their lives through miraculous intervention in their time of need.

Pastor Sarah saw her California donut shop as an opportunity to minister to those who walk through its doors, as well as to raise money for her church. When I accompanied a group of interlocutors from Long Beach to the donut shop, which was located in a primarily non-Cambodian neighborhood about an hour's drive from her church, I watched as Pastor Sarah interacted energetically with her customers of various backgrounds, addressing some in English, some in Spanish, and greeting many with a warm smile of recognition. She had operated this shop for twenty years, becoming something of a fixture in the neighborhood. I noticed at least two paintings of Jesus on the walls, in addition to a book about the life of the prophet Daniel, propped up on a shelf in the back. Pastor Sarah had in mind not only the encouragement of the Cambodian community but also the evangelization of her non-Cambodian neighbors. Just before I left Long Beach for Paris, she shared with me that she was in the process of selling her donut shop to another Christian woman. Reflecting on the two decades she had spent as the shop's proprietor, Pastor Sarah felt that she had experienced the favor of God. "God sees us," she said with conviction. "God sees our hearts. Just trust and believe.... Twenty years of donut shop, no robbery."

Sometimes, Cambodian evangelicals' endeavors to evangelize among their non-Cambodian neighbors in the United States took place through children's ministry. One of my early visits to Pastor Bona's church in Philadelphia fell on the Sunday following an annual children's program. That morning, the youth pastor, Chea preached in English, with Pastor Bona as his interpreter at the church's bilingual service. His sermonic testimony was entitled "What Can You Give?" During his message, Chea challenged the entire community, both English-speaking and Khmer-speaking, to consider the transformation that the power of Jesus could bring about for the inhabitants of the neighborhood, most of whom did not share their ethnic heritage. He read from Acts 3:1–10, in which Peter heals a man at the temple gate, saying, "I have no silver or gold, but what I have I give you; in the name of Jesus Christ of Nazareth, stand up and walk" (3:6). Moving through a series of rhetorical questions, Chea asked the congregation, "Do you believe the name Jesus can heal? Do you believe the name Jesus can restore broken families?"

Near the end of his message, Chea declared, pausing every few moments to allow space for Pastor Bona to repeat his words in Khmer:

> *The drug issues in this community, the family abuse that happens all around, the pain, can all be healed in the name of Jesus. We were in pain. We were lost, and someone saved us. That was Jesus. This is our good news. This is our gospel to share with those who are in pain. The one thing we can give this community is the love of Christ. I'm hoping we can set up a ministry that can continue to serve this community.*

This church conceived of its position in the United States as one not of passive victimhood, as much of American culture would suggest concerning refugee communities, but of influence. The older generation attempted to impact broader society, in part, by praying for the nation in which they believed God had specifically placed them following their escape from Cambodia. The strategy of the younger generation prioritized the cultivation of relationships with other young people in the neighborhood, including children.

One might infer from Chea's comments concerning the plan for a new ministry to neighborhood children that there had been inadequate support for such an endeavor. I would suggest, however, that Pastor Bona's decision to serve as interpreter during Chea's message could be taken a signal of his personal support for the young man's proposal. During my time at Pastor Bona's church, I had seen others—normally younger members of the primarily Khmer-speaking community—serve as interpreters during the bilingual worship service, but he himself was never among them. His performance of this task might be seen as an act of collaboration with Chea in encouraging the Khmer-speaking congregation to join him in working toward establishing a greater emphasis on ministry to neighborhood children irrespective of race or ethnicity.

During one of the first church services I attended at Pastor Bona's church, he declared to his congregation, "If you look at us, we are fled from Cambodia, from the Killing Fields." He then proceeded to compare his own situation, and that of his parishioners, with the Exodus story, as the Israelites had fled Egypt and found themselves poised to enter the Promised Land. Later that month, in a sermon based on 2 Chronicles 7 (the same chapter featured in Pastor Sarah's prayer), Pastor Bona elaborated further on the idea of purpose behind his community's arrival in the United States. On the screen behind him, he arranged for the biblical text to be displayed: "If my people, who are called by my name, will humble themselves and pray and seek my face and turn from their wicked ways, then will I hear from heaven and will forgive their sin and will heal their land."[26] Further down, the PowerPoint slide continued, "Referring to the Israelites then, and to us today, the ONES who are called by His Name, the ones who kno[w] Him and seek Him in the Temple of God." Pastor Bona read aloud from his slide, "If we HIS PEOPLE, placed in this land, are not going to SEEK HIM, who will? Who are we expecting to pray that God's will be done?"[27] From Pastor Bona's perspective, his community, composed almost entirely of Cambodian refugees and their children, had come to the United States not by happenstance but because God had "placed" them within their new country and intentionally positioned them to participate in its restoration.

He sought to reinforce in his community the confidence that their having fled oppression abroad did not render them helpless victims, but rather served as an indication of their special vocation as agents of transformation, which he sees reflected in the trajectory they share with the Israelites.

Of course, Cambodian Christians are not alone in their self-identification with the people of Israel. For example, enslaved African Americans in the antebellum United States frequently conceived of themselves as captives in their own Egypt, as remembered in spirituals such as "Go Down Moses," later popularized by the Harlem Renaissance singer Paul Robeson. Christians from Dalit and tribal communities in India have also connected their experiences with the Exodus story.[28] In the case of survivors of the Cambodian genocide, identification with and support for the people of Israel likely stemmed from a combination of their experiences of oppression, suffering, flight, and resettlement in addition to the Keswickian form of Christianity that Western missionaries employed by OMF and the CMA brought to Cambodia in the years prior to the genocide, and which continued to spread in the refugee camps along the Thai border. The plight of the Jewish people constituted an early mission focus of the Keswick Convention dating back to the late nineteenth century, well before the establishment of the British Mandate for Palestine. The Keswick movement, heavily influenced by premillennialism and dispensationalism, produced an expression of Christianity which anticipated the imminent return of Christ, and in which the Jews played a key role in the fulfillment of God's plans in the last days.[29]

Today, Cambodian Christian concern for the Jewish people often includes theologically infused political support for the modern nation state of Israel, as seen in the presence of the Israeli flag inside the sanctuary of church led by a Cambodian pastor in the United States. Finding in US president Donald Trump a fellow supporter of the Israeli cause, many Cambodian evangelicals' viewed Trump as one doing the work of God. Furthermore, Trump's slogan, "Make America Great Again" dovetailed with Cambodian evangelicals' fervent prayers to see the United States return to what was in their envisioning: a safer, holier version of itself. In the view of many of my interlocutors, America's return to greatness required turning away from wrongdoing in addition to prioritizing of political alignment with the state of Israel.

Describing her personal prayer practices, Pastor Sarah incorporated references to Bible verses from the Old and New Testaments, as well as to historical and present-day American civil religion.

> *I pray morning and afternoon. Every minute. I pull my mind, thinking about God. I pray for Cambodia. Like the Bible says, "If my people stop doing evil, I will hear from heaven, and I will heal their country." I pray for the United States, that God would help President Donald Trump to understand the people's needs, so that he can guide the United States toward becoming great again. Like the money says, "In God We Trust."*

This interview took place in English, but the phrase "pull my mind" corresponds to 2 Corinthians 10:5 in Khmer. In both the KHOV and KSV translations of the Bible, the word [tiɲ], which literally means "pull," but which figuratively can mean "captivate," appears in the phrase in which Paul commands the members of the church at Corinth to "take every thought captive to obey Christ."[30] Invoking 2 Chronicles 7:14, Pastor Sarah identifies God's promise to heal the land as motivation for praying for then president Trump to live up to his lofty campaign goal of making America great again. In quoting the official motto of the United States, "In God We Trust," Pastor Sarah hearkens back to a time when, in her understanding, Americans sought to center the life of the nation on faith in the God of the Bible.

While not all of my interlocutors expressed support for Trump or the state of Israel, it is worth noting that such support extended beyond the American-based Cambodian evangelical community. Véronique, an elderly Chinese Cambodian woman in France, declared over lunch one afternoon during the spring of 2019 that Trump was the "hand of God." She proudly held up a photo of Trump on her phone and told me that she hoped to speak with him someday. I conversed openly with Véronique about the difference in my own perspective, and when she asked me why I did not approve of the president, I explained, "He is against refugees."[31] In response to my objection, she squeezed my arm tightly and gently scolded me, insisting that I did not understand. With a grave expression, she said of Trump, "He helps Israel."

Despite Trump's rejection of refugees, it is at least in part through the history of flight from the Khmer Rouge that many Cambodians have developed support for Trump. On January 6, 2021, Vietnamese journalist Nga Pham of the British Broadcasting Corporation (BBC) tweeted a photo in which there could be seen at least one Cambodian flag, along with a scattering of South Vietnamese flags, flying above the sea of humanity present at the US Capitol.[32] While admittedly insufficient evidence exists to assign a religious motive—or any other specific motive, for that matter—to those who carried the flags of Cambodia and of South Vietnam during the events of this now infamous day, the presence of the flags at an event in support of a president identified with an anticommunist ideal bring to mind the generations-long history of the support conservative US politicians have enjoyed from survivors of violent communist regimes.

Regarding Israel, my Cambodian evangelical interlocutors were not deterred in their support of the modern Israeli nation state by its government's contribution toward creating refugees. Rather, they saw in Israel a community all too acquainted with the grief of oppression, the chaos of refugee flight, and the hope of reconnection that they themselves know intimately. Cambodian evangelical attraction to Trump's anticommunist rhetoric is in line with the sentiments of many immigrants and refugees who have fled oppression under communist regimes.[33] Kristin Kobes Du Mez emphasizes the connection between American evangelicalism and anticommunism, recalling that Jerry Falwell famously cautioned his followers on the Religious Right that if Americans failed to prevent communism from eliminating freedom in America, then the nation would be at risk of the same level of "atrocities committed by the Russia-backed 'Vietnamese Communists' and the 'Red China'-backed Khmer Rouge in Cambodia."[34]

By praying for the transformation of hearts and supporting political leaders they believed would aid Israel and fight communism—often interpreted as authoritarian oppression—many of my interlocutors sought to play a role in reinstating their vision of American greatness, while keeping Cambodia and the well-being of its current inhabitants always in mind. Commitment to what they saw as the betterment of US society did not entail an abandonment of the homeland, with both countries, in addition to Israel, figuring into group prayer.

A Glimpse of the Future: Digital Media in Cambodian Transnational Evangelicalism

Ever since the Cambodian diaspora came into existence, expatriates—students, interns, refugees, or otherwise—have frequently sought to maintain ties to their nation of origin. Cambodians, Christian and otherwise, even those unable to travel often or at all, historically have fostered connections with family and friends abroad through letters, phone calls, and remittances. More recently, this phenomenon has made the jump to lightspeed through digital media. This was the case even before the global outbreak of COVID-19, but in the time since I completed my fieldwork, the digital aspect of transnational Cambodian evangelicalism naturally has become more prominent, as I have explored elsewhere.[35]

Anthropologist Birgit Meyer has written about religious sensation as mediated through television and other forms of mass media, particularly in Ghana. Meyer asserts that it is "sensational forms" that are responsible for inducing religious excitement by "[making] it possible to sense the transcendental." She defines these "sensational forms" as "relatively fixed, authorized modes of invoking and organizing access to the transcendental, thereby creating and sustaining links between religious practitioners in the context of particular religious organizations."[36] Interestingly, she considers sensational forms that fall into the categories of "modern media such as print, photography, TV, film, [and] the internet" to be "media that mediate, and thus produce, the transcendental and make it available to the senses."[37] She highlights the role of differing social locations in Ghanaian Pentecostal churches' use of mass media to broadcast worship services, indicating that "religious sensations, in the sense of experiences and feelings, are organized by sensational forms, and hence are subject to social construction and power structures." Examples of this power at work in shaping the religious experience through mass media include the way in which programs broadcast over mass media are "recorded during church conventions yet edited carefully so as to ensure utmost credibility"[38] and the prominent role the pastor plays as the focal point of these programs, "featured as an embodiment—indeed an objectification—of divine power."[39] Meyer muses that from this now common broadcasting practice has arisen "a new sensational form that makes miracles happen on the television screen and seeks to reach out to a mass audience, which is invited to 'feel along' with the televised spectacle witnessed on screen." She also calls attention to the anonymity of the audience.[40]

In considering Meyer's remarks on the use of media in religious practice in her fieldwork, one might notice that the viewers essentially receive whatever the pastor and video editors decide to set before them. The church leaders responsible for editing the videos, persons perhaps as anonymous to the viewers as the viewers are to them, therefore hold a tremendous amount of power in deciding what to include, what to omit, where to focus the camera, and the like—all factors that can contribute heavily to the religious experience of those viewing the service from home.

In my fieldwork, broadcasting also played a significant role, although the power dynamics played out rather differently. In each of the four major cities to which I traveled, my interlocutors took to interactive, digital media to highlight different aspects of their corporate and individual spiritual practice. I remember one Sunday in Long Beach, when a group of older, female parishioners was preparing to ascend the stage to perform a special hymn. This in and of itself was not unexpected, as it is a common custom at many Khmer churches, both in Cambodia and in the diaspora, for there to be at least one song presented during each service by a group of female parishioners. On this occasion, one of the morning's singers, Rany, held out her smartphone and asked that I capture video of the performance for Facebook Live, in order for one of her cousins in Cambodia to have the opportunity to watch it online. Once I started recording, I noticed the tiny images representing various Facebook friends of Rany's appearing on the screen, signaling that they had just begun to view the performance. Once the song was over, I returned the phone to Rany, who did not attempt to record any other part of the service.

In Paris, Ponleu used Facebook Live multiple times per week to record herself praying, singing hymns, reading Bible passages, and preaching to a transnational, Khmer-speaking audience. I remember joining her one morning after receiving a notification on Facebook that she had just begun to broadcast. Prior to singing any given song, Ponleu was careful to announce its corresponding number in the combined Khmer hymnal to facilitate participation from home. As I prepared to participate in Ponleu's self-initiated church service, I pulled out my own copy of the hymnal, which I had ordered years earlier from a Cambodian church in California, and found the page from which Ponleu would soon begin singing. Just as I had been aware of the moment at which each of Rany's friends had started to view her video, Ponleu also knew when I had joined hers. In response, she smiled into her webcam and welcomed me verbally, by name. Over the course of the ninety minutes or so that she led her service, she called out to me multiple times, addressing me in English, French, and Khmer.

Whereas the video broadcasts Meyer describes involved careful curation on the part of a select group of authorized decision-makers, Facebook Live and similar platforms have opened new opportunities for ordinary Christians—including, notably, women—to contribute to the development of their community's transnational, religious experience. Individuals, with or without formal authority, are now able to freely record and broadcast the moments in which they desire for their networks to have the chance to participate. Some of the churches during my fieldwork allowed women to preach and, in some cases, to be ordained. Others invited the contributions of women but stopped short of providing them access to the pastorate. The level of women's involvement in church leadership typically followed denominational lines. Through Facebook Live, my female interlocutors found ways to obtain and maintain a voice for themselves within the Christian community, essentially making a pulpit out of the dining room table or backyard. The interactive nature of Facebook Live also allowed for a personal, relational touch, in contrast to the double anonymity that characterizes the churches about which Meyer has written.

Hyemin Na also calls attention to power dynamics in her analysis of digital media usage within megachurch culture in South Korea. She delineates the intensely editorial role that official producers and designers acting on behalf of a church in a suburb of Seoul play in establishing an accessible worship environment for *Canaan*, the Korean term for Christians who no longer go to church.[41] Na describes an illustrative situation in which a member of a church camera crew discussed with her his approach to filming during the service. This man "conduct[ed] the camera cuts more frequently with faster praise songs during worship, and less frequently with slower songs" in order to convey a certain spiritual "aura" or "vibe" for the sake of those who participated in the church's service by watching the video online.[42]

At the churches featured in Na's article, recognized staff and lay ministers employed digital media to shape the devotional experiences of those who wish to participate in the worshiping community from a distance, including through small groups hosted in the popular Korean messaging application Kakaotalk. Na highlights the creative work of Digital Church (the anonymized name of the church she studied), at which "the staff invited artistically talented congregants to meditate on the pastor's sermons to produce a single-image visual rendition," which the media team proceeded to make available on social media.[43] Regarding the increasingly popular practice of livestreaming, on the one hand, and the strikingly innovative tactic of presenting a sermon summary in the form of an image, on the other, the Korean churches figuring into Na's work share with Meyer's interlocutors a somewhat top-down approach to media representations of worship within the community. With my interlocutors, both in Cambodia and in the diaspora, I was intrigued to see the extent to which laypersons, without any official leadership roles in the church and without having been commissioned by church staff, felt the freedom to broadcast to their personal networks those moments they themselves thought were most pertinent.

Na concludes her article by stating that "those who produce, edit, and disseminate" the images featured in online media representations of worship services "hold a new kind of agency to shape the imagination of the community."[44] Taking her insight into consideration, I submit that the impact of the laity, including women, who tend to fill fewer positions of pastoral authority than do their male counterparts within Cambodian evangelicalism, has been essential in developing new visions of Cambodian Christian faithfulness. Through their videos of formal church services and informal proclamation sessions, several of my female interlocutors played an active role in determining the images of and perspectives on Christianity that continue to make their way around the Cambodian diaspora via the internet.

The power of digital media to amplify the role of women in the development of Cambodian evangelicalism calls attention to a reality that has existed for a long time, without much fanfare. Referring to Cambodian American churches in metropolitan Boston in the 1990s, Nancy Smith-Hefner wrote that it was women who represented "a more active presence within the church, just as they [did] in the [Buddhist] temple, although men continue to fill virtually all church leadership roles."[45] Teresa indicated in a conversation over soup and noodles one afternoon that even at her church, which had recently invited numerous women into leadership roles, it is still a struggle for such changes to take hold. For Khmer people, she explained, pastoral leadership still "looks like a charismatic man."[46] I frequently encountered the same expectation in Cambodia, even though there are denominations and other organizations there that encourage women's leadership in the evangelical context. Women outnumbered men in every church I visited during my fieldwork, a common pattern in churches all around the world,[47] but official authority typically rested with male leaders. Against that background, one can readily appreciate why the growing popularity of spiritual broadcasting over the internet among my female interlocutors demonstrates the democratizing effect of digital media within the transnational Cambodian evangelical community. It has also highlighted the perspectives of women, which heretofore had been overshadowed frequently by the men who held official power within the church.

As evangelical survivors of the Cambodian genocide—as well as their descendants—wrestle with why they survived when so many others did not, many have found solace in the concept that God saved them from death and invited them to pursue a specific purpose in life. Efforts to offer spiritual encouragement to friends and family far-flung throughout the transnational Cambodian cultural network depend heavily today on digital media, including livestreaming public and private worship services through the lens of a smartphone or laptop webcam. This has not only increased the ability of Cambodian evangelicals living in different countries to relate across international borders, but it has also provided a platform for women and laypersons to play a role in highlighting what they perceive to be the most important aspects of Christianity and to propagate their perspectives worldwide.

CONCLUSION

Conversion to Christianity has been influential in the lives of my Cambodian evangelical interlocutors, offering an opportunity to find hope, meaning, and purpose in the face of collective grief. While many of my interlocutors first recalled having experienced a belief-based conversion experience before committing to the Christian community, others remembered it the other way around. Frequently, initial interest in identifying with the Christian religion occurred out of a desire for some practical benefit such as peace within a family; the opportunity to resettle in the United States, France, or another Western nation; or upward mobility following resettlement, with a more intellectual understanding of Christian theology arising later. Another important aspect of the conversion process, which I highlight in this book, is the relational aspect—that is, a convert's understanding not only of his or her familial and communal relationships but also of his or her relationship to the Christian God. My interlocutors' faith testimonies often included anecdotes in which they believed God had intervened in their lives—sometimes, in a direct and visible way—and in response, they felt compelled to interact with God in the way they might with an intimate friend or relative. The relational aspect of conversion could either precede or follow commitment, belief, or both, but whenever it occurred, it occupied a prominent position in the conversion narrative.

Cambodia's layered religious history has contributed to the syncretic nature of its Buddhist cosmology—and, consequently, of its Christian cosmology—influenced by Brahmanism and Mahayana Buddhism, as well as by Khmer and Chinese indigenous religions. Each of these layers maintains a presence in contemporary Cambodian Theravada cosmology, with some Brahmanic deities, for example, remaining as objects of devotion associated with Buddhism, rather than with Hinduism. While there is evidence of Buddhist-Christian multiple religious belonging within the transnational Cambodian community, more common among my interlocutors was the phenomenon of multiple religious believing without multiple religious belonging. In my research, I did not encounter many individuals who openly identified as both Christian and Buddhist. Critical to my interlocutors' self-understanding as Christians was their self-understanding as non-Buddhists, although beliefs rooted in Buddhism have nevertheless remained influential in their lives postconversion. Cosmological borrowings from Buddhism have impacted the way Cambodian evangelicals have talked about Christian doctrine, including that concerning the death of Jesus and the love of God. The ways that categories of spiritual beings are drawn in Cambodian evangelicalism might appear surprising to readers most familiar with Western forms of Christianity, particularly with respect to the expansive and detailed roster of demons and other spirits Cambodian evangelicals typically regard as threats to a Christian's spiritual and physical well-being. Ultimately, Cambodian evangelical cosmology is anchored in the idea that the Christian God retains and demonstrates power over all other spirits.

My interlocutors found hope through a spirituality based on an understanding of God as available to them, particularly in the role of a loving and generous father who related to the experiences of bereavement and adoption—experiences that are both intimately familiar to the Cambodian evangelical community. In response to what they saw as the initiation of relationship on the part of God, my interlocutors sought to demonstrate loyalty to God by refraining from seeking security from any source—whether this-worldly or other-worldly—other than God. Attempting to honor this set of ideals looked different for various Cambodian evangelicals, depending on factors such as age, location, and denomination, but all agreed that the life of a Christian should look different following conversion. For some, this meant deciding never again to set foot on the Buddhist temple grounds, nor even to mention the names of Buddhist deities; others showed a greater tolerance for nuance and expressed a willingness to participate in certain events associated with Buddhist practice, with the caveat that they would articulate the boundaries as to that which they felt they could and could not do as Christians. Many spoke of the importance of demonstrating spiritual loyalty by entrusting to God all of one's resources—including both money and the time one ordinarily would spend earning it—and thereby affirming the giving of oneself to God.

Bearing in mind the importance of personal loyalty to God within Cambodian evangelicalism, my interlocutors were far from individualistic with respect to their religious expression. Through a network of relationships maintained in large part through frequent travel and digital communication—with COVID-19, of course, bringing about a decrease in the former and an increase in the latter—Cambodian evangelicals prioritize mission, including both reverse mission and the multidirectional, transnational phenomenon I have called mutual mission. In the Cambodian evangelical context, the recruitment and mentoring of new Christians often occurs within families or, just as significantly to those involved, within the familial community of the church. Westerners have often perceived Cambodian congregations and other churches founded by refugees to be insular, helpless, and too concerned with their own struggles to care about their impact on the world around them. My interlocutors, however, viewed their position in society through a different lens. Having come into contact with ministries led by Korean and Filipino expatriates, Cambodian evangelicals are no strangers to mission from the Global South. Many Cambodian evangelicals also have found hope and meaning through ministry to other members of their transnational ethnic community, as well as to their new neighbors in the nations in which they have resettled.

The initial vision of the United States as a Christian nation, envisioned by many Cambodian refugees while still in the border camps in Thailand, ultimately failed to meet expectations. In response to the violence, drug abuse, robbery, and other problems affecting the areas in which many of my interlocutors lived, they prayed and looked for other ways to serve their surrounding communities, believing that if more Americans would become Christians, then peace and safety would increase in their neighborhoods. The desire to improve American society sometimes—though not always— manifested through a sympathetic stance toward Trump's "Make America Great Again" movement, despite its track record of exclusion toward refugees.

Particularly for Cambodian evangelicals in the United States, there is often a sense of alienation from the rest of American society, including other Asian Americans, as well as from their own homeland. While trying to maintain transnational connections with friends and family, Cambodian evangelicals have found solace in the idea of a spiritual home where they belong even when they face rejection within multiple earthly communities. Even before the onset of the COVID-19 pandemic, Cambodian evangelical communities sought to overcome the geographical distances between them through digital media, especially when physical travel was difficult to accomplish. It remains to be seen the ways in which responses to the pandemic might impact the technological side of transnational Cambodian evangelicalism in the years ahead, including with respect to the amplification of women's voices.

This book offers a segue into other themes relevant to conversations within World Christianity, including South-South religious trade, the role of youth in the development of Christianity, and the utility and connotations of the term "evangelicalism" in a non-Western cultural context. Especially among my younger interlocutors, encounters with Christians from other parts of the Global South—particularly, though not exclusively, Korea and the Philippines—have been critical to the development of their religious identity. The role of South-South religious trade in the shaping of the generation of Cambodian evangelicals just now coming of age would be an interesting topic of further research.

In Cambodia itself, the active role adolescents and other young people play in church ministry is worthy of further scholarly attention, as it would be a generative point of comparison vis-à-vis Christian cultures in which church members typically must be older to hold significant influence. With the median age of the global Christian population matching that of the world—thirty years old, as of 2017[1]—it is unsurprising, perhaps, that in Christian communities with older populations throughout the world, including many of those in the United States, young people do not typically hold the same level of responsibility in the church as those in Cambodia often do.

In his recent analysis of Global South evangelicalism through the lens of the Bebbington Quadrilateral, Brian Stanley asserts that evangelicalism outside the European world and the influence of the Enlightenment has become more "immanentist." By this, Stanley conveys that Global South evangelicalism is more concerned with matters of this-worldly experience, protection, and spiritual power, and less so with those of doctrine and personal morality. Stanley claims that it therefore could be said that Global South evangelicalism "exhibits a fifth defining characteristic, namely a consistent emphasis on the tangible power of the Holy Spirit, who communicates the victory of Christ over the spirit world and the powers of darkness to the experience of believers."[2]

With respect to Stanley's suggestion, borrowed from John Maiden, of adding a fifth characteristic to the description of evangelicalism, I agree that in the Cambodian evangelical context, the influence of the Holy Spirit's power—"pneumatism," as Maiden terms it[3]—would be an accurate addition to the quadrilateral, rendering it a pentagon. Despite the fact that the majority of my interlocutors identified themselves as categorically against charismatic Christianity, the fault line between charismatic and noncharismatic evangelicalism lies in a different place in the Cambodian context than it does in the American context, and perhaps especially in the White American context. For example, my interlocutors who rejected charismatic spirituality typically did so on the basis of what they identified as excesses associated with silent listening prayer, faith healing, and glossolalia. When it came to matters of spiritual power and protection, it could be more difficult to tell the difference between charismatic and noncharismatic positions. Such terms as "materialist" or even "cessationist," especially when interpreted as a cessation not only of certain gifts of the Holy Spirit but also of nearly all supernatural activity, may not be particularly helpful in the Cambodian context. Even those among my Cambodian evangelical interlocutors who expressed skepticism toward certain approaches to the use of spiritual gifts nevertheless could be said to have maintained a concept of a populous cosmology, as opposed to the sparse cosmology of many Westerners. Individuals in the West who believe in God may possess a concept of the spiritual involving exclusively the interactions between human beings and an invisible God, with nothing more occurring in the world other than that which can be seen. Among those who advocated for the continued use of spiritual gifts such as speaking in tongues, healing, discernment, and words of knowledge, and among those who did not, the populous cosmology my interlocutors possessed led them to adopt a pneumatic approach to Christian faith based on an awareness that the power of God over other spirits remained ever present. In my interlocutors' understanding, it was the notion that God was actively intervening in their world and available for relationship that constituted the source of their hope. Thus, a key aspect of the pneumatism identified by Maiden and Stanley could be that of relationship with God and with one another.

Will the community practicing this pneumatic, relationship-centered expression of Christianity continue to see its reflection in the evangelical mirror? Only time will tell. Recent observers have noted that many White evangelicals, who constitute the majority of those self-identifying as evangelicals in the United States, have begun basing their collective identity less on certain theological perspectives—for example, the components of the Bebbington Quadrilateral—and more on membership in a distinct cultural and political community. For example, well-known evangelical leader Russell Moore recently penned an article on the rise of "unchurched evangelicals," in which he critiques the new form of cultural Christianity as that which "keeps everything about the Religious Right except the religion."[3] Certain aspects of cultural and political evangelicalism in the past several years have run counter to the interests of the Cambodian community, particularly in the United States; chief among these perhaps would be the high numbers of Cambodian American deportations under Trump's presidency and many evangelicals' support of his administration's immigration policies. Will the support for Israel and inclination toward establishing the United States as a Christian nation be enough to keep Cambodians within the fold of the new evangelicalism over the long haul? All of this remains to be seen. What we do know is that while my interlocutors exhibited adherence to the Bebbington Quadrilateral, the defining feature of their expression of Christianity had to do with connection to the Christian God, with everything else flowing out of that connection. For my interlocutors, it was in relating to God that hope was to be found.

EPILOGUE

Reflections on the Ethnographer's Identity in World Christianity

I have argued that Cambodian converts to evangelical Christianity have found, through their conversion, a profound sense of purpose, both as individuals and as a people, in the wake of large-scale tragedy. These findings are based on a combination of interviews and participant observation with Cambodian Christians in Philadelphia, Los Angeles, Paris, and Phnom Penh. Ethnography, by virtue of its relational quality, can never be purely objective. I am keenly aware, therefore, that my research process and interpretations have been shaped by each of a number of aspects of my identity, as perceived internally and interpreted externally by my various interlocutors. These factors combined to affect my reception within the various communities I visited, which in turn impacted the research itself. The entrée I was given—or denied—in any given instance, the specific individuals I had the opportunity to interview, the topics on which my interlocutors felt comfortable to elaborate in my presence, and numerous other factors related directly to the ways in which my interlocutors responded to various facets of my life.

Kirin Narayan's article "How Native Is a 'Native' Anthropologist?" offers key insights into how a researcher might situate herself within the ethnographic world while also keeping in view her specific identity as a human being. Narayan rejects the concept of the "native" anthropologist. She finds this concept problematic because she believes it implies that a "native" anthropologist cannot be a "real" anthropologist, and also because the "multiplex" nature of identity renders every researcher a "native" or insider in some respects and an outsider in others. The applicability of Narayan's analysis extends beyond the situation of those of us who, like Narayan herself, are ethnically mixed. She argues that all authors are "minimally bicultural in terms of belonging simultaneously to the world of engaged scholarship and the world of everyday life."[1] Narayan finds it "more rewarding to examine the ways in which each one of us is situated in relation to the people we study" than to attempt to determine who qualifies as a "native" anthropologist and who does not.[2]

Here, I reflect on my fieldwork and seek to situate myself as a researcher and as a person in relation to my interlocutors. I agree with Narayan that no one can be purely an insider or an outsider, to the exclusion of the other. In certain respects—for example, my religious background—my interlocutors tended to treat me as an insider. In others, such as my age, I became categorized first as an outsider and later as an insider, due to the discrepancy in the ages of my interlocutors in the United States and France versus those in Cambodia. Different behavior was required of me in each location, pertaining to my age and life stage. My ethnic ambiguity led to my being received as an insider at certain times, and as an outsider at others. My individual identity as a Christian from a Christian family, a single woman in my late twenties, and an American of both African and Asian descent undoubtedly shaped the experience, outcome, and interpretation of my fieldwork in unique ways.

Life Stage and Gender

At twenty-seven to twenty-eight years old, I was often the youngest adult in any given church service or Bible study during my fieldwork in the diaspora. This meant that when I greeted my interlocutors, I typically was expected to bow my head, press my hands together in front of my face, and otherwise display deference through the [sampeah],[3] the Cambodian analog of the greeting known in Indian societies as the *Añjali Mudra*. I frequently received requests to pick up some of my elderly interlocutors and drive them to various locations for church-related events. A different set of vocabulary is required when addressing elders, and particularly those who are only familiar with the version of the Khmer language spoken prior to the war and who have not spent much time, if any, in Cambodia since having left. In the four decades since the Cambodian genocide ended, the Khmer language has seen significant changes, such that certain words that previously were considered inappropriate are now customary, and certain words that younger people once employed regularly with their elders have fallen out of general use.

Today, [ɲam], the word for "eat" commonly used in Khmer conversation today—even in fairly formal settings—strikes some older Khmer speakers in the diaspora as overly familiar and therefore gravely disrespectful. This has to do with a change in the word's connotation over the years. Clavaud defined the following Khmer terms for "eat" in 1973 thus, in order to illustrate the complexities of translating the Bible into Khmer: [sii] "for animals and occasionally for human beings in a vulgar sense"; [piʔsaa] as "the usual term" for addressing or referring to others; [tɔtuəl tie nɔɔ] for referring to oneself; [bɑɑreʔpʰook] as a "literary" term; [cʰan] for members of the monkhood; and [saoy] for monarchs and deities. In order to illustrate the complexity involved in the attempt to highlight Christ's "dual nature," Clavaud then asks, "What word should we use for Jesus? If we take his abasement seriously we shall use the term *pisa*. If on the other hand we want to stress his kingship we shall choose the term *saoy*."[4] More recently, Christine Su, in her 2003 doctoral dissertation on Khmer identity and democracy, overlapped with Clavaud concerning the terms to be used for animals, kings, and monks, but lists [ɲam][5] as being for use between "people of equal/approximately equal status (polite),"[6] rather than as a term reserved for those considered socially inferior to the speaker. Su's assessment does indeed correspond to my experience in the field, both with regard to younger interlocutors in the diaspora, and to those of all ages in Cambodia itself.

In Cambodia, many of my interlocutors were in their twenties and thirties. Seeing me as a peer, they interacted with me in an informal, lighthearted manner. The pastor at one of my field churches in Phnom Penh encouraged his parishioners to welcome me as a friend and pick me up on their motorcycles for adventures out in the city. Indeed, several of them, both male and female, did come by for me at different times to take me to share meals at restaurants, shop at the mall, or go to the cinema. (*Avengers: End Game* and *John Wick: Chapter 3–Parabellum* were my young interlocutors' movies of choice during the spring of 2019.)

My status as a single woman also affected my reception among my interlocutors. Before beginning my fieldwork in California, I was concerned that living in neighboring Compton, rather than within Long Beach itself, might signal to my interlocutors that I was not fully committed to the community. I had in the back of my mind Nathaniel Roberts's account of his fieldwork with Dalit Christians in Chennai, India. Initially, Roberts had intended to live with his wife "in another part of town" and commute to the neighborhood in which his interlocutors lived. He eventually realized, however, that he had "hit a wall" in his understanding of his interlocutors. He began spending six nights a week living with his assistant in Anbu Nagar, the community in which he had begun his fieldwork. Relocating to Anbu Nagar made all the difference for Roberts, completely transforming his "standing among those who lived there." Having become a neighbor, albeit a temporary one, Roberts "could just hang out, like everyone else, with no purpose besides passing the time and enjoying others' company."[7]

Hoping to achieve the status of neighbor, as Roberts had managed after effecting the necessary changes in his ethnographic approach, I spent several weeks looking for suitable apartments or even individual rooms to rent in Long Beach. At last, about a month into my time in California, I did find a room for rent within walking distance of two of the churches I had been visiting. After moving into the new apartment, where I subleased a room from an elderly woman from Mexico, I was proud to demonstrate my commitment to the Long Beach community by sharing with my interlocutors that I was living within the city limits. The reactions I received upon announcing what I had considered rather victorious news failed to accomplish the intended effect. My interlocutors, especially the older, female majority, appeared perplexed and even perturbed that I would choose to live with a stranger when I had family nearby. Given that in Cambodian culture, unmarried women typically live at home with their families,[8] my attempt to build greater trust within the community resulted in my creating unnecessary confusion, if not suspicion.[9]

I soon realized that in this setting, geographical proximity would not be the primary mode by which I would communicate my commitment to my interlocutors, nor to build trust among them. I moved back into my grandmother's home and continued driving out to Long Beach multiple times per week. My grandmother and I took two Khmer-language courses together at the Mark Twain Public Library. Often, she and I were the only two students of African descent in the class. On days when I did not have any interviews or church events on the calendar, I often sat in the library and read or practiced my language skills. People I had met in class sometimes passed by the table where I was reading and waved at me. Slowly but surely, my face became somewhat known in the neighborhood. I jumped at each opportunity to participate in a Cambodian cultural event in Long Beach, and frequently,

EPILOGUE

one or more members of my family came along for the ride. My sister joined me for a gala hosted by a Cambodian community organization, after one of my Khmer-language instructors had extended an invitation to join her table at the event. As often as possible, I brought my family to Cambodian restaurants and donut shops. Whenever a pastor invited me up on the stage at a church event, I always introduced my family, for whom my interlocutors cheered heartily. My grandmother received special honor whenever she accompanied me. She was overjoyed to be singled out for an award during our final Khmer-language class shortly before I left for France.

Whereas for Roberts, living in Chennai, staying in the community where he hoped to carry out his fieldwork was essential to the establishment of trust and rapport with his interlocutors, I realized that in my case, as a single woman working with Cambodian evangelicals in Long Beach, living in close proximity to my interlocutors was not as important to the process of facilitating understanding and relationship with them as was living with my family. Introducing my grandmother, my mother, and my sister to my interlocutors demonstrated that I was not merely a researcher, but also a granddaughter, a daughter, and a sister. I could be seen in my context, even as I sought to see them in theirs. They were free to witness my interactions with my family members and ascertain something about our familial relationships, our cultural background, and our faith.

Shortly after beginning my fieldwork in California, I attended a Khmer-language service at an intercultural, multicongregational church with my mother. As the service was about to begin, a member approached us and reminded us that there would be an English service later that day. I thanked the woman and explained that my mother and I had come to the Khmer service to learn. Upon hearing this, she broke into a warm smile and hugged us, exclaiming, "Thank you for wanting to be here with us!" From that day forward, the members of this church went out of their way to seek out both me and my mother and welcome us during or after the service. On days when she was unable to join me, they always asked about her and sent their greetings.

After arriving in Paris alone in January 2019, I immediately noticed the difference in my reception. Although there were many Cambodian evangelicals in Paris who welcomed me warmly, I often struggled to establish trust in this context, especially for the first several weeks. There were likely numerous reasons for the suspicion I encountered in France, including my Americanness and concerns some of my interlocutors had with US politics, especially relating to the CIA and Guantanamo Bay. I found myself at times in the position of having to defend my presence and convince my interlocutors of my goodwill toward them and their communities. Every time I encountered a new set of interlocutors, I noticed them struggling to place me, as they asked a plethora of questions, often more about my family than about my research. Part of this apparently anxious curiosity, I imagine, had to do with my racial ambiguity, which I address in the next section, but, perhaps, part of it also had to do with their desire to figure out where I fit in the world. What was my true goal? Was I trustworthy? Where did I really come from? Why did I ask so many questions? Without any family with me, I as an individual proved difficult to understand.

Especially on those occasions when I had sent cold emails to church leaders, rather than being introduced by a mutual contact, suspicion sometimes arose concerning my true intentions. In France, when I asked a church leader about the possibility of interviewing him, he agreed to speak with me but then burst out in an expression of apparent frustration, "I don't know you. I don't know your church. I don't know your pastor." He then asked if I could send him my notes, and I agreed to send him those pertaining to his interview, if he would indeed feel comfortable to share his story with me. He willingly did so, saying that he had "nothing to hide." He asked several questions of his own, and I was grateful for the opportunity to share with him in greater detail about my background and my research. Interestingly enough, after taking the time to express his reservations and have his concerns addressed, this gentleman shared enthusiastically for nearly three hours nonstop (my maximum requested interview period was one hour). Afterward, he emailed me five paragraphs of additional details and reviewed my interview notes in Microsoft Word, using italics to draw attention to the corrections he had so meticulously made.

Ethnic Identity

By far, the most common conversation I had in Khmer pertained to my ethnic heritage. On those inevitable occasions, multiple times per week, if not per day, when people asked about my ethnicity, I learned to rattle off this answer: [Kɲom kɨɨ cie koon kat. ʔəvpuk rɔbah kɲom kɨɨ cie cən. Mdaay rɔbah kɲom kɨɨ cie cɔɔn ciet sbaek kmav]. In English, this translates to: "I am mixed (literally: mixed child). My father is Chinese. My mother is Black."[10] More often than not, it seemed that no one took particular notice of me when I entered a room filled with Khmer people. If there were settings in which the individuals present would have wanted to present a more idealized version of life because of the presence of an outsider, I imagine that I received the uncensored version more frequently, due to my ability to blend into the crowd, though not by any effort on my part. In fact, I was proactive about showing pictures of my family and identifying myself as a biracial American—but for the most part, people both in churches and on the street in Cambodian neighborhoods simply regarded me as Khmer and spoke to me with the expectation that I would know how to respond, both linguistically and culturally.

Uncomfortable conversations sometimes resulted when I explained my ethnic mix. One rather awkward moment that occurred more than once, especially in France and Cambodia, occurred when interlocutors introduced me to their friends, hesitated partway through describing my ethnic background, and then decided to mention only the Chinese part of my parentage, perhaps afraid that I myself would be embarrassed if others were to know about the African American side. I took it upon myself on such occasions to complete my own introduction, clearing up any potential misunderstanding regarding my heritage.

As I have explained, my biracial identity, and most specifically, my being of African descent, as well as of Asian descent, led to an unusual set of complicated conversations. On the one hand, my identity was inextricably linked to my family, because Khmer culture situates the individual within the nuclear family unit. I received favor because of my parents' involvement in ministry, but I also felt pressure—which I utterly rejected—to separate myself off from my African American heritage, because this aspect of my identity made some of my interlocutors uncomfortable. In this sense, there was a re-individualization that took place, following the inevitable de-individualization that frequently happens in cross-cultural encounters involving Westerners. I imagine that my light brown skin and diminutive stature—measuring just under five feet tall, the average height for a Cambodian woman[11]—contributed to my being perceived as an ethnic insider. This experience of being assumed Khmer likely had to do with a combination of factors relating to my individual, biracial heritage and my interlocutors' interpretation of my appearance.

Religious Background

As a Christian raised in an evangelical home, many of the beliefs and practices my interlocutors held were familiar to me. In retrospect, entering an ethnographic field as a coreligionist came with both benefits and detriments. Certainly, one of the most essential, if not the single most essential, ways I established trust with interlocutors was to demonstrate that I took matters of faith seriously in my own life, rather than merely for the sake of research.

Writing about her experience of undertaking multisited ethnographic fieldwork with West Indian Pentecostal churches in New York and London, Janice McLean-Farrell recalls that her identity as a fellow Christian, in addition to her Jamaican ethnicity, rendered her an "insider" in the eyes of church gatekeepers, but that her role as a researcher interested in studying the community made her an outsider.[12] McLean-Farrell notes her surprise at "finding [her]self somewhere in between an insider and an outsider in Brooklyn and London contexts," since she had expected that her "familiarity with the context and prior contact with churches before commencing fieldwork" would have positioned her "closer to the insider side of the spectrum." Participating in services, prayer meetings, and other gatherings were crucial in building trust in her interlocutors.[13] I, too, found that in most, if not all, of the congregations I visited, pastors and other gatekeepers initially sought to evaluate my trustworthiness based on an assessment of my religious background and practice.

At the first church I visited in Long Beach, the pastor, with whom I had met over lunch to describe my project and to hear any insights he might have for me, surprised me one Sunday by inviting me up on stage during the morning service. He gave me the opportunity to introduce myself, describe my project, and recruit interviewees from the front. After introducing myself, along with my grandmother, mother, and sister, who had been visiting this church with me, I shared with those in attendance that morning that I was studying Christianity around the world, and that I was working on a project about Cambodian Christianity. Trying to couch my project in words that would make sense in a church context, rather than the academic one in which I had been steeped for so long, I announced that I wanted to hear their faith testimonies—stories about how they had decided to convert to Christianity—and what their faith meant to them in the present. I explained that I wanted to be able to hear as many of their stories as possible, to be able to pass them along to others. I stopped at that point, conscious of time. I had not expected to be the center of attention even for that long and was keen not to monopolize the entire service.

What ensued took me utterly by surprise. The pastor asked me if I could talk more about my family's ministry. I did not immediately appreciate the full implications of how this topic related to my research, but I gladly obliged.

I shared about my parents' decades-long work in campus ministry during my childhood and youth, and about my father's current leadership of a church in Canada. The pastor knew, although I did not, that my family's involvement in Christian ministry would serve to establish greater trust in the community. Although I had long been aware that American culture tended to be more individualistic than many others and had made a conscious effort to prepare myself for a more community-oriented pattern of engagement during my fieldwork, I nevertheless bristled at the thought of being judged, even in a positive light, because of my parents' actions or attributes. *I am my own person*, I thought. *I should stand on my own two feet.* For the purposes of my fieldwork, however, I learned more and more that while I might feel like an individual, my interlocutors did not perceive me as such. My social location as a Christian and as the daughter of a pastor often ended up assuaging the anxieties of initially skeptical interlocutors.

Most of the time, being recognized as a coreligionist eased my entry into a variety of worship-focused events. I know that ethnographers of various stripes have famously wrestled with the ethics of participant observation during religious rituals, and specifically about what types of religious activities are appropriate for a secular or differently religious ethnographer to join. Although these questions surfaced for me regularly in Cambodian Buddhist contexts, I had no moral or ethical qualms about responding in the affirmative when interlocutors invited me to pray during Bible studies or church services, as they often did.

On a related note, however, being a coreligionist also brought about challenges of its own. Chief among these, perhaps, was that church members often forgot or misunderstood the fact that I had come to the community for research purposes, although I made repeated attempts to clarify my fieldwork aims. Perhaps especially since I was a Christian entering a Christian context, it seemed that my interlocutors often figured either that I was a missionary to Cambodia, or that, unbeknownst to me, I was called by God to become one in the future. This topic came up frequently, with church members and other acquaintances at various times inviting me to consider joining specific mission agencies in Cambodia or to acknowledge a call to missions in Cambodia more generally. One man in France was quite adamant about this and insisted that I pray about the matter. He assured me that my knowledge of the Khmer language and interest in learning about Cambodia could not be "random."

Furthermore, Christianity, and even evangelical Christianity, includes a significant amount of theological diversity, and I was not always in agreement with my interlocutors in matters of religious belief and practice. My initial inclination was to avoid bringing up points of theological discrepancy, but in cases where it seemed that failing to self-disclose would dishonor the relationship, I chose to show my cards. I felt that such moves were tremendously risky as, for example, openly identifying as an egalitarian in a church that excludes women from church leadership could lead certain interlocutors who previously had trusted me as a fellow Christian now to distance themselves from me as an object of suspicion. Prior to leaving for fieldwork, I had made up my mind that in order to acknowledge equality, or "coevalness,"[14] with my interlocutors, I could not maintain integrity while expecting them to answer my questions about their personal religious experience and identity and simultaneously refusing to allow them access to information about my own. As a result, I found myself in a number of somewhat awkward conversations about alcohol consumption, charismatic spirituality, and contemporary American politics, among other issues controversial in certain evangelical settings—I also, through these moments of discomfort, developed relationships of substance with many interlocutors.

One caveat associated with carrying out research as a coreligionist, of course, can be found in the ever-present possibility of losing certain important ethnographic revelations in a sea of faux familiarity. Certain phrases, doctrinal points, and ritual activities that have one meaning in one Christian setting can have wildly different meanings in different cultural contexts. In my efforts to take note of theological, cosmological, and other cultural differences amid scenes often very similar to those I had grown up seeing regularly in church community, one of my most effective methodological allies turned out to be the continuous study of Cambodian Buddhist thought and practice, which often signaled that there was more to what I observed than I otherwise would have known or intuited. For example, Anne's story in chapter 2, in which she prays to "the god of the sky," reads differently when one knows that Cambodian Buddhists have long identified the Hindu deity Indra as the god of the sky. In this same story, the moment at which "the man in white" announces that his job is to build "a big road" might take on another layer of significance when one takes into consideration that in Cambodian folklore, the god Indra is believed to have been a builder of roads in a previous life.[15]

If anyone else had followed my fieldwork itinerary, spending time in the same four cities, with the same set of congregations, it is quite possible that the observations, themes, and arguments that rose to the surface would have been different from those that I have set forth in this book. I imagine I would have had a rather different collection of experiences, for example, had I been older, younger, Buddhist, male, a different ethnicity, with different Institutional Review Board (IRB) arrangements, or with a higher or lower level of fluency in Khmer—the list goes on. So much of ethnography depends on the embodiment of the ethnographer, and on his or her pattern of interactions with the communities in question. I do not pretend that this work represents the whole of Cambodian Christianity, or even of Cambodian evangelicalism. My interlocutors represent only a small, though far-flung, portion of the Cambodian Christian community throughout the world. I hope that my presentation and analysis of their stories here will honor their experiences and how they strive to relate to their God of hope, as well as how they made the time to relate to me, as they risk much to do with others, the hope they have found through their faith.

Notes

Introduction

1. Snowball sampling is a method that involves seeking the assistance of current interlocutors in order to locate new ones. See Babbie, *Basics of Social Research*, 20.
2. My Institutional Review Board arrangements only allowed for interviews with people aged eighteen and older.
3. United Nations Population Fund Cambodia, "Cambodia Youth Data Sheet 2015."
4. "Cambodian Genocide Project."
5. Hamera, "Answerability of Memory," 70.
6. Peschoux and Kang, *Itinerary of an Ordinary Torturer*, 159. Kang Kech Ieu's name is also written as Kang Kek Iew, Kaing Kek Iev, or Kaing Guek Eav.
7. Maha Ghosananda, *Step by Step*, 45.
8. Zucker, *Forest of Struggle*, 14–15, 19.
9. Mortland, *Cambodian Buddhism in the United States*, 15.
10. Hefner, "Introduction," 3–44.
11. Horton, "African Conversion," 105.
12. Young, "Horton's 'Intellectualist Theory' of Conversion," 115. Young borrows the term "cognitive reorganization" from Mortanz, 156. See Young, "Horton's 'Intellectualist Theory' of Conversion," 131n17.
13. Phan, "Multiple Religious Belonging," 495–519; Davie, *Religion in Britain Since 1945*.
14. Hansen and Ledgerwood, "At the Edge of the Forest," 7.
15. Ebihara, Legerwood, and Mortland, *Cambodian Culture Since 1975*, 8.
16. Smith, "Cambodia," 130.
17. Hansen and Ledgerwood, "At the Edge of the Forest," 8.
18. Smith-Hefner, "Ethnicity and the Force of Faith"; Smith-Hefner, *Khmer American*.
19. Smith-Hefner, "Ethnicity and the Force of Faith," 25.
20. Poethig, "Visa Troubles," 199.
21. Um, *From the Land of Shadows*, 11.
22. Brinkley, *Cambodia's Curse*, 14–15.
23. Zucker, *Forest of Struggle*, 27.
24. Marston and Guthrie, *History, Buddhism, and New Religious Movements*, 5.
25. Ibid., 12, 180.
26. Mam, *Church Behind the Wire*, 162.
27. Chan and Sigrist, *Enfer où Dieu prenait soin*.
28. Clark, *Almighty is His Name*.
29. Ibid., xix.
30. Maher and Uon, *Cry of the Gecko*.

Chapter 1

1. Cormack, *Killing Fields, Living Fields*, 446, 447.
2. Ponchaud, *Cathedral in the Rice Paddy*, 72.
3. Kiernan, *Pol Pot Regime*, 298.
4. Cormack, *Killing Fields, Living Fields*, 447.
5. Clymer, *Troubled Relations*, 10.
6. Hammond, "Preparing the Scriptures in the Native Tongue," 15, CMA National Archives.
7. Cormack, *Killing Fields, Living Fields*, 447–48.
8. Clymer, *Troubled Relations*, 10.
9. Cormack, *Killing Fields, Living Fields*, 447.
10. Pye, "New Religions in East Asia," 499–501.
11. Clymer, *Troubled Relations*, 11.
12. Cormack, *Killing Fields, Living Fields*, 447, 448.
13. J. J. Piaget, "From Persecution to Freedom," 1, Annual Report Cambodian Field—1971, CMA National Archives.
14. Cormack, *Killing Fields, Living Fields*, 449.
15. Ninh, "Mobilizing Ethnic-Religious Transnationalism," 216–17, citing Ponchaud, *Cathedral of the Rice Paddy*.

16. Ponchaud, *Cathedral in the Rice Paddy*, 72. Cf. Wong, "Historical Interface," 258.
17. Ninh, "Mobilizing Ethnic-Religious Transnationalism," 216, citing Ponchaud, *Cathedral of the Rice Paddy*.
18. Dubus, *Cambodge*, 7-8. Original: *une face doublement étrangère*.
19. Ibid., 8. Original: *khmériser la liturgie, d'arriver progressivement à l'emploi unique de la langue cambodienne pour la liturgie de la Parole*.
20. Ibid.
21. Heuveline, "Demographic Analysis of Mortality Crises," 103.
22. Geldenhuys, *Foreign Political Engagement*, 180.
23. Heuveline, "Demographic Analysis of Mortality Crises," 103.
24. Ehrentraut, "Perpetually Temporary," 34, citing Goshal, Ku, and Hawk, *Minorities in Cambodia*, 20.
25. Dubus, *Cambodge*, 12, quoting Ponchaud. Original: *brutalement vidée de la grande majorité de ses fidèles*.
26. Ibid., 13.
27. Maher with Uon, *Cry of the Gecko*, loc. 2004-2009, Kindle.
28. Ninh, *Race, Gender, and Religion*, 89-90.
29. Pol Pot, born Saloth Sar, was the leader of the Cambodian communist group known as the Khmer Rouge (literally meaning "Red Khmer" in French) and the eventual prime minister of the Khmer Rouge-led government, which was dubbed Democratic Kampuchea. Chandler, *Brother Number One*, 7.
30. Widyono, *Dancing in Shadows*, 25.
31. Cormack, *Killing Fields, Living Fields*, 449.
32. Kiernan, *Pol Pot Regime*, 17, 25.
33. Ibid., 22.
34. Staffan Hildebrand, personal communication, quoted in Kiernan, *Pol Pot Regime*, 25.
35. Kiernan, *Pol Pot Regime*, 22.
36. Ibid., 16-17.
37. Cormack, *Killing Fields, Living Fields*, 449.
38. Annual Report Cambodian Field—1971, CMA National Archives.
39. Cormack, *Killing Fields, Living Fields*, 450.
40. Mam, *Church Behind the Wire*, 162.
41. "Cambodian Genocide Project."
42. Cormack, *Killing Fields, Living Fields*, 450.
43. Hinton, *Why Did They Kill?*, 1.
44. Ablin and Hood, xxxv, in Smith-Hefner, *Khmer American*, 2.
45. Hinton, *Why Did They Kill?*, 1. The word Romanized here as *Ângkar* can be found in the SEAlang Library Khmer Dictionary under its IPA rendering, /ʔaŋkaa/. This term should not be mistaken for *Angkor* (rendered in IPA as /ʔaŋkɔɔ/), meaning "capital" or "city." The latter word, /ʔaŋkɔɔ/, corresponds to the name of the medieval Khmer empire, which lasted from 802 to 1432 CE. See Miksic and Goh, *Ancient Southeast Asia*, 261.
46. Smith-Hefner, *Khmer American*, 2.
47. Hinton, *Why Did They Kill?*, 1.
48. Kiernan, "Cambodian Genocide," cited in Kissi, "Cambodia and Ethiopia," 313.
49. Kiernan, "External and Indigenous Sources," 189.
50. World Christian Database, "People: Western Cham (Cambodian)"; World Christian Database, "People: Eastern Cham (Cambodian)."
51. Taylor, *Cham Muslims of the Mekong Delta*, 6, 29, 46-47, 115.
52. Kiernan, *Pol Pot Regime*, 64, 274. Cf. Kiernan, "External and Indigenous Sources," 189.
53. Schabas, *War Crimes and Human Rights*, 730.
54. Beech, "Khmer Rouge's Slaughter in Cambodia."
55. Um, *From the Land of Shadows*, 5.
56. Nguyen, *Nothing Ever Dies*, 92.
57. Southgate, "ASEAN and the Dynamics of Resistance," 211.
58. Cormack, *Killing Fields, Living Fields*, 450.
59. Eastmond and Öjendal, "Revisiting a 'Repatriation Success,'" 40, 41.
60. Goldsworthy and Edwards, *Facing North*, 195.
61. "Khao-I-Dang"; Center for Disease Control, "International Notes Surveillance

of Health Status." For comparison, in 2021, Cambodia had a crude birth rate of 20.84 per 1,000 population, and Niger, the country with the highest crude birth rate in 2021, had an estimated 47.28 per 1,000 population. See Central Intelligence Agency, "Country Comparisons—Birth Rate."

62. Vickery, *Cambodia*, 12.

63. Cormack, *Killing Fields, Living Fields*, 451.

64. Mam, *Church Behind the Wire*, 173.

65. Rasmey and Chunakara, "Cambodia," 48.

66. Cormack, *Killing Fields, Living Fields*, 451.

67. Scheer, "New Life," 68.

68. Clark, *Almighty Is His Name*, xxi, 63.

69. Harris, *Buddhism in a Dark Age*, 166.

70. Cormack, *Killing Fields, Living Fields*, 452.

71. Vickery, *Cambodia*, 11–12. Cf. Vickery, *Cambodia*, 180–81.

72. Zucker, *Forest of Struggle*, 111.

73. Mam, "Cambodia," 182–83.

74. Mam, *Church Behind the Wire*, 173.

75. World Christian Database, "Country: Cambodia."

76. Keyes, "Why the Thai Are Not Christians," 262, 276, 268.

77. Mortland, *Cambodian Buddhism in the United States*, 77.

78. Holt, *Spirits of the Place*, 15.

79. Frederiks, "Mission or Submission," 81–83.

80. Cannell, "Introduction," 1.

81. Chow, "Demolition and Defiance," 252; Taneti, *Telugu Christians*, 4; Religion and Public Life, "Christianity in Myanmar"; Unrepresented Nations and Peoples Organization, "Hmong."

82. Bebbington, *Evangelicalism in Modern Britain*, 2–3.

83. "Your word is a lamp to my feet and a light to my path." Psalm 119:105, NRSV.

84. "For God so loved the world that he gave his only Son, so that everyone who believes in him may not perish but may have eternal life." John 3:16, NRSV.

85. "Jesus said to him, 'I am the way, and the truth, and the life. No one comes to the Father except through me.'" John 14:6, NRSV.

86. "Rejoice in the Lord always; again I will say, Rejoice." Philippians 4:4, NRSV.

87. "See, I am coming soon; my reward is with me, to repay according to everyone's work. I am the Alpha and the Omega, the first and the last, the beginning and the end." Revelation 22:12–13, NRSV.

88. Mortland, *Cambodian Buddhism in the United States*, 88.

89. Lim, "Contextualizing Ancestor Veneration," 113.

90. Du Mez, *Jesus and John Wayne*, 7.

91. Chan, *Survivors*, 239.

92. Revelation 22:12–13, NRSV.

93. Bebbington, *Evangelicalism in Modern Britain*, 2–3.

94. Zehner, "Orthodox Hybridities," 593–94.

95. Mam, "Compilation of the Khmer Indigenous Hymnal," 150. Throughout this book, I have followed the transcriptions used by Barnabas Mam and Karen B. Westerfield Tucker when referring to both the old and new CMA hymnals. For those interested in searching for detailed definitions of each term in the SEAlang Library Khmer Dictionary, the words they have transcribed as *tomnuk, domkerng, Khmer,* and *borisot* can be found under their IPA renderings— [tumnuk] ("lyrics"), [tɑmkaəŋ] ("to glorify"), [kmae] ("Khmer"), and [bɑɑreʔsot] ("holy"), respectively.

96. Westerfield Tucker, "Methodism's 'World Parish,'" 145–46.

97. Wijers, "Reception of Cambodian Refugees in France," 243–44.

98. Sucheng Chan, "Cambodians in the United States," 2.

99. Wijers, "Reception of Cambodian Refugees in France," 244.

100. Simon, "Choice of Ignorance," 65.

Chapter 2

1. World Christian Database, "Christian Growth by Region: South-Eastern Asia."

2. Davie, "Believing Without Belonging." Cf. Kasselstrand, "Nonbelievers in the Church," 275–94.

3. Horton, "African Conversion," 105.

4. Ibid., 101.

5. Ibid., 104.

6. Ibid., 102.
7. Hefner, "Introduction," 3–44. Cf. Young, "Christianity and Conversion," 449.
8. Hefner, "Introduction," 17.
9. Hann, "Anthropology of Christianity Per Se," 402.
10. Hanciles, *Migration*, 150.
11. Ibid., 150–51, quoting MacMullen, *Christianizing the Roman Empire*, 5.
12. Young, "Christianity and Conversion," 447–48.
13. Ibid., 454.
14. Ibid., 451.
15. Robbins, *Becoming Sinners*, 86–87, in Young, "Christianity and Conversion," 451.
16. Mortland, *Cambodian Buddhism in the United States*, 64.
17. Smith-Hefner, "Ethnicity and the Force of Faith," 28.
18. Ibid., 31.
19. Smith-Hefner's romanization.
20. Smith-Hefner, "Ethnicity and the Force of Faith," 31.
21. Men, "Changing Religious Beliefs and Ritual Practices," 228.
22. Appleby, *Ambivalence of the Sacred*, 129.
23. Um, *From the Land of Shadows*, 256.
24. Long and Reeves, "Dig a Hole and Bury," 75.
25. Schlund-Vials, *War, Genocide, and Justice*, 50.
26. Sloan, "Brothers' New Father," 56.
27. Bennett, "Karma After Democratic Kampuchea," 68–82.
28. Wood, "Touring Memories of the Khmer Rouge," 182.
29. Zucker, "From Soldier to Guardian Spirit."
30. New Tribes Mission, now known as Ethnos360, is an American evangelical mission organization founded in 1942 and dedicated to Bible translation and evangelism among "unreached people groups"—indigenous populations with little to no prior contact with Christianity. See "About Ethnos360."
31. Wiebe, *Visions of Jesus*, 74, 78.
32. Ricoeur, *Rule of Metaphor*, 318, quoted in Hindmarsh, "Religious Conversion," 350.
33. Ricoeur, *Rule of Metaphor*, 350.
34. Anderson, *To the Ends of the Earth*, xi.

35. Mortland, "Khmer Buddhists in the United States," 72.
36. Brinkley, *Cambodia's Curse*, 14–15.
37. Ollier, "Rapping (in) the homeland, 105.
38. Ricoeur, *Memory, History, Forgetting*, 132.
39. Luhrmann, *When God Talks Back*, xvi.
40. Ibid., 5.
41. Granqvist, "Attachment Theory and Religious Conversions," 182.
42. Smith-Hefner, "Ethnicity and the Force of Faith," 31.
43. Ricoeur, *Memory, History, Forgetting*, 132.

Chapter 3
1. Harris, *Cambodian Buddhism*, 52.
2. Ibid., 53.
3. Ibid., 256n12.
4. Leclère, *Buddhisme au Cambodge*, 263.
5. Hin and Trevor, *Cambodian Myth—History*, 18.
6. Harvey, *Buddhism and Monotheism*, 1, quoting Buddhaghosa, *Visuddhimagga*, chapter 19, paragraph 603.
7. McLellan, *Cambodian Refugees in Ontario*, 124.
8. Smith-Hefner, *Khmer American*, 44.
9. Obeyesekere, "Great Tradition and the Little," 140.
10. Ibid., 151.
11. Ebihara, *Svay*, 175.
12. Harris, *Cambodian Buddhism*, 59.
13. Eisenbruch, "Ritual Space," 285n11, cited in Harris, *Cambodian Buddhism*, 59.
14. Harris, *Cambodian Buddhism*, 60.
15. Ibid., 79.
16. Ibid., 53.
17. Langford, *Consoling Ghosts*, 64.
18. Ibid., 64, citing Edwards, "Between a Song and a Prei," 150.
19. Harris, *Cambodian Buddhism*, 58.
20. Ibid., 59.
21. Ibid., 55.
22. Ibid., 59. The terms comprising this term can be located in the SEAlang Library Khmer Dictionary under their IPA transcriptions—[hav] and [prɔliŋ], respectively.
23. Harris, *Cambodian Buddhism*, 59, citing Thompson, *Calling of the Souls*.
24. Harris, *Cambodian Buddhism*, 58.

25. Clavaud, "Problems Encountered in Translating," 421–22.

26. Klostermaier, *Hinduism*, 174.

27. This word has the meaning of both "parents" or "spirit of an ancestor." It can be found in the SEAlang Library Khmer Dictionary under its IPA rendering, [mee baa].

28. Smith-Hefner, *Khmer American*, 38–39.

29. Men, "Changing Religious Beliefs and Ritual Practices," 225.

30. Mortland indicates that the phrase "crossing the river" typically refers to giving birth and cites Anne R. Hansen in indicating that it also represents "spiritual salvation." Mortland, "Khmer Buddhists in the United States," 162n4, citing Hansen, "Crossing the River."

31. Mortland, "Khmer Buddhists in the United States," 75.

32. Harris, *Buddhism in a Dark Age*, 127–28. The Khmer word for the Pali term *sangha*, referring to the monkhood, is [sɑŋ].

33. Davidson, *Indian Esoteric Buddhism*, 200.

34. François Bizot has provided the most evidence in this direction, and his arguments are largely based on the Cambodian context. See McGovern, "Esoteric Buddhism in Southeast Asia." Cf. Harris, *Cambodian Buddhism*, 226.

35. See Zieck, *UNHCR and Voluntary Repatriation of Refugees*, 147.

36. More information about the custom in which Buddhist monks tie strings around an individual's wrist or waist for spiritual protection can be found in chapter 4.

37. McLellan, *Cambodian Refugees in Ontario*, 131.

38. Phan, "Multiple Religious Belonging," 498.

39. Smith-Hefner, *Khmer American*, 36. The word *achaa* can be located in the SEAlang Library Khmer Dictionary under the IPA transcription [ʔaacaa].

40. Ibid.

41. Pye, *Skilful Means*, 1, 9.

42. Ibid., 131.

43. Ibid., 131–32.

44. Ibid., 159.

45. Davie, *Religion in Britain Since 1945*, 5.

46. Douglas, "Changing Religious Practices among Cambodian Immigrants," 137.

47. Mortland, *Cambodian Buddhism in the United States*, 205.

48. Wong, "Buddhist-Christians in Cambodian America," 50–70.

49. SEAlang Library Khmer, Search Results, "slap."

50. Ibid., "soʔkɔət."

51. The Holy Bible in Khmer Old Version, 1 Corinthians 15:3, accessed 11 July 2019, http://biblecambodia.org/khov54/1CO15.htm#Vo.

52. SEAlang Library Khmer, Search Results, "soʔkɔət."

53. Khmer Standard Version of the Holy Bible in the Khmer Language of Cambodia, 1 Corinthians 15:3, accessed 11 July 2019, available: http://www.biblecambodia.org/khsv/1CO15.htm#Vo.

54. SEAlang Library Khmer, Search Results, "tiʔvuəŋkuət."

55. Zehner, "Orthodox Hybridities," 590.

56. Ibid., 596.

57. Ibid., 605.

58. Ibid., 606.

59. Obeyesekere, "Great Tradition and the Little," 140.

60. Zehner, "Orthodox Hybridities," 610.

Chapter 4

1. The Holy Bible in Khmer Old Version, 2 Chronicles 16:9, accessed 16 March 2020, https://biblecambodia.org/khov54/2CH16.htm#Vo; Khmer Standard Version of the Holy Bible in the Khmer Language of Cambodia, 2 Chronicles 16:9, accessed 16 March 2020, http://www.biblecambodia.org/khsv/2CH16.htm#Vo.

2. SEAlang Library Khmer, Search Results, "smɑh."

3. By "worship," Chanvatey likely intended to communicate reverence.

4. Exodus 23:13, NRSV.

5. Um, *From the Land of Shadows*, 193–94.

6. See chapter 3 for more information on the renaming of spirits after conversion to Christianity.

7. Cf. Wong, "Longing for Home," 285.

8. It was almost certainly the Mahayana, and not Theravada, form of Buddhism that Martine grew up practicing, given that

Mahayana is the prevalent form of the religion in Vietnam.

9. 1 Samuel 28:1–25, NRSV.
10. Mam, *Church Behind the Wire*, 202.
11. CMH, "I have decided to follow Jesus."
12. Zehner, "Orthodox Hybridities," 594.
13. Ibid., 593.
14. Lindhardt, "Mediating Money,"149.
15. Ibid., 151.
16. Ibid.
17. Ibid., 148, 151.
18. Lindhardt, "Mediating Money," 148.
19. Hinton, *Why Did They Kill?*, 107.
20. Ibid., 106.
21. Mortland, *Cambodian Buddhism in the United States*, 238.
22. Selka, "Morality in the Religious Marketplace," 299.
23. Ibid., 301.
24. Ibid., 298.
25. Ibid., 296.
26. A *terreiro* is a Candomblé temple. See Selka, "Morality in the Religious Marketplace," 291.
27. Selka, "Morality in the Religious Marketplace," 300.
28. Ibid., 302.
29. This story appears as part of Kham's testimony in chapter 3 of this book.
30. Selka, "Morality in the Religious Marketplace," 301.
31. The IPA transcription of this term is [ruup ʔaarak]. Each of the two words in this term can be searched independently in the SEAlang Library Khmer Dictionary.
32. Harris, *Cambodian Buddhism*, 58–59.
33. All transcriptions are Harris's. Harris, *Cambodian Buddhism*, 59.
34. Galatians 5:22–23, NRSV.
35. Kuttiyanikkal, *Khrist Bhakta Movement*, 228.
36. Rhee, "Family Structures," 233.
37. Wong, "Historical Interface," 263.
38. Egge, *Religious Giving*, 4.
39. Lindhardt, "Mediating Money," 150.
40. Ibid., 154.
41. Ibid., 157.
42. Ibid., 157–58.
43. Mauss, *Gift*, 46.
44. Bertrand, "Medium Possession Practice," 162.
45. Mortland, *Cambodian Buddhism in the United States*, 66.
46. Stark and Finke, *Acts of Faith*, 120.
47. Guthrie, "Khmer Buddhism, Female Asceticism, and Salvation," 133.
48. Penner, *Rediscovering the Buddha*, 164, 166.
49. Harris, *Cambodian Buddhism*, 74.
50. Penner, *Rediscovering the Buddha*, 164.
51. Ibid., 166.
52. Harris, *Cambodian Buddhism*, 74.
53. See Leclère, *Livre de Vesandar*, in Bowie, *Of Beggars and Buddhas*, 5.
54. Harris, *Cambodian Buddhism*, 70.
55. Bowie, *Of Beggars and Buddhas*, 4.
56. Chandler, *Facing the Cambodian Past*, 24, cited in Bowie, *Of Beggars and Buddhas*, 4–5.
57. Leclère, *Livre de Vesandar*, in Bowie, *Of Beggars and Buddhas*, 5.
58. Penner, *Rediscovering the Buddha*, 218.
59. Bauman and Young, "Minorities and the Politics of Conversion," 187.
60. National Institute of Statistics, *Cambodia Demographic and Health Survey*, 4.
61. Wong, "Historical Interface," 264–65.
62. Nichols, "Dunkin' and the Doughnut King." Cf. Ngoy, *Donut King*.
63. Sucheng Chan, *Survivors*, 147.
64. Matthew 12:9–13, NRSV. Cf. Mark 3:1–6 and Luke 6:6–11, NRSV.

Chapter 5

1. Adogame, *African Christian Diaspora*, 169.
2. Daniels, "Reterritorizing the West in World Christianity," 116.
3. Catto, "Church Mission Society and Reverse Mission," 90.
4. Mam, *Church Behind the Wire*, 54.
5. Poethig, "Visa Trouble," 197.
6. Um, *From the Land of Shadows*, 7–9, 243.
7. Ibid., 9.
8. Poethig, "Visa Trouble," 198–99.
9. Ibid., 188.
10. Ollier, "Rapping (in) the homeland," 106.
11. 1 Corinthians 12:22–25, NRSV.
12. John 17:4, NRSV.
13. John 14:1–3, NRSV.

14. Smith-Hefner, *Khmer American*, 23.
15. Ibid.
16. Ollier, "Rapping (in) the Homeland," 108.
17. Wuthnow, *Boundless Faith*, 56.
18. Pearson, *Missions and Conversions*, 98–99.
19. Ibid., citing Malkki, "Speechless Emissaries," 384–90.
20. Pearson, *Missions and Conversions*, 99.
21. Ibid., 103.
22. Ibid., 186.
23. Adogame, *African Christian Diaspora*, 169.
24. Wuthnow, *Boundless Faith*, 56.
25. Walls, "Mission and Migration," 4.
26. 2 Chronicles 7:14.
27. All emphases are Pastor Bona's.
28. Dudley-Jenkins, *Religious Freedom and Mass Conversion*, 53, 103.
29. Kommers, "Focus on the World," 3.
30. 2 Corinthians 10:5, NRSV.
31. Indeed, in 2018, the year before this conversation took place, the United States deported 110 Cambodians. By the end of 2019, the eighty more would be repatriated—including twenty-five in January, the month I arrived in France. See Narim, "US Deported 80 Cambodians."
32. Pham, "As protesters gathered outside before swarming," Twitter.
33. Kuo, "Beyond Ontologizing Asian America."
34. Du Mez, *Jesus and John Wayne*, 96–97, citing Jerry Falwell, *Listen, America!* (New York: Doubleday, 1980).
35. See Wong, "Longing for Home," 281–97.
36. Meyer, "Religious Sensations," 707.
37. Ibid., 711.
38. Ibid., 709.
39. Ibid., 710.
40. Ibid.
41. Na, "Imaging the Sacred Online," 90. Cf. Davie, "Believing Without Belonging," 79–89.
42. Ibid., 93, 94.
43. Ibid., 91–92.
44. Ibid., 96.
45. Smith-Hefner, "Ethnicity and the Force of Faith," 28.

46. In this case, the word "charismatic" denotes a character trait, rather than a theological orientation.
47. Robert, "World Christianity as a Women's Movement," 180.

Conclusion

1. Hackett and McClendon, "Christians remain world's largest religious group."
2. Stanley, "Evangelical Christian Mind," 299–300. Stanley acknowledges in a footnote, "This suggestion was made at the Baylor symposium by Dr. John Maiden of the Open University." Stanley, "Evangelical Christian Mind," 300n70.
3. Maiden, "Quadrilaterals in Waco."
4. Moore, "When the South Loosens."

Epilogue

1. Narayan, "How Native is a 'Native' Anthropologist?," 672–73, 678.
2. Ibid., 678.
3. SEAlang Library Khmer, Search Results, "sɑmpeah."
4. All transcriptions are Clavaud's. Clavaud, "Problems Encountered in Translating," 420–21. The complexities of Bible translation in the Khmer context are discussed more at length in chapter 3 of this book.
5. This term is equivalent to the one Clavaud renders *gnam*.
6. Su, "Tradition and Change," 82.
7. Roberts, *To Be Cared For*, 24.
8. Heuveline and Hong, "One-Parent Families in Contemporary Cambodia," 216–42.
9. Cf. Narayan, "How Native is a 'Native' Anthropologist?," 674. Narayan discusses in some detail the frustration she felt as a young woman at having to navigate "traditional expectations for proper behavior by an unmarried daughter" during her fieldwork in Nasik, India, and in the Himalayan foothills.
10. Even more frequently, I used a shorter form of this same sentence: [Kɲom koon kat. ʔəvpuk cən; mdaay cɔɔn ciet sbaek kmav]. I often chose the shortened version in order not to come off as stilted; since Khmer is "a prodrop language," it is customary for a recently mentioned "subject, object, or topic"

to be "omitted from the sentence," especially in informal conversation. Sak-Humphry, *Colloquial Cambodian*, 213.

11. Subramanian, Özaltin, and Finlay, "Height of Nations," Figure 1.

12. McLean-Farrell, *West Indian Pentecostals*, 192.

13. Ibid., 193.

14. Cf. Fabian, *Time and the Other*, xi. Fabian expresses concern that as long as ethnographers talk about their interlocutors as those who are "primarily . . . seen," they are "likely to persist in denying coevalness to [the] other," in that they imply that their interlocutors somehow belong to another, less sophisticated age.

15. Hin and Trevor, *Cambodian Myth*, 18.

Bibliography

Ablin, David A., and Marlowe Hood. "Introduction." In *The Cambodian Agony*. Armonk, NY: M. E. Sharpe, 1987.

"About Ethnos360: Our Mission." Ethnos360. Accessed July 11, 2021. https://ethnos360.org/about.

Adogame, Afe. *The African Christian Diaspora: New Currents and Emerging Trends in World Christianity*. London: Bloomsbury Academic, 2013.

Albera, Dionigi, and John Eade. *International Perspectives on Pilgrimage Studies: Itineraries, Gaps and Obstacles*. New York: Routledge, 2020.

Anderson, Allan. *To the Ends of the Earth: Pentecostalism and the Transformation of World Christianity*. New York: Oxford University Press, 2013.

Annual Report Cambodian Field—1971. The Christian and Missionary Alliance (CMA) National Archives. Colorado Springs, CO, US.

Appleby, R. Scott. *The Ambivalence of the Sacred: Religion, Violence, and Reconciliation*. Lanham, MD: Rowman and Littlefield.

Babbie, Earl. *The Basics of Social Research*. 4th ed. Belmont, CA: Thomson/Wadsworth, 2008.

Bauman, Chad M., and Richard F. Young. "Minorities and the Politics of Conversion: With Special Attention to Indian Christianity." In *Minority Studies*, edited by Rowena Robinson, 185–203. New Delhi: Oxford University Press, 2012.

Bebbington, David. *Evangelicalism in Modern Britain: A History from the 1730s to the 1980s*. Grand Rapids, MI: Baker Book House, 1989.

Beech, Hannah. "Khmer Rouge's Slaughter in Cambodia Is Ruled a Genocide." *New York Times*, November 15, 2018. https://www.nytimes.com/2018/11/15/world/asia/khmer-rouge-cambodia-genocide.html.

Bennett, Caroline. "Karma After Democratic Kampuchea: Justice Outside the Khmer Rouge Tribunal." *Genocide Studies and Prevention: An International Journal* 12, no. 3 (2018): 68–82.

Bertrand, Didier. "A Medium Possession Practice and Its Relationship with Cambodian Buddhism: The Grū Pāramī." In *History, Buddhism, and New Religious Movements in Cambodia*, edited by John Marston and Elizabeth Guthrie, 150–70. Honolulu: University of Hawai'i Press, 2004.

Borja, Melissa. "Speaking of Spirits: Oral History, Religious Change, and the Seen and Unseen Worlds of Hmong Americans." *Oral History Review* 44, no. 1 (2017): 1–18.

Bourdieu, Pierre. "The Forms of Capital." In *Handbook of Theory and Research for the Sociology of Education*, edited by John G. Richardson, 241–58. New York: Greenwood Press, 1986.

Bowie, Katherine A. *Of Beggars and Buddhas: The Politics of Humor in the "Vessantara Jataka" in Thailand*. Madison: University of Wisconsin Press, 2017.

Brandner, Tobias. "Cambodia (Kingdom of)." In *Encyclopedia of Christianity in the Global South*, vol. 2, edited by Mark A. Lamport, 113–17. Lanham, MD: Rowman and Littlefield, 2018.

Briggs, Charles. *Learning How to Ask: A Sociolinguistic Appraisal of the Role of the Interview in Social Science Research*. Cambridge: Cambridge University Press, 1986.

Brinkley, Joel. *Cambodia's Curse: The Modern History of a Troubled Land*. New York: PublicAffairs, 2012.

BIBLIOGRAPHY

Brown, Bill. "Thing Theory." *Critical Inquiry* 28, no. 1 (2001): 1–22.

Buddhist Institute. *Chuon Nath Khmer Dictionary*. Phnom Penh: Buddhist Institute, 1966.

Bush, Andrew. "The Implications of Christian Zionism for Mission." *International Bulletin of Missionary Research* 33, no. 3 (2009): 144–50.

"Cambodia: Fight Discrimination Amid Pandemic." Human Rights Watch, March 30, 2020. https://www.hrw.org/news/2020/03/30/cambodia-fight-discrimination-amid-pandemic.

"Cambodian Genocide Project." Yale University. Accessed December 18, 2015. http://www.yale.edu/cgp/.

Canell, Fenella. "Introduction." In *The Anthropology of Christianity*, edited by Fenella Cannel, 1–50. Durham: Duke University Press, 2006.

Catto, Rebecca. "The Church Mission Society and Reverse Mission: From Colonial Sending to Postcolonial Partnership and Reception." In *Religion on the Move!: New Dynamics of Religious Expansion in a Globalizing World*, edited by Afe Adogame and Shobhana Shankar, 81–95. Leiden: Brill, 2012.

Center for Disease Control. "International Notes Surveillance of Health Status of Kampuchean Refugees: Khao I-Dang Holding Center, Thailand, December 1981–June 1983." *Morbidity and Mortality Weekly Report*, August 12, 1983. https://www.cdc.gov/mmwr/preview/mmwrhtml/00000123.htm.

Central Intelligence Agency. "Country Comparisons—Birth Rate." The World Factbook. Accessed August 14, 2021. https://www.cia.gov/the-world-factbook/field/birth-rate/country-comparison.

Chan, Rany, and Andrée-Marie Sigrist. *L'Enfer où Dieu prenait soin de nous, ou, quatre ans sous Pol Pot*. Paris: Fayard, 1996.

Chan, Sucheng. "Cambodians in the United States: Refugees, Immigrants, American Ethnic Minority." In *Oxford Research Encyclopedia of American History*, September 3, 2015. https://doi.org/10.1093/acrefore/9780199329175.013.317.

———. *Not Just Victims: Conversations with Cambodian Community Leaders in the United States*. Urbana: University of Illinois Press, 2003.

———. *Survivors: Cambodian Refugees in the United States*. Urbana: University of Illinois Press, 2004.

Chandler, David. *Brother Number One: A Political Biography of Pol Pot*. London: Routledge, 1999.

———. *Facing the Cambodian Past: Selected Essays, 1971–1994*. Chiang Mai, Thailand: Silkworm Press, 1996.

Chow, Christie Chui-Shan. "Demolition and Defiance: The Stone Ground Church Dispute (2012) in East China." *Journal of World Christianity* 6, no. 2 (2016): 250–76.

The Christian and Missionary Alliance (CMA) National Archives. Colorado Springs, CO, US.

Clark, Randy. *Almighty Is His Name: The Riveting Story of Sophal Ung*. With Susan Thompson. Lake Mary, FL: Charisma House, 2016.

Clavaud, Jean. "Problems Encountered in Translating the New Testament into Modern Cambodian." *Bible Translator* 24, no. 4 (1973): 419–22.

Clymer, Kenton J. *Troubled Relations: The United States and Cambodia Since 1870*. DeKalb: Northern Illinois University Press, 2007.

Cone, Margaret, and Richard F. Gombrich, trans. *The Perfect Generosity of Prince Vessantara: A Buddhist Epic*. Illustrated with paintings from the Sinhalese temples. Oxford: Clarendon, 1977.

Cormack, Don. *Killing Fields, Living Fields: An Unfinished Portrait of the Cambodian Church—The Church That Would Not Die*. Crowborough, UK: OMF International, 1997.

Cornille, Catherine. *Many Mansions?: Multiple Religious Belonging and Christian Identity*. Maryknoll, NY: Orbis, 2002.

Daniels, David, III. "Reterritorizing the West in World Christianity: Black North Atlantic Christianity and the Edinburgh Conferences of 1910 and 2010." *Journal of World Christianity* 5, no. 1 (2012): 102–23.

Davidson, Ronald M. *Indian Esoteric Buddhism: Social History of the Tantric Movement*. New York: Columbia University Press, 2002.
Davie, Grace. "Believing Without Belonging: A Liverpool Case Study." *Archives de sciences sociales des religions* 38, no. 81 (1993): 79–89.
———. *Religion in Britain Since 1945: Believing without Belonging*. Oxford: Blackwell, 1994.
Davis, Erik W. *Deathpower: Buddhism's Ritual Imagination in Cambodia*. New York: Columbia University Press, 2016.
Douglas, Thomas J. "Changing Religious Practices Among Cambodian Immigrants in Long Beach and Seattle." In *Immigrant Faiths: Transforming Religious Life in America*, edited by Karen I. Leonard, Alex Stepick, Manuel A. Vasquez, and Jennifer Holdaway, 123–45. Lanham, MD: AltaMira Press, 2005.
Dubus, Arnaud. *Cambodge: La Longue marche des chrétiens khmers*. Paris: Éditions CLD, 2005.
Dudley-Jenkins, Laura. *Religious Freedom and Mass Conversion in India*. Philadelphia: University of Pennsylvania Press, 2019.
Dudley, Sandra H. "Ritual Practice, Material Culture, and Well-Being in Displacement: *Ka-thow-bòw* in a Kaenni Refugee Camp in Thailand." In *Building Noah's Ark for Migrants, Refugees, and Religious Communities*, edited by Alexander Horstmann and Jin-Heon Jung, 101–26. New York: Palgrave Macmillan, 2015.
Du Mez, Kristin Kobes. *Jesus and John Wayne: How White Evangelicals Corrupted a Faith and Fractured a Nation*. New York: Liveright Publishing, 2020.
Eastmond, Marita, and Joakim Öjendal. "Revisiting a 'Repatriation Success': The Case of Cambodia." In *The End of the Refugee Cycle?: Refugee Repatriation and Reconstruction*, edited by Richard Black and Khalid Koser, 38–55. New York: Berghahn Books, 1999.
Ebihara, May Mayko. *Svay: A Khmer Village in Cambodia*. Edited by Andrew Mertha. Ithaca, NY: Southeast Asia Program Publications, an imprint of Cornell University Press, 2018.
Ebihara, May, Judy Ledgerwood, and Carol A. Mortland. *Cambodian Culture Since 1975: Homeland and Exile*. Ithaca, NY: Southeast Asia Program Publications, 1994.
Edwards, Penny. "Between a Song and a Prei: Tracking Cambodian History and Cosmology through the Forest." In *At the Edge of the Forest: Essays on Cambodia, History, and Narrative in Honor of David Chandler*, edited by Anne Ruth Hansen and Judy Ledgerwood, 137–62. Ithaca, NY: Southeast Asia Program Publications, 2008.
Egge, James. *Religious Giving and the Invention of Karma in Theravada Buddhism*. London: Routledge, 2002.
Ehrentraut, Stefan. "Perpetually Temporary: Citizenship and Ethnic Vietnamese in Cambodia." In *Ethnic and Racial Minorities in Asia: Inclusion Or Exclusion?*, edited by Michelle Ann Miller, 28–47. New York: Routledge, 2012.
Eisenbruch, Maurice. "The Ritual Space of Patients and Traditional Healers in Cambodia." *Bulletin de l'École Française d'Extrême-Orient* 79, no. 2 (1992): 283–316.
Fabian, Johannes. *Time and the Other: How Anthropology Makes Its Object*. New York: Columbia University Press, 1983.
Frederiks, Martha. "Mission or Submission?—From Mission History Towards an Intercultural History of Christianity: Case-study The Gambia." In *Mission Revisited: Between Mission History and Intercultural Theology*, edited by Volker Küster, 81–92. Berlin: LIT Verlag, 2010.
Geldenhuys, Deon. *Foreign Political Engagement: Remaking States in the Post-Cold War World*. London: Macmillan Press, 1998.
Ghosananda, Maha. *Step by Step: Meditations on Wisdom and Compassion*. Berkeley, CA: Parallax Press, 1992.
Goldsworthy, David, and Peter G. Edwards. *Facing North: A Century of Australian Engagement with Asia*, vol. 2: *1970s to*

BIBLIOGRAPHY

2000. Melbourne: Melbourne University Press, 2000.

Goshal, Baladas, Jae H. Ku, and David Hawk. *Minorities in Cambodia*. London: Minority Rights Group, 1995.

Granqvist, Pehr. "Attachment Theory and Religious Conversions: A Review and a Resolution of the Classic and Contemporary Paradigm Chasm." *Review of Religious Research* 45, no. 2 (2003): 172–87.

Guthrie, Elizabeth. "Khmer Buddhism, Female Asceticism, and Salvation." In *History, Buddhism, and New Religious Movements in Cambodia*, edited by John Martson and Elizabeth Guthrie, 133–49. Honolulu: University of Hawai'i Press, 2004.

Hackett, Conrad, and David McClendon, "Christians Remain World's Largest Religious Group, but They Are Declining in Europe." Pew Research Center, April 5, 2017. https://www.pewresearch.org/fact-tank/2017/04/05/christians-remain-worlds-largest-religious-group-but-they-are-declining-in-europe/.

Hamera, Judith. "An Answerability of Memory: 'Saving' Khmer Classical Dance." *TDR: The Drama Review* 46, no. 4 (2002): 65–85. http://www.jstor.org/stable/1146978.

Hammond, Arthur. "Preparing the Scriptures in the Native Tongue," 15. No date. The Christian and Missionary Alliance (CMA) National Archives, Colorado Springs, CO, US.

Hanciles, Jehu. *Migration and the Making of Global Christianity*. Grand Rapids, MI: Eerdmans, 2021.

Hann, Chris. "Anthropology of Christianity Per Se." *European Journal of Sociology/Archives Européennes de Sociologie* 48, no. 3 (2007): 383–410. https://doi:10.1017/S0003975607000410.

Hansen, Anne Ruth, and Judy Ledgerwood, eds. *At the Edge of the Forest: Essays on Cambodia, History, and Narrative in honor of David Chandler*. Ithaca, NY: Southeast Asia Program Publications, 2008.

Harris, Ian. *Buddhism in a Dark Age: Cambodian Monks under Pol Pot*. Honolulu: University of Hawai'i Press, 2013.

———. *Cambodian Buddhism: History and Practice*. Honolulu: University of Hawai'i Press, 2005.

Headley, Robert K., Kylin Chhor, Lam Kheng Lim, Lim Hak Kheang, and Chen Chun. *Cambodian-English Dictionary*. Washington, DC: Catholic University Press, 1977.

Headley, Robert K., Rath Chim, and Ok Soeum. *Cambodian-English Dictionary*. Chantilly, VA: Dunwoody Press, 1997.

Hefner, Robert W. "Introduction." In *Conversion to Christianity: Historical and Anthropological Perspectives on a Great Transformation*, edited by Robert W. Hefner, 3–44. Berkeley: University of California Press, 1993.

Heuveline, Patrick. "The Demographic Analysis of Mortality Crises: The Case of Cambodia, 1970–1979." In *Forced Migration and Mortality*, edited by Charles B. Keeley and Holly E. Reed, 102–29. National Research Council, Commission on Behavioral and Social Sciences and Education, Committee on Population, and Roundtable on the Demography of Forced Migration. Washington, DC: National Academies Press, 2001.

Heuveline, Patrick, and Savet Hong. "One-Parent Families in Contemporary Cambodia." *Marriage and Family Review* 52, no. 1–2 (2016): 216–42. https://www.ncbi.nlm.nih.gov/pmc/articles/PMC5042329/.

Hindmarsh, Bruce. "Religious Conversion as Narrative and Autobiography." In *The Oxford Handbook of Religious Conversion*, edited by Lewis R. Rambo and Charles E. Farhadian. Oxford: Oxford University Press, 2014.

Hin, Thon, and Gerald Trevor. *Cambodian Myth—History: Khmer Texts in Prajum Roeung Breng Khmer (Book 5)*. Phnom Penh: Editions Angkor, 2012.

Hinton, Alexander. *Why Did They Kill?: Cambodia in the Shadow of Genocide*.

Berkeley: University of California Press, 2005.

Holmes, Paul, and Steve Farnfield. "Overview: Attachment Theory, Assessment and Implications." In *The Routledge Handbook of Attachment Theory*, edited by Holmes and Farnfield, 1–10. London: Taylor and Francis Group, 2014.

Holt, John C. *Spirits of the Place: Buddhism and Lao Religious Culture*. Honolulu: University of Hawai'i Press, 2009.

Horstmann, Alexander, and Jin-Heon Jung, eds. *Building Noah's Ark for Migrants, Refugees, and Religious Communities*. New York: Palgrave Macmillan, 2015.

Horton, Robin. "African Conversion." *Africa: Journal of the International African Institute* 41, no. 2 (April 1971): 85–108.

Hunt, Luke. "Cambodia Backs Vaccinations as COVID-19 Case Load Soars." *Voice of America*, July 1, 2021. https://www.voanews.com/covid-19-pandemic/cambodia-backs-vaccinations-covid-19-case-load-soars.

Ide, Kanako. "Living Together with National Border Lines and Nationalisms." In *The Palgrave Handbook of Global Citizenship and Education*, edited by Ian Davies, Li-Ching Ho, Dina Kiwan, Carla L. Peck, Andrew Peterson, Edda Sant, and Yusef Waghid, 133–48. New York: Palgrave Macmillan, 2018.

"I have decided to follow Jesus." *The Canterbury Dictionary of Hymnology*. Canterbury Press. Accessed January 30, 2023. http://www.hymnology.co.uk/i/i-have-decided-to-follow-jesus.

"INFEMIT." International Fellowship for Mission as Transformation. Accessed April 22, 2021. https://infemit.org/.

Johnson, Sarah, and Vutha Srey. "Thousands of Cambodians Go Hungry in Strict Lockdown Zones." *Guardian*, May 13, 2021. https://www.theguardian.com/global-development/2021/may/13/thousands-of-cambodians-go-hungry-in-strict-lockdown-zones.

Kasselstrand, Isabella. "Nonbelievers in the Church: A Study of Cultural Religion in Sweden." *Sociology of Religion* 76, no. 3 (2015): 275–94.

Keyes, Charles. "Why the Thai Are Not Christians: Buddhist and Christian Conversion in Thailand." In *Conversion to Christianity: Historical and Anthropological Perspectives on a Great Transformation*, edited by Robert W. Hefner, 259–84. Berkeley: University of California Press, 1993.

"Khao-I-Dang." Columbia Center for New Media Teaching and Learning. Accessed December 18, 2015. http://forcedmigration.ccnmtl.columbia.edu/khao-i-dang.

Kiernan, Ben. "External and Indigenous Sources of Khmer Ideology." In *The Third Indochina War: Conflict Between China, Vietnam and Cambodia, 1972–79*, edited by Odd Arne Westad and Sophie Quinn-Judge, 187–206. London: Routledge, 2006.

———. *The Pol Pot Regime: Race, Power, and Genocide in Cambodia Under the Khmer Rouge, 1975–79*. New Haven: Yale University Press, 2003.

Kissi, Edward. "Cambodia and Ethiopia." In *The Specter of Genocide: Murder in Historical Perspective*, edited by Robert Gellaty and Ben Kiernan, 307–24. Cambridge: Cambridge University Press, 2003.

Kitiarsa, Pattana. "Beyond Syncretism: Hybridization of Popular Religion in Contemporary Thailand." *Journal of Southeast Asian Studies* 36, no. 3 (2005): 461–97.

———. *Mediums, Monks, and Amulets: Thai Popular Buddhism Today*. Chiang Mai, Thailand: Silkworm Books, 2012.

Klostermaier, Klaus. *Hinduism: A Short History*. London: Oneworld Publications, 2000.

Kommers, Johan. "Focus on the World: The Keswick Convention and Mission." *In die Skriflig* 49, no. 1 (2015): art. #1931, 1–10.

Kong, Arey. "Cambodia's February 20 Community Event COVID-19 Cases Soar to 137, Bringing Total Tally to 633." *Khmer Times*, February 24, 2021. https://www.khmertimeskh.com/50817535/cambodias-february-20

-community-event-covid-19-cases-soar-to-137-bringing-total-tally-to-633/.
Kong, Ken. "From Genocide to Kingdom-building in Cambodia." In *Refugee Diaspora: Missions Amid the Greatest Humanitarian Crisis of Our Times*, edited by Sam George and Miriam Adeney. Littleton, CO: William Carey Publishing, 2018.
Kuo, Henry. "Beyond Ontologizing Asian America." *Political Theology Network*, July 29, 2021. https://politicaltheology.com/beyond-ontologizing-asian-america/.
Kuttiyanikkal, Ciril J. *Khrist Bhakta Movement: A Model for an Indian Church?: Inculturation in the Area of Community Building*. Münster: LIT Verlag, 2014.
Langford, Jean M. *Consoling Ghosts: Stories of Medicine and Mourning from Southeast Asians in Exile*. Minneapolis: University of Minnesota Press, 2013.
Leclère, Adhémard. *Le Bouddhisme au Cambodge*. Paris: E. Leroux, 1899.
———. *Le Livre de Vesandar, le roi charitable*. Paris: E. Leroux, 1902.
Leer-Helgesen, Arnhild. *Negotiating Religion and Development: Identity Construction and Contention in Bolivia*. London: Routledge, 2020.
Lim, David S. "Contextualizing Ancestor Veneration: An Historical Review." *International Journal of Frontier Missiology* 32, no. 3 (2015): 109–15.
Lindhardt, Martin. "'If You Are Saved You Cannot Forget Your Parents': Agency, Power, and Social Repositioning in Tanzanian Born-Again Christianity." *Journal of Religion in Africa* 40, no. 3 (2010): 240–72.
———. "Mediating Money: Materiality and Spiritual Warfare in Tanzanian Charismatic Christianity." In *The Anthropology of Global Pentecostalism and Evangelicalism*, edited by Simon Coleman and Rosalind I. J. Hackett, 147–60. New York: New York University Press, 2015.
Long, Colin, and Keir Reeves. "Dig a Hole and Bury the Past in It." In *Places of Pain and Shame: Dealing with "Difficult Heritage,"* edited by William Logan and Keir Reeves, 68–81. London: Routledge, 2009.
Louis XV. "V. A Slave Code of a Catholic King: 16. from the Code Noir of King Louis XV of France, 1724." In *American Catholics and Slavery, 1789–1866: An Anthology of Primary Documents*, compiled and edited by Kenneth J. Zanca, 23–27. Lanham, MD: University Press of America, 1994.
Lovelace, Pastor Joshua J. *From Seedtime to Harvest: The History of the Assemblies of God in Cambodia*. Eugene, OR: Wipf and Stock, 2019.
Luhrmann, T. M. *When God Talks Back: Understanding the American Evangelical Relationship with God*. New York: Alfred A. Knopf, 2012.
Luhrmann, T. M., and Rachel Morgain. "Prayer as Inner Sense Cultivation: An Attentional Learning Theory of Spiritual Experience." *Ethos* 40, no. 4 (2012): 359–89.
MacMullen, Ramsay. *Christianizing the Roman Empire*. New Haven: Yale University Press, 1984.
Maher, Brian. *Cry of the Gecko*. With Uon Seila. Centralia, WA: Gorham Printing, 2012. Kindle.
Maiden, John. "Quadrilaterals in Waco: Reflections on the 'Evangelicals and the Bible' Symposium." Contemporary Religion in Historical Perspective, The Open University, October 1, 2019. http://www.open.ac.uk/blogs/religious-studies/?p=944.
Malkki, Liisa. *Purity and Exile: Violence, Memory, and National Cosmology Among Hutu Refugees in Tanzania*. Chicago: University of Chicago Press, 1995.
Mam, Barnabas. "Cambodia." In *Christianity in East and Southeast Asia*, edited by Kenneth R. Ross, Francis Alvarez, and Todd M. Johnson, 175–86. Edinburgh: Edinburgh University Press, 2020.
———. *Church Behind the Wire: A Story of Faith in the Killing Fields*. Chicago: Moody Publishers, 2012.
———. "Compilation of the Khmer Indigenous Hymnal and Khmer Discipleship

Materials." In *Church Partnerships in Asia: A Singapore Conversation*, edited by Michael Nai-Chiu Poon, 146–53. Singapore: Trinity Theological College, 2011.

Marston, John, and Elizabeth Guthrie. *History, Buddhism, and New Religious Movements in Cambodia*. Honolulu: University of Hawai'i Press, 2004.

Mast, Jason L., and Jeffrey C. Alexander, eds. *Politics of Meaning / Meaning of Politics: Cultural Sociology of the 2016 US Presidential Election*. Cham, Switzerland: Palgrave Macmillan, 2019.

Mauss, Marcel. *The Gift*. New York: W.W. Norton, 2010.

McGovern, Nathan. "Esoteric Buddhism in Southeast Asia." *Oxford Research Encyclopedia of Religion*, October 26, 2017. https://oxfordre.com/religion/view/10.1093/acrefore/9780199340378.001.0001/acrefore-9780199340378-e-617.

McLean-Farrell, Janice. *West Indian Pentecostals: Living Their Faith in New York and London*. New York: Bloomsbury, 2016.

McLellan, Janet. *Cambodian Refugees in Ontario: Resettlement, Religion, and Identity*. Toronto: University of Toronto Press, 2009.

Men, Chean Rithy. "The Changing Religious Beliefs and Ritual Practices Among Cambodians in Diaspora." *Journal of Refugee Studies* 15, no. 2 (2002): 222–33.

Meyer, Birgit. "Religious Sensations: Why Media, Aesthetics, and Power Matter in the Study of Contemporary Religion." In *Religion: A Concept*, edited by Hent de Vries, 704–23. New York: Fordham University Press, 2008.

Miksic, John N., and Geok Yian Goh. *Ancient Southeast Asia*. London: Routledge, 2017.

Miller, Amanda. "Development Through Vocational Education: The Lived Experiences of Young People at a Vocational Education, Training Restaurant in Siem Reap, Cambodia." *Heliyon* 6, no. 12, E05765 (2020): 1–10.

Milne, Sarah, and Sango Mahanty. "The Political Ecology of Cambodia's Transformation." In *Conservation and Development in Cambodia*, edited by Sarah Milne and Sango Mahanty, 1–27. London: Taylor and Francis, 2015.

Moore, Russell. "When the South Loosens Its Bible Belt." *Christianity Today*, August 11, 2022. https://www.christianitytoday.com/ct/2022/august-web-only/russell-moore-white-evangelicals-bible-belt-south-church.html.

Morris, Stephen J. *Why Vietnam Invaded Cambodia: Political Culture and the Causes of War*. Stanford: Stanford University Press, 1999.

Mortanz, Toby. "In the Land of the Lions: The Ethnohistory of Bruce G. Trigger." In *The Archaeology of Bruce Trigger: Theoretical Empiricism*, edited by Ronald Williamson and Michael S. Bisson, 142–73. Montreal: McGill–Queen's University Press, 2006.

Mortland, Carol A. *Cambodian Buddhism in the United States*. Albany: State University of New York Press, 2017.

———. "Khmer Buddhists in the United States: Ultimate Questions." In *Cambodian Culture since 1975: Homeland and Exile*, edited by May M. Ebihara, Carol A. Mortland, and Judy Ledgerwood, 72–90. Ithaca, NY: Southeast Asia Program Publications, 1994.

Na, Hyemin. "Imaging the Sacred Online: Digital Media Productions of Progress at a Megachurch in Korea," *Journal of World Christianity* 10, no. 1 (2020), 84–100.

Narayan, Kirin. "How Native Is a 'Native' Anthropologist?" *American Anthropologist* 95, no. 3 (1993): 671–86.

Narim, Khuon. "US Deported 80 Cambodians Last Year: Report." *Khmer Times*, February 11, 2020. https://www.khmertimeskh.com/689595/us-deported-80-cambodians-last-year-report/.

National Institute of Statistics, Directorate General for Health and ICF International. *2014 Cambodia Demographic and Health Survey Key Findings*. Rockville, MD: National Institute of Statistics, Directorate General for Health and ICF International, 2015.

BIBLIOGRAPHY

Net, Wanna. "Khmer Language: Fonts and Romanization." *EthnoMed*, University of Washington, January 1, 2008. Accessed March 1, 2020. https://ethnomed.org/culture/cambodian/khmer-language.

Ngoy, Ted. *The Donut King: The Rags to Riches Story of a Poor Immigrant Who Changed the World*. Phnom Penh: Ted Ngoy, 2018.

Nguyen, Viet Thanh. *Nothing Ever Dies: Vietnam and the Memory of War*. Cambridge, MA: Harvard University Press, 2016.

———. *The Refugees*. New York: Grove Press, 2017.

Nichols, Greg. "Dunkin' and the Doughnut King." *California Sunday*, November 2, 2014. https://story.californiasunday.com/ted-ngoy-california-doughnut-king/.

Ninh, Thien-Huong T. "Mobilizing Ethnic-Religious Transnationalism Through Humanitarian Assistance: Vietnamese Catholic US–Cambodia Relations." In *Migration, Transnationalism and Catholicism: Global Perspectives*, edited by Dominic Pasura and Marta Bivand Erdal, 209–34. New York: Palgrave Macmillan, 2016.

———. *Race, Gender, and Religion in the Vietnamese Diaspora: The New Chosen People*. New York: Palgrave Macmillan, 2017.

Obeyesekere, Gananath. "The Great Tradition and the Little in the Perspective of Sinhalese Buddhism." *Journal of Asian Studies* 22, no. 2 (1963): 139–53.

Office of International Religious Freedom. "2020 Report on Religious Freedom: Cambodia." United States Department of State, May 12, 2021. https://www.state.gov/reports/2020-report-on-international-religious-freedom/cambodia/.

Ollier, Leakthina Chau-Pech. "Rapping (in) the Homeland: Of Gangs, Angka, and the Cambodian Diasporic Identity." In *Expressions of Cambodia: The Politics of Tradition, Identity and Change*, edited by Leakthina Chau-Pech Ollier and Tim Winter, 101–16. London: Routledge, 2006.

Ong, Aihwa. "Guns, Gangs, and Doughnut Kings." In *Buddha Is Hiding: Refugees, Citizenship, the New America*, edited by Ong, 229–52. Berkeley: University of California Press, 2003.

Pearson, Thomas. *Missions and Conversions: Creating the Montagnard-Dega Refugee Community*. New York: Palgrave Macmillan, 2009.

Penner, Hans H. *Rediscovering the Buddha: Legends of the Buddha and Their Interpretation*. Oxford: Oxford University Press, 2009.

Pham, Nga (@ngahpham). "As protesters gathered outside before swarming the #Capitol building, you can see the yellow flags of the old Saigon regime. Many Vietnamese Americans, mainly of the older generation, Are ardent Trump supporters." Twitter, January 6, 2021. https://twitter.com/ngahpham/status/1346961442906415110.

Phan, Peter C. "Multiple Religious Belonging: Opportunities and Challenges for Theology and Church." *Theological Studies* 64, no. 3 (2003): 495–519.

Piaget, J. J. "From Persecution to Freedom." Annual Report Cambodian Field—1971. The Christian and Missionary Alliance (CMA) National Archives. Colorado Springs, CO, US.

Poethig, Kathryn. "Visa Trouble: Cambodian American Christians and Their Defense of Multiple Citizenship." In *Religions/Globalizations: Theories and Case*, edited by Dwight N. Hopkins, Lois Ann Lorentzen, Eduardo Mendieta, and David Batstone, 187–202. Durham: Duke University Press, 2001.

Ponchaud, François. *La Cathédrale de la rizière*. Paris: Éditions CLD, 2006.

———. *The Cathedral in the Rice Paddy: 450 Years of History of the Church in Cambodia*. Translated by Nancy Pignarre and the Bishop Salas Cambodian Catholic Center. Paris: Espace Cambodge, 1990.

———. *L'Impertinent du Cambodge: Entretiens*. With Dane Cuypers. Paris: Megellan and Cie, 2013.

Pye, Michael. "New Religions in East Asia." In *The Oxford Handbook of New Religious*

Movements, edited by James R. Lewis, 491–513. Oxford: Oxford University Press, 2008.
Qasmiyeh, Yousif M., and Elena Fiddian-Qasmiyeh. "Refugee Camps and Cities in Conversation." In *Rescripting Religion in the City: Migration and Religious Identity in the Modern Metropolis*, edited by Jane Garnett and Alana Harris, 131–43. Surrey, UK: Ashgate, 2013.
Rambo, Lewis R., Steven Bauman, and Jiazhi Fengjiang. "Toward a Psychology of Converting in the People's Republic of China." *Pastoral Psychology* 61, nos. 5–6 (2012): 895–921.
Rasmey, Van Arun, and Mathews George Chunakara. "Cambodia." In *Asian Handbook for Theological Education and Ecumenism*, edited by Hope Antone, Wati Longchar, Hyunju Bae, Huang Po Ho, and Dietrich Werner, 470–99. Eugene, OR: Wipf and Stock, 2013.
Ray, Reginald A. *Buddhist Saints in India: A Study in Buddhist Values and Orientations*. Oxford: Oxford University Press, 1993.
Religion and Public Life. "Christianity in Myanmar." Glossary of Terms, Harvard Divinity School. Accessed September 1, 2022. https://rpl.hds.harvard.edu/faq/christianity-myanmar.
Rhee, Helen. "Family Structures: Early Church." In *The Oxford Encyclopedia of the Bible and Gender Studies, Volume 1: ASI-MUJ*, edited by Julia M. O'Brien. Oxford: Oxford University Press, 2014.
Ricoeur, Paul. *Memory, History, Forgetting*. Translated by Kathleen Blamey and David Pallauer. Chicago: University of Chicago Press, 2004.
———. *The Rule of Metaphor*. Translated by Robert Czerny. Toronto: University of Toronto Press, 1977.
Robbins, Joel. *Becoming Sinners: Christianity and Moral Torment in a Papua New Guinea Society*. Berkeley: University of California Press, 2004.
Robert, Dana L. "World Christianity as a Women's Movement." *International Bulletin of Missionary Research*, 30, no. 4 (2006): 180–88.
Roberts, Nathaniel. *To Be Cared For: The Power of Conversion and Foreignness of Belonging in an Indian Slum*. Berkeley: University of California Press, 2016.
Ryle, Jacqueline. *My God, My Land: Interwoven Paths of Christianity and Tradition in Fiji*. Farnham, UK: Ashgate, 2012.
Sak-Humphry, Chhany. *Colloquial Cambodian: The Complete Course for Beginners*. London: Routledge, 2016.
Schabas, William. *War Crimes and Human Rights: Essays on the Death Penalty, Justice and Accountability*. London: Cameron May Publishers, 2008.
Scheer, Catherine. "New Life in an Expanding Market Economy: Moral Issues Among Cambodia's Highland Protestants." In *New Religiosities, Modern Capitalism, and Moral Complexities in Southeast Asia*, edited by Juliette Koning and Gwenaël Njoto-Feillard, 65–88. New York: Palgrave Macmillan, 2017.
Schiocchet, Leonardo. "Palestinian Steadfastness as Mission." In *Building Noah's Ark for Migrants, Refugees, and Religious Communities*, edited by Alexander Horstmann and Jin-Heon Jung, 209–34. New York: Palgrave Macmillan, 2015.
Schlund-Vials, Cathy. *War, Genocide, and Justice: Cambodian American Memory Work*. Minneapolis: University of Minnesota Press, 2012.
SEAlang Library Khmer Dictionary. Accessed December 1, 2019. http://www.sealang.net/khmer/dictionary.htm.
Selka, Stephen. "Morality in the Religious Marketplace: Evangelical Christianity, Candomblé, and the Struggle for Moral Distinction in Brazil." *American Ethnologist* 37, no. 2 (2010): 291–307.
Shellnut, Kate. "Evangelicals for Social Action Leaves Behind 'Evangelical' Label." *Christianity Today*, September 15, 2020. https://www.christianitytoday.com/news/2020/september/evangelicals-for-social-action-name-change-christian.html.
Simon, Patrick. "The Choice of Ignorance: The Debate on Ethnic and Racial

Statistics in France." In *Social Statistics and Ethnic Diversity*, edited by Patrick Simon, Victor Piché, and Amélie A. Gagnon, 65–87. IMISCOE Research Series. Cham, Switzerland: Springer, 2015.

Sloan, Bronwyn. "The Brothers' New Father." *Far Eastern Economic Review* 167, no. 2 (January 15, 2004).

Smith-Hefner, Nancy J. "Ethnicity and the Force of Faith: Christian Conversion Among Khmer Refugees." *Anthropological Quarterly* 67, no. 1 (1994): 24–37. http://yeshebi.ptsem.edu:2079/stable/3317275.

———. *Khmer American: Identity and Moral Education in a Diasporic Community*. Berkeley: University of California Press, 1999.

Smith, T. O. "Cambodia." In *The Routledge History of Genocide*, edited by Cathie Carmichael and Richard C. Maguire. London: Routledge, 2015. https://www.routledgehandbooks.com/doi/10.4324/9781315719054.ch9.

Southgate, Laura. "ASEAN and the Dynamics of Resistance to Sovereignty Violation: The Case of the Third Indochina War (1978–1991)." *Journal of Asian Security and International Affair* 2, no. 2 (2015): 200–221.

Spiro, Melford. *Buddhism and Society: A Great Tradition and Its Burmese Vicissitudes*. New York: Harper and Row, 1970.

Stanley, Brian. "The Evangelical Christian Mind in History and Global Context." In *Every Leaf, Line, and Letter: Evangelicals and the Bible from the 1730s to the Present*, edited by Timothy Larsen, 276–302. Downers Grove, IL: IVP Academic, 2021.

Stark, Rodney, and Roger Finke. *Acts of Faith: Explaining the Human Side of Religion*. Berkeley: University of California Press, 2000.

Subramanian, S. V., Emre Özaltin, and Jocelyn E. Finlay. "Height of Nations: A Socioeconomic Analysis of Cohort Differences and Patterns Among Women in 54 Low- to Middle-Income Countries." *PLoS One* 6, no. 4: e18962 (2011). https://doi:10.1371/journal.pone.0018962.

Su, Christine M. "Tradition and Change: Khmer Identity and Democracy in the 20th Century and Beyond." PhD diss., University of Hawai'i, 2003.

Swearer, Donald K. *The Buddhist World of Southeast Asia*. Albany: SUNY Press, 2010.

Tambiah, Stanley J. *Buddhism and the Spirit-Cults of North-East Thailand*. Cambridge: Cambridge University Press, 1970.

Taneti, James. *Telugu Christians: A History*. Minneapolis: Fortress Press, 2022.

Taylor, Philip. *Cham Muslims of the Mekong Delta: Place and Mobility in the Cosmopolitan Periphery*. Singapore: NUS Press, 2007.

Thomas, Sonja. "Feminist Ethnography and 'Studying Up' in World Christianity Studies." Presentation at the World Christianity Conference, Princeton Theological Seminary, Princeton, NJ, March 29, 2019. https://www.youtube.com/watch?v=z5pQO-Q4w2U.

Thompson, Ashley. "The Future of Cambodia's Past: A Messianic Middle-Period Cambodian Royal Cult." In *History, Buddhism, and New Religious Movements in Cambodia*, edited by John Marston and Elizabeth Guthrie, 13–40. Honolulu: University of Hawai'i Press, 2004.

Um, Khatharya. *From the Land of Shadows: War, Revolution, and the Making of the Cambodian Diaspora*. New York: New York University Press, 2015.

United Nations Population Fund Cambodia. "Cambodia Youth Data Sheet 2015." February 25, 2016. https://cambodia.unfpa.org/sites/default/files/pub-pdf/Flyer_Cambodia_Youth_Factsheet_final_draft_%28approved%29.pdf.

Unrepresented Nations and Peoples Organization, "Hmong: Religious Persecution Continues in Vietnam." April 18, 2019. https://unpo.org/article/21467#:~:text=In%20Vietnam%2C%20Hmong%20Christians%20continue,defend ing%20national%20unity%20and%20security.

Vickery, Michael. *Cambodia: 1975–1982*. Boston: South End Press, 1984.

Walls, Andrew. "Mission and Migration: The Diaspora Factor in Christian History." *Journal of African Christian Thought* 5, no. 2 (2002): 3–11.

Westerfield Tucker, Karen B. "Methodism's 'World Parish': Liturgical and Hymnological Migrations in Three Ecclesiastical Generations." In *Liturgy in Migration: From the Upper Room to Cyberspace*, edited by in Teresa Berger, 131–54. Collegeville, MN: Liturgical Press, 2012.

Widyono, Benny. *Dancing in Shadows: Sihanouk, the Khmer Rouge, and the United Nations in Cambodia*. Lanham, MD: Rowman and Littlefield, 2008.

Wiebe, Phillip. *Visions of Jesus: Direct Encounters from the New Testament to Today*. Oxford: Oxford University Press, 1997.

Wijers, G. D. M. "The Reception of Cambodian Refugees in France." *Journal of Refugee Studies* 24, no. 2 (2011): 239–55.

Wong, Briana. "Buddhist-Christians in Cambodian America." *Studies in World Christianity* 25, no. 1 (2019): 50–70.

———. "The Historical Interface Between Buddhism and Christianity in Cambodia, with Special Attention to the Christian and Missionary Alliance, 1923–1970." *Buddhist-Christian Studies* 40 (2020): 255–71.

———. "Longing for Home: The Impact of COVID-19 on Cambodian Evangelical Life." *Studies in World Christianity* 26, no. 3 (2020): 281–97.

———. "'We Believe the Bible': Cambodian Women in Christian Leadership, 1953–Present." *Indonesian Journal of Theology* 9, no. 1 (2021): 32–40.

Wood, Timothy Dylan. "Touring Memories of the Khmer Rouge." In *Expressions of Cambodia: The Politics of Tradition, Identity and Change*, edited by Leakthina Chau-Pech Ollier and Tim Winter, 181–92. London: Routledge, 2006.

World Christian Database. Center for the Study of Global Christianity. Accessed March 16, 2020. https://www.worldchristiandatabase.org/.

Wuthnow, Robert. *Boundless Faith: The Global Outreach of American Churches*. Berkeley: University of California Press, 2009.

Young, Richard Fox. "Christianity and Conversion: Conceptualization and Critique, Past and Present, with Special Reference to South Asia." In *The Oxford Handbook of Christianity in Asia*, edited by Felix Wilfred, 444–57. Oxford: Oxford University Press, 2014.

———. "Horton's 'Intellectualist Theory' of Conversion, Reflected on by a South Asianist." In *Beyond Conversion and Syncretism: Indigenous Encounters with Missionary Christianity, 1800–2000*, edited by David Lindenfeld and Miles Richardson, 115–34. New York: Berghahn Books, 2011.

Zehner, Edwin. "Orthodox Hybridities." *Anthropological Quarterly* 78, no. 3 (2005): 585–617.

Zieck, Marjoleine. *UNHCR and Voluntary Repatriation of Refugees: A Legal Analysis*. The Hague: Martinus Nijhoff Publishers, 1994.

Zucker, Eve Monique. *Forest of Struggle: Moralities of Remembrance in Upland Cambodia*. Honolulu: University of Hawai'i Press, 2013.

———. "From Soldier to Guardian Spirit: Cultural Resilience Through Re-enchantment." The Asia Dialogue, University of Nottingham. Asia Research Institute, August 10, 2017. https://theasiadialogue.com/2017/08/10/from-soldier-to-guardian-spirit-cultural-resilience-through-re-enchantment/.

Index

activism, 25, 29
   See also quadrilateral, evangelical
adoption, 8, 104–7, 113–14, 121, 144, 147
   See also father, God as
African American culture, 99, 130, 135, 155
age, 4, 36–37, 118, 150–54
   See also youth
Aladura culture, 46
alcohol, 32, 77, 113, 158
Alliance Chrétienne et Missionnaire de France. *See* Christian and Missionary Alliance
ancestor spirits, 27, 50, 66, 73–74
   See also spirits
angels, 65, 68, 69, 76
   See also spirits
Angkor Wat, 35, 66
añjali mudra (hand gesture), 150
Anlong Veng, 53
anthropology of Christianity, 23
anticommunism, 137
   See also communism
Assemblies of God, 21
attachment theory, 61
Austin (TX), 62
Australia, 22, 33
autogenocide, 19
   See also genocide

bakus (hindu priests), 66
baptism, 26, 31, 44, 45, 95, 117
Battambang, 13, 21
BBC, 136
"believing without belonging," 8, 43, 83
"belonging without believing," 43
Benedictine monastery, 15
bhajan, 99
Bible, Hebrew, 68
   See also Old Testament
Bible, Khmer
   and cosmology, 84
   versions of: controversy regarding, 84, Khmer Old Version, 84, 91, 121, 122, 136; Khmer Standard Version, 84, 91, 121
   See also translation, Bible

Bible reading
   in church, 36, 133, 134; bilingual, 36
   as an individual practice, 96, 97, 113, 120
   in a small group, 42, 113
   via digital media, 139
Bible schools
   CMA Bible School in Battambang, 13
   Phnom Penh Bible School, 56, 120
biblicism, 24–27
   See also quadrilateral, evangelical
Bilāwal rāga, 99
border, Cambodian-Thai, 7, 10–11, 16, 20–21, 45, 78–79, 121, 135
Boston (MA), 51–52, 141
Brahma, 66–70
   See also Brahmanical deities
Brahmanical deities, 66–70, 99, 144, 158
   Brahma, 66–70
   Ganeś, 70
   Indra, 66–68, 158
   Sakka, 99
   Śiva, 66
   Umā, 66
   Visnu, 66
Brahmanism, 7, 66, 68, 69, 70, 72, 144
   See also Brahmanical deities
British Broadcasting Company, 136
Buddhaghosa, 68
Buddhism
   Mahayana, 8, 65, 81, 144
   Theravada, 8, 22, 65–70, 78, 80–81, 85–86, 108, 144; cosmogony and, 67; "great" and "little" traditions, 69; Khmer identity and, 22; Khmer religious cosmology and, 66–71; prayer and, 66
   See also monks, Buddhist
Buddhist Lent, 108
Burma. *See* Myanmar

Calvinists, 12
Cambodia
   Battambang, 13, 119
   Kampong Cham provence, 14
   Kep provence, 15
   Kratie provence, 70

INDEX

Phnom Penh, 1–2, 4, 12–14, 16–17, 20–21
    as protectorate of France, 12
    Pursat provence, 119–20
    Takeo provence, 124
    US carpet-bombing of, 6, 16, 19
Cambodian Civil War, 14, 16, 22, 34, 132
Cambodian cultural identity. *See* cultural identity, Cambodian
Cambodian flag, 35, 136
Cambodian Genocide. *See* genocide, Cambodian
Canada, 80, 121, 157
Candomblé, 101, 102, 166n26
Caodai (religion), 13
Catholicism, 6, 8, 12–18, 42, 54–56, 97
celibacy, 78
    See also monks, Buddhist
Cham (ethnic group), 18–19
charismaticism, 32–33, 59, 93, 100–101, 147, 158
    See also Pentecostalism
Chennai (India), 152–53
Chhang, Youk, 59
China Inland Mission. *See* OMF International
Christian and Missionary Alliance, 13–15, 17, 24, 29–31, 105, 112, 121, 135
Christian Contemporary Music, 28
Church of the Nazarene, 26, 30
cigarettes. *See* smoking
Civil War, Cambodian, 14, 16, 22, 34, 132
clothing, 33–34, 37–38, 57
    waistbands and wristbands, protective, 79, 101, 103
    white clothing, figures wearing, 57, 66, 67, 68, 76, 158
Cochinchina, 14
coevalness, 158, 168n14
Cold War, 6
communion, 31
    See also Lord's Supper
communism, 10, 13, 15–17, 29, 53–54, 62, 137, 162n29
    See also anticommunism
Communist Party of Kampuchea. *See* Khmer Rouge
Compain, Alice, 31
conversion
    associated risks, 49–50
    motivations for, 7, 51–59, 129
    stages of, 41–48
    See also deconversion
conversionism, 24–25
    See also quadrilateral, evangelical
cosmogony, 67–68
    See also creation

cosmology, Khmer religious
    components of, 66
    heavens, 10, 30, 68–69, 84–87, 126–29, 134–36
    hells, 85–87
    hybridity, 80, 85–87
    karma, 5, 45, 51, 54, 59, 83–84, 108, 110; merit, 8, 82, 108, 110; rebirth, 51, 67, 83, 86–87
    multiple religious believing without multiple religious belonging, 83, 144
    multiple religious belonging, 80, 82–83, 91, 102, 110, 144
    See also spirits
COVID-19, x, 6, 115, 138, 145, 146,
creation, 67–68, 82
creationism, 30
crucicentrism, 24, 29
    See also quadrilateral, evangelical
cultural identity, Cambodian
    Buddhism and, 22, 49, 51
    Christianity and, 91
    preservation of, 34–37

Dalits, 24, 135, 152
Damnatio memoriae, 91
Day of Remembrance (formerly Day of Hate, Day to Remain in Anger), 52
death, Khmer translations of, 84
deconversion, 51–52
    See also conversion
deliverance, 103
    See also exorcisms
demons, 65, 85–87, 144
    See also spirits
Democratic Kampuchea, 11, 18, 59, 78
dhamma (dharma), 101
    See also Buddhism
diaspora, 22, 30–37, 131–42
digital media, 139–42
    Facebook, 139; Facebook Live, 9, 139–40; Facebook Messenger, 3, 9
    Google Hangouts, 123
    Internet, 115, 138, 141
    Skype, 124
disability, 79
discipleship, 116–18, 125
disloyalty, 94, 102, 107
    See also loyalty
Documentation Center of Cambodia, 59
Dominicans (Catholic order), 12
donut shops, 112, 129, 132–33, 153
double religious belonging, 80
    See also multiple religious belonging

181

INDEX

dreams, 75–77, 79
Duch (Kang Kech Ieu), 5
Easter, 94
Egypt, 134–35
Ellison, David, 13
English language, 18, 36–37, 44, 55, 95, 122, 133, 139
 See also language
entrepreneurship
 donut shops, 112
 guest house, 96–97
 lumber business, 26
 sewing business, 113
Ethnos360. See New Tribes Mission
eucharist. See communion
evangelicalism, cultural expressions of
 Cambodian, 24–30
 Thai, 30, 85–88
 White American, 27–28, 147
Exodus (biblical book), 91, 134–35
exorcism, 70–71, 74–75, 87, 103
 See also praying
Extraordinary Chambers in the Courts of Cambodia. See Khmer Rouge Tribunal

Facebook, 139
 Facebook Live, 9, 139–40
 Facebook Messenger, 3, 9
 See also digital media
Falwell, Jerry, 137
fashion. See clothing
father, God as, 60–61, 65, 90, 103–7, 114, 116, 119, 127
filial piety, 27, 127–28
Filipino, 145
 See also Philippines, the
finances
 faith and, 104, 109–14
 foreign financial impact on Cambodian churches, 33
 transnationalism and, 123
flags
 Cambodian, 35, 136
 Israeli, 135
 South Vietnamese, 136–37
Focus on the Family, 28
food
 festive, 93
 conversion and, 7, 41
 offerings of, 71–72, 75, 82, 106, 109, 113
 (see also offerings)
 post-church meals, 34–35
 vehicle for cultural preservation, 37–38

forced marriages, 53–54, 78
 See also Khmer Rouge
forgiveness
 for one's own actions, 29, 38, 45, 51–52, 54, 67, 82–84, 87
 forgiveness of others, 103, 104
Foursquare Church, 21
French language, 18, 35, 36, 42, 45, 122, 127
 See also language
fruit (as religious offering), 104, 106, 107, 109
fruit of the spirit, 104
funerals, 50, 92

Ganeś, 70
 See also Brahmanical deities
gangs, 129–30
gender
 egalitarianism, 158
 ethnography and, 151–52, 167n9
 See also women in ministry
Geneva Convention, 19
 See also genocide, Cambodian
genocide, Cambodian, 1, 3–5, 9–11, 17–22, 29, 52–53, 57–62, 141
 autogenocide, 19
Ghana, 138
ghosts, 71, 74, 75, 92
 See also spirits
gift-giving, 106–10
 See also tithing
glossolalia, 33, 147
 See also speaking in tongues
Google Hangouts, 123
 See also digital media

Hammond, Arthur, 13, 105
Hammond, Fred, 99
heavens, 10, 30, 68–69, 84–87, 126–29, 134–36
 See also cosmology, Khmer religious
hells, 85–87
 See also cosmology, Khmer religious
Heng Samrin, 20
Hinduism, 65, 67–68, 144
Hindustani language, 99
 See also language
Holi, 94
Holidays, 94
 Buddhist Lent, 108
 Christmas, 56, 94, 98
 Easter, 94
 Holi, 94
 Khmer New Year, 93–94
 Thanksgiving, 94
Holy Spirit, 32, 65, 68, 77, 79, 92, 146, 147

fruit of the, 104
gifts of the, 32, 147
See also spirits
Hun Sen, 21
hybridity, 80, 85–87
See also cosmology
hymnals, 31, 34, 38, 98, 139, 163n95
controversy regarding, 98
See also singing

incense, 72, 82
See also prayer: Buddhist prayer
independence, Cambodian, 13
India, 24, 70, 104, 108, 135, 150, 152, 167n9
Indra, 66–68, 158
See also Brahmanical deities
intellectualist theory, 7, 45–47
internet, 115, 138, 141
See also digital media
Iringa (Tanzania), 100, 106
Israel (nation state), 29, 135–37, 148
Issaraks, 13

January 6, 2021. *See* United States Capitol Building, storming of
Judaism, 108, 112, 135

Kampong Cham, 14
See also Cambodia, provinces of
Kang Kech Ieu (Duch), 5
Kat kal chaol, 91
Kep, 15
See also Cambodia, provinces of
Keswick Convention, 17, 29, 65, 91, 135
Khao-I-Dang Holding Center. *See* refugee: refugee camps
Khmer Evangelical Church, 14, 15, 17
Khmer Kraom (ethnic group), 13
Khmer language, 13–14, 35–38, 42, 45, 72, 122, 150–53
development of, 150–51
See also language
Khmer New Year, 93–94
Khmer Rouge (Communist Party of Kampuchea): 3–5, 9–10, 15–21, 52–53, 57–59, 83, 122, 136–37
forced marriages under, 53–54, 78
Khmer Rouge Tribunal, 19, 52
killing fields. *See* genocide, Cambodian
Kingdom of Cambodia. *See* Cambodia
Kingston (ON), 80
Korea, 21, 119, 120, 140, 145, 146
Kratie, 70
See also Cambodia, provinces of

labor camps, 18, 42, 53, 57, 58
language, 3, 36, 38, 55, 72, 85
language acquisition, 44, 55, 95, 119, 152–53
language as barrier, 29, 25, 62, 130–31
language interpretation, 36, 45, 133–34
English language, 18, 36–37, 44, 55, 95, 122, 133, 139
French language, 18, 35, 36, 42, 45, 122, 127
Hindustani language, 99
Khmer language, 13–14, 35–38, 42, 45, 72, 122, 150–53; development of, 150–51
Pali language, 69, 78, 81, 84, 86
Sanskrit language, 68, 69
Spanish language, 132
Thai language, 85
Vietnamese language, 14, 35
Living Hope in Christ Church (LHCC), 21
Lon Nol, 15–16
Long Beach, 10, 34, 35, 38, 130, 151–53
Lord's Supper, 62
See also communion
Los Angeles, 1, 149
love
and the ancestors, 73
of God, 89–90, 105–7
Bible translation term, 105
in ministry, 119, 133
Lowell (MA), 10, 51, 130
loyalty, 8, 50, 75, 87–94, 98–103, 111, 114, 144–45
See also disloyalty
Ly, Prach (PraCh), 126

Madagascar, 13
Māghamānab, 66
See also Indra
Malaysia, 18, 21
marriage, 53–54, 55, 78, 82, 110
forced marriages, 53–54, 78 (*See also* Khmer Rouge)
mass media, 138
material religion, 100–101
meditation, 93–94
Mekong Delta, 18
memorization (of Scripture), 103
mentorship, 20, 33, 97, 117, 145
See also discipleship
Merit, 8, 82, 108, 110
See also karma
Methodists, 3, 21, 30
United Methodist Church, The, 3
migration, Adamic and Abrahamic, 132

183

ministry
    healing as, 101
    transnational, 115–18
    women in, 9, 31, 37, 98, 139–42, 146, 158
    See also mission
mission
    mutual mission, 6, 8, 9, 20, 115–42
    reverse mission, 118, 128–37, 145
    South-South mission: Chinese, 86; Filipino, 33, 145; Indian, 99; Korean, 145
    Western mission, 11–15, 17, 20–21, 120, 121, 130, 135
Missions Étrangères de Paris, 14
music. See singing
monks, Buddhist, 49, 52–53, 69–70, 72, 78–82, 86, 101, 151
    novitiate of boys, 108
    sangha (monkhood), 78, 108, 151
Montagnard-Dega community, 131
Moses, 94
Mount Meru, 69
multiple religious believing without multiple religious belonging, 83, 144
    See also cosmology, Khmer religious
multiple religious belonging, 80, 82–83, 91, 102, 110, 144
    See also cosmology, Khmer religious
Myanmar, 24

National Assembly (of Cambodia), 15
National United Front of Kampuchea (FUNK), 15
nature spirits, 66
    See also spirits
Nazarene, Church of the, 26, 30
New Apostolic Church, 21
New Life Fellowship Phnom Penh, 21
New Testament, 13, 15, 27, 32, 36, 84, 135
New Tribes Mission, 56, 164n30
nidhi (power), 78
Nigeria, 46
North Vietnam, 15, 20
    See also Vietnam

Oakland (CA), 130
offerings, 36, 42, 71–73, 99, 102, 104, 106, 109
Old Testament, 13, 15, 27, 36
    See also Hebrew Bible
OMF International, 17, 31, 135
orixás, 101–2
orthodoxy
    in evangelical Protestantism, 51, 85–87
    in Theravada Buddhism, 66, 70, 81, 85–86

ostracism, 41, 49
Overseas Mission Fellowship. See OMF International

Pali Canon, 69, 81, 86
Pali language, 69, 78, 81, 84, 86
    See also language
pandemic. See COVID-19
parable of the raft, 81
parachurch organizations, 27, 33
Paris, 34, 36, 153–54
Passover, 94
Pentecostalism, 59, 100, 138, 156
    See also charismaticism
Philadelphia, 34, 38, 123
Philippines, the, 2, 33, 120, 146
    See also Filipino
Phnom Penh, 1–2, 4, 12–14, 16–17, 20–21
Phnom Penh Bible School, 56
Pneumatism, 147
    See also charismaticism
Pol Pot, 3, 7, 10, 15–21, 91, 162n29
Portuguese (nationality), 12
Povo de santo, 101–2
praCh, 126
praying
    asking for another's conversion, 96–97
    blessing one's nation, 134–37
    compared with discipleship, 116
    exorcising spirits, 70–71, 74–75, 87, 103
    facing resistance, 26, 49
    form of activism, 29
    individual, 60, 67, 90, 98, 113, 120, 135–36
    group, 70, 91, 113
    healing, 32, 68, 101
    pastoral, 113
    requesting personal assistance, 119
    seeking divine revelation, 43, 54, 67, 125
    via digital media, 139
    viewed as unidirectional, 93–94
    viewed as bidirectional, 60, 97, 113
    within Buddhism, 66, 90
preaching, 31, 36–38, 45, 56, 83, 103, 111, 133
    gender and, 139
Presbyterians, 21
Protestantism, 8, 12, 14, 16, 21, 54–55, 65
    See also evangelicalism
Providence (RI), 51
Pursat, 119–20
    See also under Cambodia

quadrilateral, evangelical, 24, 146, 147, 148
    activism, 25, 29
    biblicism, 24–27

conversionism, 24–25
crucicentrism, 24, 29
Quakers, 30, 31

raft, parable of, 81
Ramousse, Yves, 14
Ratanakiri, 56
rationalization and rationality, 46
Reading (PA), 55
reading of the Bible. *See* Bible reading
rebirth, 51, 67, 83, 86–87
    See also karma
reference group theory, 46–47
refugees
    resettlement of, 20–21, 34, 44, 55, 62, 67, 129, 132; and identification with Israel, 133–37
    repatriation of, 20, 167n31
    sponsorship of, 55, 82, 112, 129
    stereotypes of, 131
refugee camps, 11, 20–22, 38, 58, 128, 135, 145
    I-Dang Holding Center, 26, 31, 54;
    Site II, 67
    in interlocutor testimonies, 42, 54–55, 61–62, 78–79, 83, 86, 129; Buriram, 44–45; Khao-
Religious Society of Friends (Quakers), 30, 31
reverse mission, 118, 128–37, 145
    See also mission
revivals, religious
    period of revival prior to the Cambodian genocide, 17
    refugee camp revivals, 21–22, 128
    revival meeting in Long Beach, California, 94
ritual objects, destruction of, 119–20
rup arak (female spirit medium), 102
    See also spirit mediums
Russey Keo (district in Phnom Penh), 14

Sabbath, 112, 113
sacrifice (ritual), 102, 106
Sakka, 99
    See also Brahmanical deities
Saloth Sar. *See* Pol Pot
salvation, 29, 51, 84, 85, 113, 122, 165n30
Sam, Sarin, 31
sangha (monkhood), 78, 108, 151
    See also monks, Buddhist
Sanskrit language, 68, 69
    See also language
Satan, 30, 65, 73, 74, 75, 82, 92, 98
    See also spirits
Seventh Day Adventist Church, 30

Shivalinga, 72
Sihanouk, Norodom, 6, 13, 14, 15, 16, 17
Singapore, 17, 21
Singing, 36–38, 44, 62, 86, 98–99, 125, 139, 140
    See also hymnals
Sisowath Monivong, 13
Śiva, 66
    See also Brahmanical deities
skillful means, 81
sky, God of the, 57, 58, 66, 67, 158
Skype, 124
    See also digital media
soteriology, 51, 83
    See also salvation
South Vietnam, 13, 15
    flag of, 136
    See also Vietnam
Southern Baptist Convention, 21, 30
Spanish language, 132
    See also language
spirits
    ancestor spirits, 27, 50, 66, 73–74
    angels, 65, 68, 69, 76
    associated with Brahmanical deities and folk heroes, 66–70
    belief in, 77, 87, 91–92
    demons, 65, 85–87, 144
    ghosts, 71–72, 74–76
    Holy Spirit, 32, 65, 68, 77, 79, 92, 146, 147
    nature spirits, 66
    Satan, 30, 65, 73, 74, 75, 82, 92, 98
    souls, 70, 74
    See also spirit mediums
souls, 70, 74
    See also spirits
speaking in tongues, 33
    See also glossolalia
spirit mediums, 87, 97, 100, 102
    rup arak (female spirit medium), 102
Sri Lanka, 69, 108
Stockton, California, 130
survivor's guilt, 7, 39, 59
Switzerland, 21

Taing Chhirc, 17
Taiwan Presbyterian Church, 27
Takeo, 124
    See also under Cambodia
temples, Buddhist, 51–53, 69, 79, 82, 90, 92, 96, 144
    Angkor Wat, 35, 66
    Preah Vihear, 78
    Wat Vihear Thom, 70
terreiro (Candomblé temple), 102, 166n26

INDEX

Thailand, 10–11, 13, 20, 22, 55, 85–88, 91, 108
    See also border, Cambodian-Thai
Thai language, 85
    See also language
theophany, 7, 57, 66
tithing, 110
Tomnuk Domkerng. *See* hymnals
Tomnuk Khmer Borisot. *See* hymnals
torture, 5, 21
translation, Bible
    historical efforts in Cambodia, 13, 15, 105
    Khmer cosmology and, 84
    See also Bible, Khmer
Trinity (doctrine), 30, 85
Trump, Donald, 115, 135, 136, 137, 145, 148
Tu Duc, 12, 14
Tuol Sleng Prison, 5
Tweet (Twitter post), 136

Umā, 66
    See also Brahmanical deities
UNHCR, 42
United Bible Society, 15
United Methodist Church, The, 30
    See also Methodists
United Nations High Commissioner for Refugees (UNHCR), 42
United States capitol building, storming of, 24, 136
upward mobility, 44, 143
    See also language: language acquisition

VeggieTales, 28
Vessantara Jataka, 8, 108, 109, 110
Vichy France, 13

Vietnam, 6, 12–16, 18–22, 24, 42, 96, 131, 165–66n8
    North Vietnam, 15, 20, 21
    South Vietnam, 13, 15; flag of, 136–37
    war in (*see* Vietnam War)
Vietnamese ethnicity, 94, 136
    relationship with Catholicism, 14–15
Vietnamese language, 14, 35
    See also language
Vietnam War, 6, 21, 131
    Viet Cong, 16
    Vietminh, 13
Vineyard Church, 60
Visnu, 66
    See also Brahmanical deities

waistbands and wristbands, protective, 79, 101, 103
    See also clothing
Wat Vihear Thom, 70
    See also temples, Buddhist
white clothing, figures wearing, 57, 66, 67, 68, 76, 158
    See also clothing
women in ministry, 9, 31, 37, 98, 139–42, 146, 158
    See also ministry
World Christian Database, 40
World Christianity, 23, 118, 128, 132, 146, 149
worship, 33–37, 74, 91–92, 98, 113, 134, 140–42, 165n3

Youk Chhang, 59
youth, 4, 36, 42, 133, 146
    See also age